On Poets and Poetry

On Poets & Poetry

William H. Pritchard

SWALLOW PRESS   ATHENS, OHIO

Swallow Press / Ohio University Press, Athens, Ohio 45701
www.ohioswallow.com

To obtain permission to quote, reprint, or otherwise reproduce or distribute material
from Swallow Press / Ohio University Press publications, please contact our rights and
permissions department at (740) 593-1154 or (740) 593-4536 (fax).

Printed in the United States of America
Swallow Press / Ohio University Press books are printed on acid-free paper ⊚ ™

16 15 14 13 12 11 10 09   5 4 3 2 1

Library of Congress Cataloging-in-Publication Data
Pritchard, William H.
  On poets and poetry / William H. Pritchard.
    p. cm.
  Includes bibliographical references and index.
  ISBN 978-0-8040-1114-3 (hc : alk. paper) — ISBN 978-0-8040-1115-0 (pb : alk. paper)
  1. English poetry—20th century—History and criticism. 2. American poetry—20th
century—History and criticism. 3. English-speaking countries—Intellectual life—20th
century. 4. Criticism. I. Title.
  PR610.P75 2009
  821'.91209—dc22

                                                        2009014774

For Christopher Ricks

Gifted with so fine an ear

Contents

The Middle Generation

3. THREE CRITICS OF POETS AND POETRY

Preface

Fifty years ago I published my first essay for the *Hudson Review*, an omnibus poetry chronicle that attempted to come to terms with fifteen or so poets, whose books ranged from undistinguished slim volumes to the collected poems of Louis MacNeice, which I admired. I had taught poems, mostly twentieth-century ones, in various courses, had completed a dissertation on Robert Frost, but had scarcely gone public with my critical wares and was nervous about the venture. The worry was not assuaged when the head man in Amherst College's Department of English, a man who regarded publication by his colleagues with some suspicion, asked me why I felt I had to do this. He professed himself sorry for the poor poets I had taken exception to and extended his sympathies to me in case they should respond with physical threats of harm. But his lack of enthusiasm for my decision to be a public critic—not just an English teacher at a small New England college—failed to deter me from pursuing a career of writing essays, reviews, and a few books, often about poets and poetry. Over the years I found myself dealing less often with contemporary poets, but rather seeking opportunities to write about older ones. These "older" ones can now include the American and English array of modernists and traditionalists who flourished in the fifty years stretching roughly from 1914 to 1965 (just before my reviewing career began), from Frost and Eliot to Larkin and Lowell.

Many of the pieces that follow here issue from the invitation to review a book, most likely a biography of a poet or a collection of his poems. The foremost literary critic of the last century, T. S. Eliot, wrote hundreds of such reviews, most of which have never been available in book form (that situation will gradually be corrected) with the result that one must search out the pages of magazines like the *Egoist* or *Athenaeum* to read what he had to say about Stendhal, Henry Adams, Kipling, and numerous others. At the peril of inviting comparison with Eliot, it appears to me that, unlike the scholarly essay which must justify itself by bringing out a new aspect of a writer's work or correcting the inadequate interpretation of earlier critics, reviews are bound by no such rules. The reviewer is not only free but expected to take the book at hand as a chance to direct attention to central issues. As a critic he may speak to large matters of a poet's achievement, comparing the writer with contemporaries and predecessors in an effort to capture his or her distinctness. Under the confines of a thousand-word limit—or in more spacious situations double or treble that length—he can embrace limits as a provocation to speak out, sometimes doubtless recklessly, in order to elicit something essential about his subject. The great reviewer Randall Jarrell put it most extravagantly in "The Age of Criticism" when he declared that "taking the chance of making a complete fool of himself—and, sometimes, doing so—is the first demand that is made upon any real critic: he must stick his neck out just as the artist does, if he is to be of any real use to art."

The contents of this book are divided into three sections: the first consists of seven essays, two of which—on Dryden and Hardy—are reconsiderations of a poet's achievement; but so in a smaller way are those provoked by a book for review, on Milton, Wordsworth, Tennyson. The attempt in all of them, indeed in all the pieces in this collection, is to address an audience wider than an academic one. In my classrooms the students with whom I read and discuss poems are not by a long shot exclusively "English" oriented; similarly, I would presume that not all readers of my criticism are subscribers to academic periodicals like *Modern Language Notes* or *English Literary History*. The notion that one can address a broader-based, if still small, audience of intelligent nonspecialists—however vain a notion—helps keep me going. Frost once said about his poems that he had no desire for them to be "caviare to the crowd. . . . I want to reach out, and would if it were a thing I could do by taking thought."

Reaching out to the "crowd" of intelligent readers is even more evident in the book's second section where I take up, in brief reviews, a number of important English and American poets of the last century. Over the past few decades poets such as Frost, Stevens, Auden, Lowell, and Larkin have been preserved and more fully presented through collections of their work, biographies, letters, and other prose, or by canonization in the Library of America. My notion is that the poets considered in part 2 can be thought of as in conversation with one another, helped along by my juxtapositions and judgments.

In the third section I consider three twentieth-century critics who figure for me as among the most exciting and valuable commentators on poets and poetry from that century. Two of them, Eliot and Donald Davie, were indeed poet-critics; the third, Hugh Kenner, did not write poetry, although it looks from his writing as if he did just about everything else. William Empson once said about Eliot that he, Empson, couldn't say just how much of his mind Eliot had invented; Eliot, Kenner, and Davie surely invented much of my own. In his invaluable, long-out-of-print anthology of poems, *The Art of Poetry*, Kenner wrote, "The chief requisite for criticism is not analytic skill but a trained sensibility." Those three critics trained my sensibility.

What keeps it in training is still the classroom, where I continue to make the attempt to know literature—to know a poem—freshly. Early in my career as a teacher and a writer, I discovered the following sentences of R. P. Blackmur, ones I have returned to frequently. Blackmur is speaking of how we go about, in Pound's phrase, making it new, and claims:

> The institution of literature, so far as it is alive, is made again at every instant. It is made afresh as part of the process of being known afresh; what is permanent is what is always fresh, and it can be fresh only in performance—that is, in reading and seeing and hearing what is actually in it at this place and this time . . . the critic brings to consciousness the means of performance.

Those final words always seem to demand rereading, as with so many of Blackmur's sentences, but I take it that the teacher likewise "brings to consciousness"—to his students and himself—"the means of performance":

the verbal invitations to our eyes and (above all) our ears that issue from the poem. Selfishly, the classroom is central to my life because it is the only place where something like a conversation can be started about a poem of Ben Jonson's, Shakespeare's *Cymbeline*, or a novel by Henry James. One doesn't expect to have such a conversation when dining at a friend's or even when passing the time with a professional colleague. They might not have read or been reading the right book at the right time; for that to happen, something like a captive audience of more or less agreeable students is necessary.

Denis Donoghue, who has reflected much on the teaching of literature, recently took a gloomy look at those students and their relation to "English." As a beginning teacher, he said, his assumption was that the merit of reading great works consisted in the access they gave to "deeply imagined lives other than their own." He thinks this assumption no longer has broad currency, its appeal having lost its persuasiveness:

> Students seem to be convinced that their own lives are the primary and sufficient incentive. They report that reading literature is mainly a burden. Those students who think of themselves as writers and take classes in "creative writing" to define themselves as poets or fiction writers, evidently write more than they read, and regard reading as a gross expenditure of time and energy.

However things go on at NYU, where Donoghue has long been established, his charge has the ring of overstatement; at least I know that neither my better nor my more ordinary students would sign on to such a declaration. Donoghue, however, has a point when he goes on to say that many people feel confident enough in talking about fiction—novels and stories—but are more or less tongue-tied when it comes to poetry. Doubtless this condition has something to do with their desire, as he says, to "come to themes and issues directly, without the hesitations enforced by considerations of form, structure, and style."

This bears out my experience that students come from secondary school prepared to think of poetry as a very deep art indeed, and that their task is to penetrate its depths and arrive at something called the real meaning. Thus Frost's "Stopping by Woods on a Snowy Evening," with its snowflakes and harness bells, is "really" about death, perhaps about suicide. In other words, the poem's enchanting surface ("The only other sound's the sweep / Of easy wind and downy flake") exists only to be seen through to something beyond or under it. If there is a single principle holding these essays on poets and poetry together, it is that style needs to be attended to, not just at the beginning of our reading but continuously, and that readers should invest in an engagement, sometimes a prolonged one, with the surface of a poem—with its events that can be seen and heard as they reveal themselves over time.

Acknowledgments

I am grateful to the following for reading all or parts of this collection, and for their useful, encouraging comments: Paul Alpers, Christopher Benfey, Warner Berthoff, Patrick McGrath, Roger Sale, and David Sofield. Marietta Pritchard continues to be my first editor and critic.

As in the past, Susan Raymond-Fic was indispensable in transforming the typed manuscript and converting disarray into order.

Thanks to David Sanders for taking on this project, and to Nancy Basmajian for scrupulously editing it.

Once more I am indebted to the late Frederick Morgan and to Paula Deitz for giving me the chance, in *Hudson Review*, to write at length about some of these poets.

The book is dedicated to a great critic of poets and poetry from whom I have learned much.

ONE

Essays on Older Poets

Dryden Rules

Waller was smooth; but Dryden taught to join
The varying verse, the full resounding line,
The long majestick march, and energy divine.

Pope, "Epistle to Augustus"

Writing to Philip Larkin more than sixty years ago, Kingsley Amis delivered one of his frequent literary critiques of English poets, this one of John Dryden:

I have stopped reading Dryden. He is very like Chaucer, isn't he? I mean, however hard you try, you cannot *see what people mean* who admired them. Now, I see what people *mean* (though I don't *agree* with them) who like *Donne* or *Pope* or *Wordsworth*, or *Keats*, or even *Milton*, but I cannot with Dryden. A second-rate fucking journalist ("Oh?"). A SECOND-RATE FUCKING JOURNALIST ("Oh").

Amis showing off for Larkin, of course.[1] But then there was C. S. Lewis pronouncing as if from on high: "Dryden fails to be a satisfactory poet because being rather a boor, a gross, vulgar, provincial, misunderstanding mind, he yet constantly attempts those kinds of poetry which demand the *cuor gentil*."[2] And on the occasion of Dryden's tercentenary in 2000, the Oxford don Barbara Everett, one of the shrewdest living critics of poetry, noted with regard to Dryden's low public esteem, "Perhaps the few readers of poetry who still exist need an intensity of verse that Dryden never cared to supply." She acknowledged that after decades of teaching she

First published in the *Hudson Review* 58, no. 4 (Winter 2006): 541–67 has found that "only the rarest of able pupils has agreed to try Dryden, has indeed (it sometimes seems) heard of him."[3] My own experience tallies with Everett's: in decades of teaching I have supervised but a single honors essay by a student on the writer—that one, as with Everett, by the rarest of able pupils. If Dryden is not read with enthusiasm and admiration in college classrooms, where is such reading likely to occur?

It occurred most memorably in the eloquent testimony of one of his first and perhaps his finest critics, Samuel Johnson. In his "Life of Pope," in *Lives of the Poets*, Johnson made a famous, extended comparison between the characteristics of Pope's and Dryden's verse containing formulations such as the following:

> Dryden's page is a natural field, rising into inequalities, and diversified by the varied exuberance of abundant vegetation; Pope's is a velvet lawn, shaven by the scythe, and leveled by the roller. . . . If the flights of Dryden therefore are higher, Pope continues longer on the wing. If of Dryden's fire the blaze is brighter, of Pope's the heat is more regular and constant. Dryden often surpasses expectation, and Pope never falls below it. Dryden is read with frequent astonishment, and Pope with perpetual delight.

At the end of the parallel, Johnson hopes it will be found just, then makes the following confession:

> If the reader should suspect me, as I suspect myself, of some partial fondness for the memory of Dryden, let him not too hastily condemn me; for meditation and enquiry may, perhaps, shew him the reasonableness of my determination.

As a young man Johnson contemplated writing a biography of Dryden, so the "partial fondness" might be accounted for solely on that ground, and surely the modern reader, contemplating Johnson's parallel, should feel no need to choose one of these poets over the other. Yet this particular reader after considerable ventures into studying and teaching both poets (Johnson's "meditation and enquiry") has become convinced of the reasonableness of Johnson's determination. The pages to follow attempt to give an account of that conviction.

No one in the last century, unless it be Mark Van Doren—whose 1920 book on Dryden was the occasion for T. S. Eliot's short but trenchant review essay—has written more sympathetically about the poet than Eliot; yet in thinking about Dryden's status as a great English writer, sentences from another of Eliot's essays come to mind, his even more trenchant one about Ben Jonson. That essay begins by stating bluntly, "The reputation of Jonson has been of the most deadly kind that can be compelled upon the memory of a great poet":

> To be universally accepted; to be damned by the praise that quenches all desire to read the book; to be afflicted by the imputation of the virtues which excite the least pleasure; and to be read only by historians and antiquaries—this is the most perfect conspiracy of approval.

Except for the first attribution of universal acceptance—Dryden's acceptance is probably less than universal—the terms fit Dryden equally well: "a poetic practitioner who learned from Jonson" (Eliot's words) and who provided the first significant criticism of Jonson's work. The "virtues" imputed to Dryden—his refashioning of English prose from, in Samuel Johnson's words, brick to marble; his skill as political satirist and arguer in verse; his services as a creative translator of the Latin poets, of Boccaccio, and of Chaucer—are acknowledged more by lip service than by responsive attention to the prose and poetry in which those virtues are embodied.

His posthumous career, however, may be distinguished from Jonson's in that it is marked, as Jonson's was not, by a series of excellent commentaries from readers who were not merely "historians and antiquaries" but discerning critics whose accounts of the writer's work on various fronts remain fresh and useful in the twenty-first century. A list of these would begin with Johnson's Life and continue with the biographical and critical commentary in Walter Scott's great edition of 1808. Near the end of the closing decades of the nineteenth century, George Saintsbury revised Scott's edition and contributed an excellent small book on Dryden to the English Men of Letters series; at roughly the same time John Churton

Collins in England and James Russell Lowell in this country wrote substantial essays on him. The classicist A. W. Verrall's *Lectures on Dryden* was published in 1914 after Verrall's death; six years later came Van Doren's book (his dissertation at Columbia University), by all odds the fullest, most perceptive treatment of Dryden's contribution as a man of letters. Eliot's review essay followed the next year, and in 1932 he published the valuable *John Dryden: The Poet, the Dramatist, the Critic,* three talks given for the BBC. The second half of the last century saw an outpouring of books about every aspect of Dryden, the latest examples of which are two further volumes in the excellent Longman's Annotated English Poets series, taking Dryden up to 1696, and a volume of essays devoted to him in the Cambridge Companion series. Dryden has fared well at the hands of the professoriat, most of whose writing about and editing of him has been exemplary. That still leaves the question of whether such a conspiracy of approval includes readers who read him—in F. R. Leavis's words about Donne—as we read the living.[4]

There is, of course, no argument about the ambitious variety of Dryden's literary performances. The editor of the *Cambridge Companion* notes

> the rapidity and fluency with which Dryden managed the thousands of pages of verse and prose—prologues, epilogues, and plays; songs, satires, state poems, and panegyrics; commendatory verse and elegies; epitaphs, epistles, odes, essays, dedications, prefaces, biographies, and a raft of translations from ancient and modern languages.

In this essay I shall treat none of these modes of verse or prose adequately, and shall completely ignore Dryden's plays, which, lively as they were felt to be at the time, are unlikely to attract curious readers of today. And I begin with an autobiographical memory of being introduced to the writer when, as an Amherst College senior, I audited Reuben Brower's course titled "Pope to Tennyson." In fact Brower began, briefly, with Dryden, indeed Dryden at his best, with the allusive satire of *Mac Flecknoe* and *Absalom and Achitophel,* and the elegiac grandeur of "To the Memory of Mr. Oldham." I brought no experience of Virgil to my reading of these poems, and they were hard going, more so than the ones by Pope that followed. But I believed in Brower, if not yet in Dryden, and tried to imitate my teacher's way of reading and responding. Not until graduate school and beyond did I catch a foothold to the point where I could begin to read Dryden with pleasure, perhaps even to understand Eliot's pronouncement in his essay that "to enjoy Dryden means to pass beyond the limitations of the nineteenth century into a new freedom." A heady claim: was I experiencing anything like it?

Brower's training as a classicist as well as a close reader of English poetry (he studied at Cambridge with Richards and Leavis) made him an ideal critic of what he liked to call Dryden's "allusive irony," a better term he thought than the usual "mock heroic" for the poet's particular technique. In his long out-of-print Dryden selection in the Laurel Poetry series (price thirty-five cents), Brower considered passages from *Mac Flecknoe* in order to show that "[t]he surface magnificence of Dryden's jokes is essential to his way of expressing high scorn, of imparting greatness to his opponents while deftly letting them down." These observations were made apropos of the famous couplets about Shadwell, the inheritor of his father Flecknoe's kingdom of Dullness:

Besides, his goodly fabric fills the eye,
And seems designed for thoughtless majesty:
Thoughtless as monarch oaks that shade the plain,
And, spread in solemn state, supinely reign.

Brower said about the word "supinely" that it sounds "deceptively noble, in its Latinity" until we realize that Shadwell's reign is rather unlike that of the monarch oaks he's been compared to, since his "goodly fabric" is displayed from flat on his back.

Brower noted that Dryden's fusion of venom and majesty made for satire that was the opposite of the "slovenly butchering of a man" Dryden alluded to in the long essay from his final decade, the "Discourse Concerning the Original and Progress of Satire." The reference to the "slovenly butchering of a man" occurs in what the editor of his critical essays, George Watson, has called one of the finest moments in Dryden's prose:

How easy it is to call rogue and villain, and that wittily! But how hard to make a man appear a fool, a blockhead, or a knave, without using any of those opprobrious terms! To spare the grossness of the names, and to do the thing yet more severely, is to draw a full face, and to make the nose and cheeks stand out, and yet not to employ any depth of shadowing. This is the mystery of that noble trade which yet no master can teach to his apprentice; he may give the rules, but the scholar is never the nearer in his practice. Neither is it true that this fineness of raillery is offensive. A witty man is tickled while he is hurt in this manner, and a fool feels it not. The occasion of an offence may possibly be given, but he cannot take it. If it be granted that in effect this way does more mischief—that a man is secretly wounded, and though he be not sensible himself, yet the malicious world will find it for him—yet there is still a vast difference betwixt the slovenly butchering of a man, and the fineness of a stroke that separates the head from the body and leaves it standing in its place. A man may be capable, as Jack Ketch's wife said of his servant, of a plain piece of work, a bare hanging; but to make a malefactor die sweetly was only belonging to her husband.

From the notes to this passage in the Longman edition we learn that Jack Ketch, public hangman from around 1663 (he died in 1686), was notorious for his botching of public executions, so perhaps Mrs. Ketch was partial. Watson suggests in his note on the passage that it seems as much an aspiration on Dryden's part as a true description of his art, since Dryden's satires are more political and sometimes abusive than the ideal account lets on.

Yet even so qualified, this description of the satirist that Dryden conceived himself to be rose out of his actual practice in the great satires of more than a decade previous, most notably *Mac Flecknoe* and *Absalom and Achitophel.* The standard account of Dryden's progress and discovery of his true gift as a poet contrasts these vivid, ironically voiced poems with the panegyrical strain he practiced earlier in ones such as the *Heroic Stanzas* on Cromwell (1658), the celebration of Charles's restoration (*Astraea Redux,* 1660), and the historical poem about England's sea wars with the Dutch and the great fire of London (*Annus Mirabilis,* 1667). The declamatory, mono-voiced soliloquizing in the heroic plays he wrote during the sixties, culminating in the two-part *Conquest of Granada* (1672), would also seem inimical to the tonal complexity of the humorous poems to come. But something surprising happens in *Annus Mirabilis,* when Dryden subtly complicates his heroicizing of the English fleet. In his preface to the poem he announced that "the adequate delight of heroic poesy" was constituted by certain "descriptions or images, well wrought." These "beget admiration . . . as the images of the burlesque, which is contrary to this, by the same reason beget laughter." Dr. Johnson admired the poem, although he felt that in it Dryden "seems not yet fully to have formed his versification, or settled his system of propriety." Johnson quoted some quatrains from the sea fight in which the English pursue the Dutch:

> Like hunted castors, conscious of their store,
> > Their waylayed wealth to Norway's coasts they bring;
> There first the north's cold bosom spices bore,
> > And winter brooded on the eastern spring.

> By the rich scent we found our perfumed prey,
> > Which flanked with rocks did close in covert lie;
> And round about their murdering cannon lay,
> > At once to threaten and invite the eye.

Here as in other places in the poem, Johnson declared, "the sublime [is] too often mingled with the ridiculous." He was bothered by Dryden's itch to illustrate everything with a simile that would supposedly win our admiration. Such constant solicitation may make the wonder cease, and perhaps a similar thought occurred to the poet.

Whatever his state of mind, there is a moment in the Anglo-Dutch battle that is richly predictive of the satirist to come. The "haughty Belgians," as Dryden calls them, with their different styles of ship construction, direct their fire at the sails of the English ships with the following result:

> And as the built, so different is the fight:
> > Their mounting shot is on our sails designed;
> Deep in their hulls our deadly bullets light,
> > And through the yielding planks a passage find.

> Our dreaded admiral from far they threat,
> > Whose battered rigging their whole war receives:

> All bare, like some old oak which tempests beat,
>   He stands, and sees below his scattered leaves.

> Heroes of old, when wounded, shelter sought,
>   But he, who meets all danger with disdain,
> Ev'n in their face his ship to anchor brought,
>   And steeple-high stood propped upon the main.

Dryden terms the admiral's behavior "excess of courage," such as to make his foes temporarily withdraw in awe. But more is going on in the presentation: the editor notes, with respect to the bareness of the weatherbeaten oak, its leaves brought down by the assault, that it recalls an item from the *London Gazette* recounting that "[t]he Duke had all his Tackle taken off by Chain-shot, and his Breeches to his Skin were shot off." Dryden here adapts a passage from the fourth book of the *Aeneid* where—in an earlier translation from the seventeenth century—we hear of tempests, the old oak, and scattered leaves. In his book about the poem, Michael McKeon asserts that "Dryden converts the ridiculous destruction of Albemarle's breeches into an occasion for celebrating his manliness."[5] But this is to presume that the movement is one way only, from "low" subject to high epic celebration. One could just as well look at the portrait of Albemarle as mock heroic, a nice mixture, to use Johnson's terms, of the "sublime mingled with the ridiculous," or, in Dryden's words, "images of the burlesque that beget laughter."

The elegance of Dryden's portrayal of the admiral may be brought out by contrast with some lines from another poem about Albemarle's receiving what Pepys referred to as "a little hurt in the thigh." The author of "Third Advice to a Painter," now attributed to Andrew Marvell and published the year before *Annus Mirabilis*, puts it this way:

> But most with story of his hand or thumb
> Conceal (as Honor would) his Grace's bum,
> When the rude bullet a large collop tore
> Out of that buttock never turn'd before.
> Fortune, it seem'd, would give him by that lash
> Gentle correction for his fight so rash,

But should the Rump perceiv't, they'd say that Mars
Had now reveng'd them upon Aumarle's arse.

The Longman editor says that these lines "less sympathetically" record
the incident; put positively, why not say that Dryden's more sympathetic
portrayal of the admiral is remarkably satisfying for its cool fusion of the
heroic and the bathetic, done without batting an eye. From here it is but
a step to the lines in *Mac Flecknoe* where Shadwell is compared to monarch
oaks spread in solemn state and supinely reigning. Or to that other pas-
sage Brower singled out as a great instance of Dryden's allusive irony in its
presentation of Flecknoe and his chosen heir:

> The hoary prince in majesty appeared,
> High on a throne of his own labours reared.
> At his right hand our young Ascanius sate,
> Rome's other hope, and pillar of the state:
> His brows thick fogs, instead of glories, grace,
> And lambent dullness played around his face.

The current editor brings out, as did Brower, the Virgilian echoes in "Rome's
other hope" ("*spes altera Romae*"; *Aeneid*, xii) and in "lambent dullness played
around his face" ("*Lambere flamma comas et circum tempora pasci*"; *Aeneid*, ii).

Further help in distinguishing Dryden's mode of satiric attack, espe-
cially from Pope's, is provided by George Saintsbury in an impressionistic
disquisition on how the couplet works in *Absalom and Achitophel*:

> It must be always well in hand, serious without passion, and dis-
> dainful without loss of temper. Everywhere in the measure, as well
> as in the sense, perfect command has to be manifested: the poet
> cannot afford to miss a hit, to fire in the air, to boggle anything;
> and he does not. It is almost enough to say that the passage of
> Pope's satire which most reminds us of Dryden is the character of
> Atticus, and that the principal thing which reminds us that it is not
> Dryden is the deadly earnest of it—the absence of the Olympian
> quality. Pope attacks on the level, or from below, and sometimes
> from behind; Dryden always from above.

This is too absolute to fit some of the "low" touches in *Mac Flecknoe*—
"Echoes from Pissing Alley 'Shadwell' call,/And 'Shadwell' they resound
from Aston Hall"—but will do for other ones where dullness is enlarged
and glorified. (Some editors following the miscellany of 1684 print "Sh——"
rather than "Shadwell," thus bringing out the excrementitious theme. But
Dryden originally spelled out his whole name.) And although Eliot in his
essay doesn't mention Saintsbury he may well have had him in mind when
he (Eliot) contrasted Dryden's style of portraiture with Pope's:

> When Pope alters, he diminishes; he is a master of miniature. The
> singular skill of his portrait of Addison, for example, in the *Epistle
> to Arbuthnot*, depends upon the justice and reserve, the apparent
> determination not to exaggerate. The genius of Pope is not for
> caricature. But the effect of the portraits of Dryden is to transform
> the object into something greater . . .
>
> > A fiery soul, which working out its way,
> > Fretted the pigmy body to decay,
> > And o'er informed the tenement of clay.
>
> These lines are not merely a magnificent tribute. They create the
> object which they contemplate.

What Saintsbury calls Dryden's "Olympian" quality is related to or per-
haps just another way of talking about the magnificence Eliot found in
these lines from the character of Achitophel/Shaftesbury in *Absalom*. But
before considering the lines in the larger context of the portrait, we may
note the amazing high spirits, the positive *geniality* of the verse in *Absalom*
at its best—most splendidly in the opening lines:

> In pious times, ere priestcraft did begin,
> Before polygamy was made a sin,
> When man on many multiplied his kind,
> Ere one to one was cursedly confined;
> When nature prompted, and no law denied
> Promiscuous use of concubine and bride;
> Then Israel's monarch, after heaven's own heart,
> His vigorous warmth did variously impart

> To wives and slaves: and wide as his command
> Scattered his maker's image through the land.

The alliterative play that gives life and voice to the lines; the when . . . when . . . then sequence that wheels us precipitously into Israel's monarch; the complete confidence of rhythm; the sudden full-stop after "wives and slaves" in the next to last line—these are a few of the qualities that contribute to magnificence. Admittedly David/Charles II is a "good" character here, but he is presented through the man-of-the-world jaunty knowingness of Dryden, which presentation is really not different in kind from the way the "bad" guys are treated in their turn.

Probably the greatest single portrait in all Dryden's gallery is of Achitophel, and here geniality, disdain, or the Olympian quality Saintsbury identifies is replaced by something even richer. Everyone admires the passage, but its special fineness has not I think been enough remarked upon. We know that Dryden added some lines later in the portrait to mitigate his adverse judgment of his villain by admitting that Shaftesbury's record as Lord Chancellor was creditable. But the unforgettable sequence of lines from which Eliot extracted the triplet about Achitophel's "fiery soul" precedes the added lines and can be experienced as a whole. The plotters against David/Charles are introduced beginning at line 150:

> Of these the false Achitophel was first:
> A name to all succeeding ages cursed.
> For close designs and crooked counsels fit,
> Sagacious, bold, and turbulent of wit;
> Restless, unfixed in principles and place,
> In power unpleased, impatient of disgrace.
> A fiery soul, which working out its way
> Fretted the pigmy body to decay,
> And o'erinformed the tenement of clay.
> A daring pilot in extremity:
> Pleased with the danger, when the waves went high
> He sought the storms; but for a calm unfit
> Would steer too nigh the sands to boast his wit.
> Great wits are sure to madness near allied,

And thin partitions do their bounds divide:
Else why should he, with wealth and honour blessed,
Refuse his age the needful hours of rest?
Punish a body which he could not please,
Bankrupt of life, yet prodigal of ease?
And all to leave what with his toil he won
To that unfeathered, two-legged thing, a son:
Got while his soul did huddled notions try,
And born a shapeless lump, like anarchy.
In friendship false, implacable in hate,
Resolved to ruin or to rule the state;
To compass this the triple bond he broke,
The pillars of the public safety shook,
And fitted Israel for a foreign yoke.

The more Dryden writes about Shaftesbury the less he understands him; or, to use the English equivalent of the Latin *admirare,* the more he wonders at him—at why he did what he did. This comes through most strongly after the famous alliance of great wits with madness and the question that follows: "Else why should he . . . Punish a body which he could not please,/Bankrupt of life, yet prodigal of ease?" No subsequent abuse of the ill-made son and heir ("that unfeathered, two-legged thing") will make the questions any more answerable. Dryden's satiric portraits regularly eschew any attempt at getting what Eliot called, in his essay on Ben Jonson, the human, "third" dimension—but this one is an exception. As for the famous triplet that Eliot says "creates the object that it contemplates," Christopher Ricks in his brilliantly resourceful essay "Dryden's Triplets" (from the *Cambridge Companion*) sees the lines as a "corporeal triplet" that conjures up "in all his damaged and damaging energy" the life of Shaftesbury:

A fiery soul, which working out its way
Fretted the pigmy body to decay,
And o'er informed the tenement of clay.

Ricks writes:

> Dryden's triplet animates not only a soul but a body, and then, through the body of the verse itself, it works that of which it speaks. For the soul of the lines can be seen and heard to be working out its way, out through the acknowledged restraint, even while fretting to decay the body of the couplet—more, while over-informing the tenement that is the couplet-form itself.

Here Ricks gives Eliot's claim substantial life.

2.

Dryden the literary and political satirist has had more justice done to him than the other Drydens Steven Zwicker names in the *Cambridge Companion* introduction. His prose has received many tributes, none more telling than the "masculine" vigor and directness informing the biographical pages of Scott's edition. It is sometimes forgotten that Matthew Arnold in "The Study of Poetry," just before he produced the patronizing claim that Dryden and Pope were classics of English prose rather than of English poetry, paid handsome tribute to Dryden the prose writer by contrasting him with two of his predecessors. Arnold quotes sentences from George Chapman (the Elizabethan dramatist and translator of Homer), calling them "intolerable," then does the same for Milton, whose prose he judges "obsolete." He then quotes part of the first sentence from Dryden's postscript to the reader, appended to his 1697 translation of the *Aeneid:* "What Virgil wrote in the vigour of his age, in plenty and at ease, I have undertaken to translate in my declining years; struggling with wants, oppressed with sickness, curbed in my genius, liable to be misconstrued in all I write." How similar this is, rhythmically, to the cadences of Dryden's couplets—their balance, their energy-within-restraint. Arnold says justly that "here at last we have the true English prose, a prose such as we would all gladly use if we only knew how." Eliot confirms this in his BBC talks on Dryden, noting that in the two hundred–odd years since his death (Eliot was writing in 1932), "hardly a word or a phrase has become quaint and obsolete."

Dryden the translator has been the subject of Charles Tomlinson's effort to establish him not only as himself a great one, but as responsible for the important conviction that translation is—in Tomlinson's words to his introduction to *The Oxford Book of Verse in English Translation*—"essentially a compromise between the original texts and the present interests and capacities of a given writer." Dryden believed that the translator must be a poet, and that the extremes of "metaphrase"—dogged literalism in following the original—and "imitation" of the "free" sort later practiced among others by Pound and Robert Lowell, were to be avoided. If asked to fix on a single instance of Dryden's empathetic skill as a reader and "bringer-over" of a predecessor's language, I would choose his treatment of Lucretius, of whose *De Rerum Natura* he translated various sections. In the preface to *Sylvae* (1685), a volume containing renderings of Virgil, Lucretius, Theocritus, and Horace, Dryden turns from remarks about translating Virgil to describe what's distinctive about Lucretius:

> If I am not mistaken, the distinguishing character of Lucretius (I mean of his soul and genius) is a certain kind of noble pride, and positive assertion of his opinions. He is everywhere confident of his own reason, and assuming an absolute command not only over his vulgar reader but even his patron Memmius. For he is always bidding him attend, as if he had the rod over him, and using a magisterial authority while he instructs him. From his time to ours I know none so like him as our poet and philosopher of Malmesbury. This is that perpetual dictatorship which is exercised by Lucretius, who though often in the wrong yet seems to deal *bona fide* with his reader, and tells him nothing but what he thinks.

Dryden's translation of the latter part of the third book of *De Rerum Natura*, "Against the Fear of Death," begins thus:

> What has this bugbear death to frighten man,
> If souls can die, as well as bodies can?
> For, as before our birth we felt no pain
> When Punic arms infested land and main,
> When heaven and earth were in confusion hurled
> For the debated empire of the world,

Which awed with dreadful expectation lay,
Sure to be slaves, uncertain who should sway:
So, when our mortal frame shall be disjoined,
The lifeless lump uncoupled from the mind,
From sense of grief and pain we shall be free;
We shall not feel, because we shall not be.

Here is the "perpetual dictatorship," the "positive assertion of his opinions" Dryden singles out in the preface as central to the Lucretian style. It's hard to talk about pace, but these lines are typical of the brisk, strong continuity of movement Dryden is so adept at creating—the conjunctives "for" and "when" and "So" contributing to the sweep of inevitable argument. Some later lines consider the many things that will be swept away with death (*tot praemium vitae*):

"Ah wretch," thou criest, "ah! miserable me,
One woeful day sweeps children, friends, and wife,
And all the brittle blessings of my life!"
Add one thing more, and all thou say'st is true:
Thy want and wish of them is vanished too,
Which well considered were a quick relief
To all thy vain imaginary grief.
For thou shalt sleep and never wake again,
And quitting life, shall quit thy living pain.
But we thy friends shall all those sorrows find
Which in forgetful death thou leav'st behind;
No time shall dry our tears, nor drive thee from our mind.

The final alexandrine gives extra force to how the dead one's memory lengthens on in those who remain to grieve, even as he himself has been set free. A modern reader can't but think of Philip Larkin's response to this attitude toward death in the lines from "Aubade" that scornfully invoke "specious stuff" like

No rational being
Can fear a thing it will not feel, not seeing
That this is what we fear—no sight, no sound,

> No touch or taste or smell, nothing to think with,
> Nothing to love or link with,
> The anaesthetic from which none come round.

Still, that "specious stuff" caught Larkin's attention, provoking perhaps the poem's finest moment; Dryden's Lucretius makes the idea something—almost—other than specious.

On the basis of the two long poems of historical and religious controversy he wrote during the 1680s, *Religio Laici* (1682) and *The Hind and the Panther* (1687), Dryden is often praised for being a better arguer in verse than his successor Pope managed to be in his *Essay on Man*.[6] Yet no part of his work has fallen more into oblivion—always excepting for the specialists—than these two poems. Scott, whose wise comments on each are to be found in his introductory notes to them, observed about Dryden in *The Hind and the Panther:* "He launched forth into a tide of controversy, which, however furious at the time, has long subsided, leaving his poem a disregarded wreck, stranded upon the shores which the surges once occupied." Compared to the partisan responses elicited by *Mac Flecknoe, Absalom and Achitophel,* and *The Medal,* the attempt of *Religio Laici* to mediate among contending religious factions in a plain-speaking, noninflammatory manner in fact attracted neither "admiration nor censure" (Scott's words). And if for Scott, a little over a hundred years after Dryden's death, the controversies felt distant, what of the reader two hundred years later who finds herself a student in a course titled Major English Writers? Needless to say, the professor who has room for four or five classes on the poet must give short shrift to these longer poems, and he will do this probably by mentioning the relatively famous bits that stand out in them—for example, the opening lines of *Religio Laici:*

> Dim as the borrowed beams of moon and stars
> To lonely, weary, wandering travellers
> Is reason to the soul; and as on high
> Those rolling fires discover but the sky
> Not light us here, so reason's glimmering ray
> Was lent, not to assure our doubtful way,
> But guide us upward to a better day.

—an unlikely "romantic" comparison for Arnold's classic of an age of prose and reason to be capable of, given exquisite pace by virtue of its enjambed lines. Or there is the autobiographical excursus early in *The Hind and the Panther:*

> My thoughtless youth was winged with vain desires,
> My manhood, long misled by wandering fires,
> Followed false lights; and when their glimpse was gone,
> My pride struck out new sparkles of her own.

But admiring the sequences from which these lines are taken is rather a different matter from following, in an informed way, the particularities of political and religious dispute in late seventeenth-century England of which both poems are full.

Although it is the case—at least for this reader—that one flags in each of the two poems when the explanatory notes at the bottom of pages in the Longman edition move up toward the page's top, the wonder of the versification is often enough to carry us over rough spots. Speaking of *The Hind and the Panther* (though similar claims could be made for *Religio Laici*), Scott wrote of that versification:

> It never falls, never becomes rugged; rises from the dignified strain
> of the poetry; sinks into quaint familiarity, where sarcasm and hu-
> mour are employed; and winds through all the mazes of theological
> argument, without becoming either obscure or prosaic.

To my judgment, the finest sequence in *The Hind and the Panther* is from its third and last book, two hundred and some lines known as the Fable of the Swallows. The fable is related, with some malicious intent, by the Panther (representing the Anglican church) to the Hind (the Roman Catholic church) as they discuss matters theological at the Hind's modest domicile. It is "about" the situation of Catholics and Catholic clergy under the present king, the Catholic James II, and the Longman note warns that it presents "a complex challenge to the reader." Instead of meeting that challenge, I wish to point out, with reference to two passages from the fable, the distinguished quality of the versification by which Dryden carries his allegory; since whatever his contemporaries were able to make of it in terms of contemporary issues, the object of our attention is essentially the action of the verse itself as it creates a fully convincing representation.

The first passage characterizes the swallows' nature; the second recounts their ill-advised decision to delay their flight south (Catholic laity and clergy are being warned by the Panther not to become overconfident or aggressive under James's reign else they will meet a sad end). The Panther begins her tale this way:

> The Swallow, privileged above the rest
> Of all the birds, as man's familiar guest,
> Pursues the sun in summer brisk and bold,
> But wisely shuns the persecuting cold;
> Is well to chancels and to chimneys known,
> Though 'tis not thought she feeds on smoke alone.
> From hence she has been held of heavenly line,
> Endued with particles of soul divine.
> This merry chorister had long possessed
> Her summer seat, and feathered well her nest:
> Till frowning skies began to change their cheer,
> And time turned up the wrong side of the year;
> The shedding trees began the ground to strow
> With yellow leaves, and bitter blasts to blow.
> Sad auguries of winter thence she drew,
> Which by instinct, or prophecy, she knew:
> When prudence warned her to remove betimes
> And seek a better heaven, and warmer climes.

Eliot in his essay contrasts Dryden's verse with Swinburne's, finding that the two bear an antithetical resemblance to one another:

> Swinburne was also a master of words, but Swinburne's words are all suggestion and no denotation; if they suggest nothing, it is because they suggest too much. Dryden's words, on the other hand, are precise, they state immensely, but their suggestiveness is often nothing.

The precision of Dryden's words can be seen, in the passage just quoted, by how subtly and firmly it avoids staying in the same key—as any stanza of Swinburne relentlessly does—but registers different kinds of denoting. There are the verbs, given added strength when they initiate a line, as in "Pursues the sun" or "Endued with particles"; there is the neat double-edge—referring both to the weather and the political climate—of "persecuting cold"; there is the combination of the informal with the poetic—compare the offhand humor of "And time turned up the wrong side of the year" with "Sad auguries of winter thence she drew." It may be too much to claim about these few lines that they "state immensely," but the way they state is powerful and assured.

The other sequence occurs near the end of the fable, as the swallows, lulled into false security by Martin, a bold, ambitious bird representing the Catholic party at James's court, encounter inclement weather that brings disaster. The friendly sun is eclipsed by the moon, to the swallows' disconcertion:

> The crowd, amazed, pursued no certain mark,
> But birds met birds, and jostled in the dark;
> Few mind the public in a panic fright,
> And fear increased the horror of the night.
> Night came, but unattended with repose,
> Alone she came, no sleep their eyes to close,
> Alone and black she came, no friendly stars arose.
>
> What should they do, beset with dangers round,
> No neighbouring dorp, no lodging to be found,
> But bleaky plains, and bare unhospitable ground?
> The latter brood, who just began to fly,
> Sick-feathered, and unpractised in the sky,
> For succour to their helpless mother call;
> She spread her wings, some few beneath 'em crawl,
> She spread 'em wider yet, but could not cover all.
> T' augment their woes, the winds began to move
> Debate in air for empty fields above,
> Till Boreas got the skies, and poured amain

His rattling hailstones mixed with snow and rain.

The joyless morning late arose, and found
A dreadful desolation reign around,
Some buried in the snow, some frozen to the ground:
The rest were struggling still with death, and lay
The Crows' and Ravens' rights, an undefended prey.

The horror of the night, magnified by the allusion to *Aeneid* IV, strikingly pervades the whole scene. It's doubtful, in the face of such a relentlessly vivid creation, that we remember this is the Panther speaking, with malice in her method; rather we admire the resourceful verse, studded with triplets and alexandrines, that hammers things home. This is as close to a poetry of pure *action*, suggesting nothing but stating immensely (to recur to Eliot's words), as can be found in all of Dryden, and it is a pity so few readers, if they begin *The Hind and the Panther* at all, are likely to reach this section of the third book.

3.

All, all of a piece throughout.

Dryden, "The Secular Masque"

One of Dryden's recent critics, Greg Clingham, on the evidence of Johnson's life, notes that Johnson thought Dryden a great poet especially in his translations, an attitude prevalent in the eighteenth and early nineteenth century among such poets and critics as Congreve, Dennis, Pope, Joseph Warton, Churchill, Scott, Wordsworth, and Keats. Dryden's major work after the "Glorious" revolution of 1688 consisted of translations, most notably that of the *Aeneid* and the volume of *Fables, Ancient and Modern* published the year of his death. These, along with such poems as the epistles to Congreve, to Sir Godfrey Kneller, to the Duchess of Ormond, and to his cousin John Driden (the latter two both included in *Fables*) are works, Clingham points out, "directly concerned with historicity, the translatability of the past, and political authority in a world in which the individual is open to forces more powerful than the self."[7] We may add that Dryden's concern for these large issues is compelling and attractive in a manner quite other than is to be found in his previous work, whether celebratory and panegyrical (*Astraea Redux, Annus Mirabilis*) or satiric (*Mac Flecknoe, Absalom and Achitophel*) or discursive (*Religio Laici, The Hind and the Panther*). The new manner is predominately retrospective, elegiac, self-deprecating, sometimes self-exculpating—one appropriate to a writer entering his seventh decade and, with the accession of William putting an end to the Stuart reign, a writer who has lost his positions as Poet Laureate and Royal Historiographer.

This manner can be felt in Dryden's prose, as in the sentence Arnold quoted from the postscript to the *Aeneid* about the adverse conditions under which the poet wrote ("struggling with wants, oppressed with sickness, curbed in my genius"). As a single illustration of Dryden's prose excellence, I would select the passage from his preface to *Fables,* in which humorous detachment and passion movingly combine. He hopes the mixture of translations (Chaucer, Boccaccio, Ovid, Homer) and original poems of his own will not be condemned by his readers:

> But if they should, I have the excuse of an old gentleman who, mounting on horseback before some ladies, when I was present, got up somewhat heavily, but desired of the fair spectators that they would count fourscore and eight before they judged him. By the mercy of God, I am already come within twenty years of his number; a cripple in my limbs, but what decays are in my mind the reader must determine. I think myself as vigorous as ever in the faculties of my soul, excepting only my memory, which is not impaired to any great degree; and if I lose not more of it, I have no great reason to complain. What judgment I had, increases rather than diminishes; and thoughts, such as they are, come crowding so fast upon me that my only difficulty is to choose or to reject, to run them into verse or to give them the other harmony of prose.

The volume appeared some weeks before he died, but no passage from it is more redolent of life.

The elegiac mode was of course congenial to Dryden from the beginning of his career, with "On the Death of Lord Hastings" and the *Heroic Stanzas* on Cromwell. It reached greatness in the poem memorializing

Oldham, and if there is anything to be said against that poem ("From the perfection of such an elegy we cannot detract," wrote Eliot), it might be that the classicizing, beautiful as it is, wears itself somewhat self-consciously:

> Once more, hail and farewell; farewell thou young,
> But ah too short, Marcellus of our tongue;
> Thy brows with ivy, and with laurels bound;
> But fate and gloomy night encompass thee around.

This is done very much after the high Roman fashion, with Catullus and Virgil strongly on display. Two years later, in the Pindaric ode "To the Memory of Anne Killigrew," the concluding stanza pulls out all the stops by wielding triumphant echoes of the famous words from 1 Corinthians about the last judgment when the trumpet shall sound and the dead be raised incorruptible:

> When in mid air the golden trump shall sound
>   To raise the nations under ground;
> When in the valley of Jehosaphat
> The judging God shall close the book of fate,
>   And there the last assizes keep
>   For those who wake and those who sleep[.]

The tone is pure exultation and fervor; as with the Oldham elegy there is no room for less exalted contemplation.

But as seen in the prose passage above quoted from *Fables*, wit and seriousness may go hand in hand (their co-presence is felt in the fable of the swallows from *The Hind and the Panther*), and they do so effectively in a number of instances from Dryden's last decade. When he returned to the stage after an absence of some years with *Don Sebastian* (1689), he informed readers in his preface that "the English will not bear a thorough tragedy; but are pleased that it should be lightened with under-parts of mirth." George Watson glosses "thorough tragedy" as a play that observes the three unities; but it may also suggest that Dryden is less interested in providing simple "admiration," as with the heroic poem, than in cultivating a more mixed mode of response. Since, as he remarked famously in *An*

Essay of Dramatic Poesy, Shakespeare had the most "comprehensive soul" of all writers, a way of achieving comprehensiveness and inclusiveness would be, like Shakespeare, to write tragicomedy—to include "under-parts of mirth" in the tragedy.

The poem of Dryden's where comprehensive soul is most fully and beautifully achieved is one for which my fondness and admiration has grown to the extent that I may claim too much on its behalf for Dryden generally. No matter, since it is such a shining example of human nature, of the mellowing years producing their autumnal harvest. "To My Dear Friend Mr. Congreve" has been used by Walter Jackson Bate to illustrate what he calls "the burden of the past," felt as Dryden looks back early in the poem to "the giant race before the flood," those dramatists from the early seventeenth century who produced the strong but rude poetry that the Restoration wits, himself included, both refined and diluted: "Our age was cultivated thus at length, / But what we gained in skill we lost in strength." We are invited to believe that the coming of Congreve, whose second play *The Double Dealer* was about to be produced, meant the rectifying of any loss and the flowering of a new poetic age:

> In him all beauties of this age we see:
> Etherege's courtship, Southerne's purity,
> The satire, wit, and strength of manly Wycherley.

One can as I do admire Congreve's work, especially his yet to be written *The Way of the World* published the year Dryden died, yet feel that Dryden is laying it on pretty thick here—that Congreve's slender shoulders can hardly bear the weight of ideal significance placed on them by the poet who imagines him as the true descendant and inheritor of his own (Dryden's) genius.

Absorbing as is the literary-historical scenario of the poem's first half, it grows into something even deeper and more affecting. Dryden wishes his own "laurel" had descended to Congreve instead of to the Shadwell he had mocked in *Mac Flecknoe*. He attempts the long, futuristic view:

> Yet this I prophesy: thou shalt be seen
> (Though with some short parenthesis between)

High on the throne of wit; and seated there
Not mine (that's little) but thy laurel wear.
The first attempt an early promise made;
That early promise this has more than paid.
So bold, yet so judiciously you dare,
That your least praise is to be regular.
Time, place, and action may with pains be wrought,
But genius must be born, and never can be taught.
This is your portion, this your native store;
Heav'n that but once was prodigal before,
To Shakespeare gave as much; she could not give him more.

Here is the consummation of the familiar style as practiced by Dryden, and Ben Jonson's presence is so much felt in it that Eliot's calling Dryden "a poetic practitioner who had learned from Jonson" seems if anything an understatement. The passage evokes Jonson the epistolary and elegiac poet generally, but especially the tone and passion of his great poem to Shakespeare. Near that poem's end, Jonson emphasises the importance of both nature and art, native genius and hard work, in producing a poet worthy of the laurel:

For a good poet's made as well as born;
And such wert thou. Look how the father's face
Lives in his issue: even so, the race
Of Shakespeare's mind and manner brightly shines
In his well-turnèd and true-filèd lines.

Dryden's own well-turned and true-filed lines quoted above are less the mark of "genius" than of the artful adapation of a speaking voice so as to produce maximum nuance and implication. One notes the two parenthetical insertions: one of them acting out the very "short parenthesis" it predicts Congreve will surmount; both of them enriching the tone and flexibility of speech. That tone grows warmer, more insistent, in the triplet concluding with Shakespeare: its repeated urgings ("This is your portion, this your native store") are followed by the satisfying stress on the next line's first word—Heav'n that but once was prodigal before"—then an enacting of that prodigality with the alexandrine completing the triplet by way of demonstrating Shakespeare's (and Congreve's) amplitude:

> This is your portion, this your native store;
> Heav'n that but once was prodigal before,
> To Shakespeare gave as much; she could not give him more.

Dryden's magnanimity comes through here, and if magnanimity is too strong a word for the impulse that fills the poem (is "urbanity" a better one?), it may still be distinguished from the comparative lack of such quality in Dryden's great successor. Pope's "Epistle to Dr. Arbuthnot" is admittedly a very different poem from the one to Congreve but—and at much greater length—it performs the retrospective taking stock of a career, a clearing of the decks with respect to friends and enemies that bears some similarity to Dryden's. The most memorable things in "Arbuthnot" are the devastating, in their different ways, portraits of Atticus and Sporus, along with the poem's brilliant opening, with its creation of the beleaguered poet harassed by bad writers and bores of all sorts. But when Pope, responding to the admittedly nasty attacks on him, turns to self-justification, a note of advertised self-righteousness—sometimes to the point of shrillness—is heard:

> Not Fortune's Worshipper, nor Fashion's Fool,
> Not Lucre's Madman, nor Ambition's Tool,
> Not proud, not servile, be one Poet's praise
> That, if he pleas'd he pleas'd by manly ways;
> That Flatt'ry, ev'n to Kings, he held a shame,
> And thought a Lye in Verse or Prose the same:
> That not in Fancy's Maze he wander'd long,
> But stoop'd to Truth, and moraliz'd his song.

Near the end of the poem Pope rises to impassioned defenses of his dead father and soon to die mother: one couplet addresses James Moore Smyth, an enemy, as follows:

> That Harmless Mother thought no Wife a Whore,—
> Hear this! and spare his Family, *James More!*

Clearly the Arbuthnot epistle doesn't worry about decorum.

By contrast, the poem to Congreve ends with a relatively quiet series of declarations behind which one feels a great deal stirring:

> Maintain your post; that's all the fame you need,
> For 'tis impossible you should proceed.
> Already I am worn with cares and age,
> And just abandoning th'ungrateful stage:
> Unprofitably kept at heaven's expense,
> I live a rent-charge on his providence:
> But you, whom every Muse and Grace adorn,
> Whom I foresee to better fortune born,
> Be kind to my remains; and O defend,
> Against your judgement, your departed friend!
> Let not th'insulting foe my fame pursue,
> But shade those laurels which descend to you;
> And take for tribute what these lines express:
> You merit more; nor could my love do less.

It's useful to think again of Jonson in his farewell "Ode to Himself" ("Come, leave the loathèd stage/And the more loathsome age"), also of the dying Hamlet's request to Horatio that he absent himself from felicity awhile in order to tell the world Hamlet's story. But really the sequence of lines is so complete, its assured breadth of statement so final, that we are moved simply to take them in, registering the moment rather than criticizing it. In *Practical Criticism* I. A. Richards remarks about one of the poems he gave out to his students for comment—Donne's sonnet "At the Round Earth's Imagined Corners"—that "It is in the nature of some performances that they leave the spectator feeling rather helpless." By comparison with Donne's evocation of the last judgment and his supplication to the Lord, Dryden's conclusion seems to be hardly a performance at all. Yet there may be a similarity felt in the spectator-reader's sense that there is no more to say.

To treat the end of the Congreve poem as Dryden's final note to his career as poet, playwright, and man of letters is a premature attempt at closure, since he would go on to write the poem to Kneller, the lovely ode on the death of Henry Purcell, "Alexander's Feast" (which Dryden thought his best work), the translations of Virgil, the *Fables*, and the century-ending "Secular Masque" ("'Tis well an old age is out/And time to begin a new"). In particular, the achievement of the *Fables* is such as to demand book-length treatment.[8] This essay will be content rather with quoting some sentences from a letter Dryden wrote two years before he died, one of the small collection of seventy-seven letters a twentieth-century editor put together decades ago. The most attractive ones are from near the end of his life when he addressed his twenty-six-year-old married cousin, Martha Steward, in a manner combining gallantry, flirtation, and humor. Gout-ridden—elsewhere he refers to himself as "an old cripple"—Dryden says he and his son, also indisposed, are going to try the waters at Bath:

> In the meantime, betwixt my intervalls of physique and other remedies which I am useing for my gravell, I am still drudging on: always a Poet, and never a good one. I pass my time sometimes with Ovid, and sometimes with our old English poet, Chaucer; translating such stories as best please my fancy; and intend besides them to add something of my own: so that it is not impossible, but ere the summer be pass'd, I may come down to you with a volume in my hand, like a dog out of the water, with a duck in his mouth. As for the rarities you promise, if beggars might be choosers, a part of a chine of honest bacon wou'd please my appetite more than all the marrow puddings; for I like them better plain, having a very vulgar stomach.—

"Dryden was not one of the *gentle bosoms*," said Dr. Johnson, memorably. Fifty years' worth of ungentle drudging without flagging produced a body of work full of surprises and discoveries for a twenty-first-century reader determined to seek them out.

NOTES

1. *The Letters of Kingsley Amis*, ed. Zachary Leader (London: HarperCollins, 2000), 96.
2. C. S. Lewis, "Shelley, Dryden, and Mr. Eliot," in *Rehabilitations* (London: Oxford University Press, 1939), 1–34. It's of some interest that Lewis's characterization of

boorishness and provinciality would for some eyes (John Betjeman's, for example) apply to rough-hewn "Jack" Lewis himself. Dryden's detractors make for some strange bedfellows. Ezra Pound's contribution to the critical "debate" was to aver that he "of all men, don't want Johnnie Dryden dug up again," and that Eliot's endeavors in the writer's behalf only strengthened his resolve "Never, never again, to open either John Dryden, his works or any comment upon them." Rather than calling him, as Lewis did, a "boor," Pound settled for "a lunk-head." (*Literary Essays of Ezra Pound*, ed. T. S. Eliot [London: Faber and Faber, 1954], 70).

3. Barbara Everett, "Unwritten Masterpiece," *London Review of Books*, 4 January 2001.

4. *The Poems of John Dryden*, ed. Paul Hammond: vol. 1, 1649–1681; vol. 2, 1682–1685 (London: Longman, 1995). *The Poems of John Dryden*, ed. Paul Hammond and David Hopkins, vol. 3, 1686–1693; vol. 4, 1693–1696 (London: Longman, 2004). *The Cambridge Companion to John Dryden*, ed. Steven N. Zwicker, 300 pp. (Cambridge: Cambridge University Press, 2004). All quotations from Dryden's poetry are from the Longman edition. Quotations from his prose are from *Of Dramatic Poesy and Other Critical Essays*, ed. George Watson, 2 vols. (London: Everyman's Library, 1962).

5. Michael McKeon, *Politics and Poetry in Restoration England* (Cambridge, MA: Harvard University Press, 1975), 53.

6. But for a recent eye-opening treatment of how "thought" goes on in poetry, see Helen Vendler's *Poets Thinking* (Cambridge, MA: Harvard University Press, 2004). Her first chapter is about the *Essay on Man*.

7. Greg Clingham, "Another and the Same: Johnson's Dryden," in *Literary Transmission and Authority: Dryden and Other Writers*, ed. Earl Miner and Jennifer Brady (Cambridge: Cambridge University Press, 1993), 121–59. See also Eric Griffiths's fine essay on Dryden and his predecessors, "Dryden's Past," *Proceedings of the British Academy* (1994): 113–49.

8. It has received it in Cedric D. Reverand's *Dryden's Final Poetic Mode: The Fables* (Philadelphia: University of Pennsylvania Press, 1988).

Milton according to Fish

F. R. Leavis once declared that the Sitwells belonged to the history of publicity rather than of poetry; there is some danger that the literary critic and theorist Stanley Fish may be suffering a similar fate. The publicity materials accompanying his book on Milton[1] from Harvard University Press include recent news items about Fish's life as Dean of the College of Liberal Arts and Sciences at University of Illinois, Chicago. Add to that a profile in the June 11 *New Yorker* subtitled "The enfant terrible of English lit grows up" and beginning with a cutely irreverent paragraph informing us that Professor Fish is, among other things, a loudmouth, a show-off, and a surpassingly delightful human being. How can any mere critic and theorist live up to this image?

Of course he brought it on himself and has been not undesigning in a career of provocations. Think of some of the essay and book titles he has thrown in our faces: "What Is Stylistics and Why Are They Saying Such Terrible Things About It?"; "Doing What Comes Naturally"; "Is There a Text in This Class?"; "There's No Such Thing as Free Speech, and It's a Good Thing, Too"; most notoriously, since everyone seems to have heard about it even if not read it, "The Unbearable Ugliness of Volvos." When you remember that his first book was modestly and accurately titled *John Skelton's Poetry* (1965) you realize what a long way Fish has come in the playing stakes for academic celebrity. The titles are the equivalent of his Jaguar sports car, announcing that—whatever I am, whatever you call me—I'm not *boring*. And indeed he is the only academic I know of who has committed himself in print (from the "Volvos" essay) to the proposition that *"Academics like to eat shit, and in a pinch they don't care whose shit they eat."* The observation, uttered one hundred years or so after Matthew

First published in *New England Review* (Fall 2001): 177–85 (as "Fish Contemplating a Bust of Milton")

Arnold, suggests how far men of letters have come in cultivating the informal style.

Although over the past two decades Fish has published essays of literary criticism—mostly on Milton, a number of which make up the body of *How Milton Works*—he hasn't published a book of such criticism since *The Living Temple* (1978), a study of George Herbert's poetry. Instead there have appeared four thick collections of essays dealing with matters of interpretive activity, with theory as observed in literary and legal studies, with politics, with the First Amendment and other matters. His rationale for professing literature is to be found in "Why Literary Criticism Is Like Virtue," one of the elegant lectures that make up his short book *Professional Correctness* (1995). Having made his influential mark as a literary interpreter of Milton's *Paradise Lost* (*Surprised by Sin*, 1967), and of various seventeenth-century writers (*Self-Consuming Artifacts*, 1972), he may have decided that his "interventions" could be more effectively carried out by arguing with this or that theoretical or practical fallacy—as if merely writing about the experience of reading George Herbert were relatively tame stuff.

The new book is long (600 pages), weighty, and unremitting in its pursuing and capturing of Milton's method and meanings in, mainly, the *Nativity Ode, Comus, Lycidas, Paradise Lost, Paradise Regained, Samson Agonistes,* and in a number of the prose tracts, especially "An Apology against a Pamphlet," "Of Prelatical Episcopacy," and "Aeropagitica." References to scores of Milton's critics show that Fish has read everything written about every aspect of the poet's production, and his agreements and dissents are scrupulously set down. Part of the book's weightiness comes from testimony on the back jacket that is of a piece with the other swollen Harvard publicity: no less than six prestigious contemporaries vie with one another in making the largest claims about its importance: "a dazzling, rigorous, and unutterably strange attempt to follow the great seventeenth-century poet" (Stephen Greenblatt); "I cannot think of a more impressive work of literary interpretation published in the past forty or so years" (Frank Lentricchia); "The indispensable book on Milton for all succeeding generations" (Victoria Kahn). We know about the nature of blurbs; still, these seem particularly all-stops-out.

As I write, *How Milton Works* has been subjected to salient critiques by four respected names: Frank Kermode, Helen Vendler, A. D. Nuttall, and John Carey. (We won't count the anonymous one in *Publishers Weekly* advising, improbably, that interested readers "stash this volume in their beach bag.") Kermode in the *New York Times Book Review* called it a "very distinguished book" that "should restore Milton to the center of critical interest" (but has he ever left it?), although he thinks Fish's understandings of *Paradise Regained* and *Samson* are deficient.[2] What Kermode calls Fish's "forensic" mode may be characterized as follows: he devotes himself repeatedly to establishing Milton as a single-minded presenter, both in prose and verse, of a world in which human beings are free to acknowledge and embrace the truth of God's absolute command. Having embraced this truth, they then see the world through a single perspective—from the inside out, as it were. Alternatively and since they are free to explore, they may become empiricists, may try out ideas and stories and make their choices on the basis of what they see or taste or reason—in other words they are free to fall, since they have started from the outside and only gotten "in" to confusion, anarchy, and sin. They are celebrators of the devil's party, whether they know it or not.

Helen Vendler in the *New Republic* finds it all monotonously single-minded (she says the book should be titled *Milton's One Idea*) and is also appalled by its neglect of Milton's poetry—of the aesthetic motive in his work. Kermode noted in passing that Fish doesn't seem interested in the "sensuous, expansive side of Milton," and Vendler expands on this in a more severe manner, citing instances where Fish's summary or paraphrase of Milton's lines coarsens, indeed cancels out their effect.[3] Vendler's example is the beginning of *Lycidas:*

> Yet once more, O ye laurels, and once more
> Ye myrtles brown, with ivy never sere,
> I come to pluck your berries, harsh and crude,
> And with forced fingers rude,
> Shatter your leaves before the mellowing year.

Fish "translates" this into the following language:

I'm "crude," I'm "rude," I'm speaking before my turn and without regard for your timetable, I'm shattering your leaves before the mellowing years—but the apology is also a boast: I *can* be crude, I *can* be distinctively unpolished, I *can* be out of sync with your rules and conventions . . . It's payback time; you've disturbed my season—I'm going to disturb yours. So there!

Vendler says such writing demonstrates that Fish "does not care much for the poetry of Milton's poetry." One takes her point; yet it is of interest that this "paraphrase" occurs, not in Fish's essay of twenty years ago (*"Lycidas:* A Poem Anonymous") that forms chapter 7 of the current book, but rather in the long opening chapter, "How Milton Works," which Fish wrote only recently. This suggests that he has felt it necessary to up the ante, to be more "outrageous" in challenges to and guyings of his audience, to disturb and annoy readers like Vendler who care about Milton's poetry in more aesthetic ways than Fish does. His business, rather, is with arguments, with Milton as the constructor of the argument of *Lycidas.* Fish was quoted in the *Chicago Tribune* as remarking, apropos of the oppressiveness of old-fashioned academic culture, "I despise certain forms of aestheticism. . . . There's a tendency for some people in the academy to be infatuated with the fineness of their sensibilities—to regard themselves and their friends as paragons of taste." No reason to hold him too closely to these words, but they help explain why a natural predisposition to arguing—something he is very good at—has been bolstered by a prejudice against the aesthetic.

When *Surprised by Sin* was reprinted a few years back, Fish wrote a long preface that began by saying what, in his own judgment and that of other Milton scholars, the book had accomplished.[4] Previous to its appearance, Fish said, criticism of *Paradise Lost* had been divided into two warring, irreconcilable (so it seemed) camps. The Christian, orthodox reading (C. S. Lewis, Douglas Bush) saw the poem as holding that disobedience to God brought misery, while obedience led to the righteous life, to salvation; the dissidents (Blake, Shelley, A. J. Waldock, William Empson) in one way or another made Milton of the devil's party insofar as the living parts of the poem were Satan's and later the fallen Adam and Eve's, while the dead parts were the pronouncements of God and his Son. Fish sees himself as having healed this split and reconciled the camps by proposing that *Paradise Lost* "is a poem about how its readers came to be the way they are." By shifting attention from "the words on the page to the experience they provided"—by focusing on the reader's response—we see that the poem's method

> is to provoke in its readers wayward, fallen responses which are then corrected by one of several authoritative voices (the narrator, God, Raphael, Michael, the Son). In this way . . . the reader is brought to a better understanding of his sinful nature and is encouraged to participate in his own reformation.

He then quotes the Miltonist William Kerrigan, who said that the book was influential in that it permitted the "pious reader" to "entertain potentially rebellious attitudes knowing that, as a sign of his fallenness, these attitudes already *confirm* the doctrinal argument of the poem and therefore have a piety all their own."

What puzzles me about Fish's account when I attempt to square it with my own reading of *Paradise Lost* are the assumptions it makes about "the reader," this figure who, presumably, is "brought to a better understanding of his sinful nature" and "encouraged to participate in his own reformation." Am I, should I try to become, this reader? Did he exist back in 1667, one of a "fit audience though few"? Did I, previous to being enlightened by Fish's book, belong to either the Christianizing or the Devil's party, thus acting out my own small part in The Milton Controversy? M. L. Abrams once wrote, speaking of the kind of word-by-word, line-by-line reading Fish advocated in *Self-Consuming Artifacts*, that with the best will in the world and no matter how hard he tried, he failed to become the sort of reader Fish was advocating.

I don't think my difficulty with Fish's way of reading *Paradise Lost* is attributable to the fact that (or *merely* that) I'm not a professional Miltonist or seventeenth-century scholar, and thus can't properly be trusted as knowing where I stand in the professorial Milton debate. I first read Milton as a college senior and over the past twenty-five years have regularly "taught" him (*Comus, Lycidas, Paradise Lost*) for three weeks in my semester course in major English writers. I find the challenge, excitements, and rewards of reading and teaching *Paradise Lost* as strong as those I've experienced with any writer, perhaps stronger. But those challenges and excitements are much too various and particular to be generalized or classified in the terms provided by a book like *Surprised by Sin.* Nor did that book permit me, for the first time, to "reconcile" my strong responses to the fallen poetry of Satan, our grandparents, and sometimes the blind bard himself, with the judgmental, corrective, authoritative voice of the Christian epic poet. Having never written a book nor an essay on John Milton, I don't feel the professional scholar's need to make a synthetic argument, to tie things up, to have a "view" of Milton in the large.

Here are some sentences from the new book that taken together provide a sense of what Fish's overall view looks like:

> Milton criticism sometimes offers us the choice between an absolutist poet with a focused vision and a single overriding message and a more tentative, provisional poet alert to the ambiguities and dilemmas of the moral life. The truth is that Milton is both, and is so without either contradiction or tension. (7)

> As I describe them, Milton's tracts and poems are always engaged in an act of containment. Centrifugal forces—named, variously, Satan, Comus, Chaos, Chance, the Prelates, the Confuter, Belial, Mammon, Moloch, Beelzebub, Sin, Death, Dalila, Adam, Eve, and, sometimes, Milton—are struggling to get out, to set up their own shop, to nominate their own values, to establish their own empire, to write their own literature, to draft their own laws, to go their own way, to have their own circuitous paths; and always they are reined in. (7)

> Much of the drama of Milton's poetry consists of confrontations between these two ways of being in the world . . . one that regards every situation as a space of new possibilities and new meanings, the other that regards every situation as a space to be filled with certainties already known and inscribed with the single meaning everything always displays. (44)

> The entire poem [*Paradise Lost*] on every level—stylistic, thematic, narrative—is an act of vigilance in which any effort, large or small,

to escape its totalizing sway is detected and then contained. Every
movement outward from a still center must be blocked; every ve-
hicle of that movement must be identified for what it is and then
stigmatized as a form of idolatry. (492)

These quotations should demonstrate, first of all, the vigor of Fish's
prose, a vigor that—as in many of his essays—carries us along not so
much through head-nodding assent to his "points" as by the crisp, un-
shakable confidence of the sentences that make them. Taken together,
and with many others added, they do not seem to me, for all their steady
driving-in of an overriding way of reading Milton, to deprive and denude
the writings of their magnificent energy, their human passion. Quite the
opposite, since there is ample room, within these principles, for the active,
individual reader (as I try to be) to discover and rediscover Milton's
consummate art. Yet A. D. Nuttall in the *London Review of Books* (June
21, 2001) finds that Fish's book is based on a misreading of Milton;
that such a "monochrome" or "exclusionist" reading of the poet deprives
his poetry of nothing less than the "this-worldy matter" that, for Nut-
tall, makes it rich. Nuttall thinks that Fish treats all the wanderings of
those who are members of the devil's party as thoroughly unreal, and
only "there" in the poems and pamphlets to set off, by contrast, the
absolute truth of God's will. So one specialist in the field accuses another
specialist in the same field of whole-scale misreading. How could such a
blindness occur, in relation to Milton or to any poet? If, as Nuttall claims,
Fish's Milton is indeed "monist, authoritarian, obscurantist, a completely
closed mind," then such an account might justly be called, as Nuttall calls
it, "absurd."[5]

But is that in fact the case? Realizing the danger of arguing from the
evidence of a particular passage to a view of the whole, I would direct
Nuttall to a paragraph exactly halfway through *How Milton Works*, from
a chapter on *Paradise Lost* ("With Mortal Voice: Milton Defends against
the Muse"). There Fish directs his attention to the epic narrator at the
opening of book VII when that narrator returns from the war in heaven
to "narrower bound / Within the visible Diurnal Sphere; / Standing on Earth,
not rapt above the Pole." Addressed to the heavenly muse, Urania, Milton
implores that Urania not "fail" him, even as he prepares to narrate the

poem's second half, which will centrally concern the fall—the failure—
of Adam and Eve. He prays for her continued protection ("More safe I
sing with mortal voice") yet also acknowledges the dire possibility that
he may fall "on th'Aleian Field . . . /Erroneous there to wander and
forlorn." Fish argues at the end of his chapter that this acknowledgment
of mortality has everything to do with Milton's awareness that "a mortal
voice . . . is a voice that can have a *career*," and that to have a career is to be
distinct from, however given over to, God or Urania—or from the angel
Abdiel, who even among angels is distinguished for the unquestioning ac-
ceptance with which he "gladly" obeys God's orders and decrees. Fish says
that "being Abdiel is being just one thing"—as Christ declares himself
to be, and "what Milton sometimes claims to be" when he announces (in
"An Apology against a Pamphlet"), "I conceav'd my selfe to be now not
as mine own person." Fish ends his account with this shrewd, and I should
say ultimately just, appraisal of Milton the poet:

> But even here [referring to "I conceav'd my selfe to be now not as
> mine own person"] the language betrays him: he *conceives* himself
> to have a corporate identity, but the act of conceiving, of thinking
> about himself in that way, is performed at a distance from what it
> contemplates; and so he fails of his claim and of his goal. But is
> it his goal? Does not a part of him want to fail, want to fall and
> wander erroneous and desolate on the plain, so that he can make
> his way, make his mark, make his career, speak with a mortal
> voice, a voice that sounds only because it is far from home, from
> *patria*, in exile, but a voice that sounds a note the exile loves as he
> loves himself?

Just so, and it suggests to me why *Paradise Lost*, along with *Lycidas*, is the
height of Milton's achievement.

My problem with *How Milton Works* is not that (*pace* Nuttall) it gets
Milton wrong, but that it doesn't get him right enough, since it is in-
sufficiently attentive to and caring of (in Vendler's words) "the poetry
of Milton's poetry." At this conclusion of his two chapters on *Comus*,
for example, Fish tells us that Milton "works out the implications of his
Christian Neo-Platonism with a precision and rigor that extends to the

smallest detail of the verse." Yet the forty-seven pages he has just devoted to the poem almost programmatically avoid describing such detail. From reading Fish you would never know that the marvelously varying tempo of *Comus* includes blank verse, octosyllabic couplets, and elaborately rhymed songs. In another chapter he admits it is disconcerting and frustrating to read *Paradise Regained* because we want the Son to *do* something, at least explain himself more fully. But, Fish tells us, this is all anticipated by Milton, whose poem is about how the Son, wholly subordinate to his Father's will, provides a critique of dramatic self-expression. The trouble with this way of justifying the Son's language is that it takes no account of the aesthetic objections, raised by Christopher Ricks four decades ago, to the unsatis-fying "over-emphatic" repetition found in those speeches.[6]

Such disregard of what for want of a better word I call "aesthetic" questions can also be seen in what Fish *doesn't* say about, doesn't attempt to explore in some of what, by common consent, are the greatest mo-ments in Milton's poetry. I adduce just two, the first from *Paradise Lost IX*, when Adam, learning that Eve has eaten of the tree, exclaims "How art thou lost, how on a sudden lost,/Defaced, deflowered, and now to death devote?"—then resolves to throw in his lot with hers:

> How can I live without thee, how forgo
> Thy sweet converse and love so dearly joined,
> To live again in these wild woods forlorn?
> Should God create another Eve, and I
> Another rib afford, yet loss of thee
> Would never from my heart; no no, I feel
> The link of nature draw me: flesh of flesh,
> Bone of my bone thou art, and from thy state
> Mine never shall be parted, bliss or woe.

It takes a very resistant reader indeed to remain detached from the quality of feeling expressed in these lines ("Love," A. J. Waldock called it), but in *Surprised by Sin* Fish remained resolutely armored and protected from falling for or with them. He finds all the reasons Adam gives for doing what he does, "equally specious" and "irrelevant": "The question 'How can I live without thee?' is answered by Adam himself. He can live without her as he has before ('to live *again*'). As a serious query this cry has no more force than Eve's obviously rhetorical address in book XI, to her flowers: 'from thee, how shall I part?'" Fish's words for Adam's whole speech are stern ones: "willful self-deception." In *How Milton Works* he makes no direct comment on the moment, presumably understanding it as just one of many illustrations of the "vain contest" Milton sees their fallen minds engaged in at the end of book IX.

My second instance is from the great sequence in *Lycidas* just preceding the triumphant instruction to the shepherds to "Weep no more" over the death of Lycidas, now risen to heavenly heights. The speaker has been summoning up "every flower that sad embroidery wears," directing them to "strew the laureat hearse where Lycid lies." He then, looking at what he has just done, calls it "false surmise" and turns his attention another way:

> Ay me! Whilst thee the shores, and sounding seas
> Wash far away, where'er thy bones are hurled,
> Whether beyond the stormy Hebrides
> Where thou perhaps under the whelming tide
> Vist'st the bottom of the monstrous world;
> Or whether thou to our moist vows denied,
> Sleep'st by the fable of Bellerus old,
> Where the great vision of the guarded mount
> Looks toward Namancos and Bayona's hold;
> Look homeward angel now, and melt with ruth.
> And, Oh ye dolphins, waft the hapless youth.

In his first essay on Milton (1936), T. S. Eliot said about these lines that "for the single effect of grandeur of sound, there is nothing finer in poetry." A later critic of the poem, Paul Alpers, in the best essay on *Lycidas* I know, suggests why, for all its grandeur of sound, the lines are something more.[7]

> The entire mode of this passage is one of imagination and surmise. Even its grammar is suspended—the uncertain scope and connection of "whilst" initiating what is the real "flow" of the passage, its speculative identifications. The intricate syntax and the delicate solicitude of a word like "perhaps" do not represent a mind assaulted or horror-stricken, and if being "unillusioned" is at issue,

the most poignant detail of the passage—imagining that Lycidas *visits* the bottom of the monstrous world—is as deeply illusioned as anything in the poem. These lines prove what the flower passage seemed to disprove—the adequacy of poetic imagination.

Alpers is concerned to describe the richness of what Milton does for Lycidas here; by contrast, Fish in his two sections on the poem in *How Milton Works* argues that there's no connection between the voice that speaks these lines and the (new) voice that says "Weep no more, woeful shepherds, weep no more." All he finds in the passage quoted above is a "current of despair conveyed verbally by a concatenation of words beginning with w"; and he finds it "evidence of a vision that is superior even if it is (realistically) dark." Alpers's essay appeared twenty years ago and contained an extended critical disagreement with Fish's reading of the poem; Fish has not deemed it necessary to respond in the new book.

But the more important failing is Fish's refusal—as with the "How can I leave thee" speech of Adam—to make anything of, to *do* anything with the poetry of Milton's poetry. Owning, as he surely does, an original mind, an ability to do things with words, and a lifelong devotion to Milton's work, I can't believe that he could fail to say interesting things (in his own words on *Comus*) about the smallest detail of Milton's verse. Perhaps it's that those fears he expressed in the interview of sounding like English teachers who prided themselves on "fineness of sensibility" are still around to inhibit him. Yet surely it takes a very fine sensibility indeed to read Milton well and to show us in the most delicate and precise ways how the poet works. For all Fish's combative liveliness and impressive command of Milton scholarship, he doesn't perform that task.

NOTES

1. Stanley Fish, *How Milton Works* (Cambridge, MA: Harvard University Press, 2001).

2. Kermode's review provoked the Harvard University Press publicity machine into action once more, when Fish's publisher, Lindsay Waters, wrote a plaintive letter to the *New York Times Book Review* claiming that Kermode had missed what was "grandly poetic" in Milton. Waters suggested, improbably, that "Milton no longer makes sense to the English."

3. It's not that Fish's words coarsen especially *Milton's* verse. A recent essay of his on Donne, a poet he says he has never liked, announces his discovery that "Donne is sick and his poetry is sick. . . . Donne is bulimic, someone who gorges himself to a point beyond satiety, and then sticks his finger down his throat and throws up." One imagines possibilities for extending such diagnostic language to other poets (Emily Dickinson? Walt Whitman?). "Masculine Persuasive Force: Donne and Verbal Power" in *Soliciting Interpretation: Literary Theory and Seventeenth-Century English Poetry*, ed. Elizabeth D. Harvey and Katharine Eisaman Maus (Chicago: University of Chicago Press, 1990), 223.

4. *Surprised by Sin: The Reader in* Paradise Lost, 2nd ed. (Cambridge, MA: Harvard University Press, 1998).

5. The English Miltonist John Carey came to the same conclusion as Nuttall (*Sunday Times* [London], June 24, 2001).

6. Christopher Ricks, "Over-Emphasis in *Paradise Regained*," *ELH* 28, no. 4 (1961),: 701–4. Neither this essay nor Ricks's *Milton's Grand Style* is referred to in *How Milton Works*.

7. Paul Alpers, "*Lycidas* and Modern Criticism," *ELH* 49, no. 2 (1982): 468–96. Also in Alpers, *What Is Pastoral?* (Chicago: University of Chicago Press, 1996) but without the section about Fish.

Johnson's *Lives*

W e should begin with the title in full: *The Lives of the Most Eminent English Poets; With Critical Observations on Their Works,* by Samuel Johnson. The author once remarked to Boswell that he was engaged in writing "little Lives, and little Prefaces, to a little edition," an enterprise set in motion by a consortium of London booksellers. The "little edition" was to consist of fifty-two English poets in an anthology designed to fend off competition from a Scottish publisher, John Bell, who had brought out a comparable anthology. Johnson's accompanying "lives" or prefaces—he used both terms to describe his contributions— would be a key attraction in the competition. It took him four years to complete the task, and in 1781 the *Lives* were first published independently of the poems and poets they introduced. Now the remarkable Roger Lonsdale, already a distinguished eighteenth-century scholar, has, as a crowning achievement, edited them for Clarendon Press in a four-volume boxed set for which the cliché "magisterial" scarcely begins to suggest the project's immensity.[1]

Its dimensions deserve to be enumerated. Running to 1,981 pages total, the editor's commentary and textual notes easily outstrip Johnson's own pages, especially in the fourth volume (190 pages of Johnson, 327 of Lonsdale), where the "Life of Pope" is especially heavily annotated. Lonsdale's admirable predecessor as an editor of *Lives of the Poets* was George Birkbeck-Hill, who in 1905 brought out, also under the Clarendon Press imprint, a three-volume edition. The main difference between the earlier and the latest edition is that Birkbeck-Hill—to whom Lonsdale records his debt—placed his footnotes at the bottom of each page with numbers in the text to tell us when we might look down for further illumination. Birkbeck-Hill also placed marginal numerals to mark the beginning of

First published in the *Hudson Review* 60, no. 1 (Spring 2007): 25–35 each of Johnson's new paragraphs, as does Lonsdale. But Lonsdale places his notes at the end of each volume so one is not directed at specific points to consult a note. And though he gives no explanation for this decision, it may be that since he annotates each and every one of Johnson's paragraphs—usually to the teeth—he is inviting us always to turn to the back.

So a reader of *Lives* in its entirety has to decide how much attention to give the always pertinent annotation. Eager to learn more about Milton or Dryden, I'm not so eager about William King or Richard Duke, the latter of whose poems, Johnson wrote, "are not below mediocrity; nor have I found much in them to praise." Duke is dispatched by Johnson in less than a page; Lonsdale, in much smaller print, provides two pages of commentary in his standard format: Composition, Sources, Publication, Modern Sources—and gives notes, as always, to each paragraph of the seven Johnson wrote. The proportion of annotation to text is navigable in such a tiny compass, but becomes not such clear sailing when Abraham Cowley's forty-one pages receive forty-nine of annotation. The "Life of Cowley" was thought by Johnson to be his best, since he was proud of the lengthy set-piece in which he adversely criticizes the Metaphysical Poets (especially Cowley and Donne). But the once-alive Cowley is now dead as a poet. "Who now reads Cowley?" asked Alexander Pope, rhetorically, a half-century after Cowley's death. Who now is impelled to attend to forty pages of commentary on a poet no one reads?

Further indications of the scope of Lonsdale's undertaking: volume one consists of 400 pages, only a quarter of which are made up of the first three lives—Cowley, Denham, and Milton—in Johnson's series. The volume is kicked off by a masterly introduction of 185 pages, which surely rivals (in length) any introduction to any book I'm aware of. It is occupied mainly with the project's origin; with the alternately dilatory and rapid pace at which Johnson composed the essays; with the persons who were his editorial assistants and the main sources he consulted. Lonsdale proceeds "to outline the trajectory of the *Lives* and to trace Johnson's explicit and implicit assumptions and preoccupations." This involves a chronological run-through of the whole list of poets by way of qualifying the received notion that Johnson was unambiguously devoted to celebrating the "elegance" and "correctness" that emerged in the Restoration and reached its apex in the poetry of Pope. Persuasively, Lonsdale finds that Johnson did not simply hold such an assumption; that rather he was

> haunted, first, by a growing suspicion that some older kinds of poetic "vigour" and mental "comprehension" had simultaneously been sacrificed, and, secondly, by an awareness that the civilized poetic qualities he himself valued had unaccountably come to seem insipid and outdated to his younger contemporaries.

It is an interesting coincidence to note that the year 1783, when the final, revised version of *Lives* was published and Johnson's six-year labor ended, is also the year in which William Blake published his first book—his only conventionally produced one—of poems. The last poem in *Poetical Sketches,* "To the Muses," looked sadly at contemporary poets and addressed them reprovingly:

> How have you left the antient love
>   That bards of old enjoy'd in you!
> The languid strings do scarcely move!
>   The sound is forc'd, the notes are few!

Blake was preparing to move the strings to notes not yet heard.

Viewing the list of fifty-two poets from Cowley to Lyttleton, we might ask how, even two and more centuries ago, this could have passed as a reasonable list of the most eminent English poets. The official answer is that no poet who wrote before the Restoration was included (no Donne, no Spenser) nor any poet still alive (no Cowper, no Chatterton). Johnson's friend, Oliver Goldsmith, had died but was omitted for reasons of copyright; the satirist Charles Churchill, praised by Yvor Winters but otherwise unread, was also omitted, either for the same reasons or because, as Mrs. Thrale claimed, Johnson didn't want him in. So essentially these most "eminent" English poets were selected by the booksellers from a span of about a hundred years, and it is hardly surprising that most of them are unknown to serious readers of poetry in 2007. No women are represented, not even Anne Finch, Countess of Winchilsea, or Lady Mary Wortley Montague, scourge in her verse of both Swift and Pope.

(Lonsdale has edited an Oxford edition of eighteenth-century women poets.) One of the longest lives here is also the earliest written, Johnson's sixty-nine-page account of his friend of youthful days, Richard Savage. The "Life of Savage," longer than any of the others except Dryden's and Pope's, has, unsurprisingly, a personal, autobiographical note absent from the other lives—except for the one of William Collins, which contains the lovely sentence "Such was the fate of Collins, with whom I once delighted to converse, and whom I yet remember with tenderness."

Johnson's *Lives*, written as he tells us "in my usual way, dilatorily and hastily, unwilling to work and working with vigour and haste," has come down to us as in effect the great writer's last will and testament. It is his supreme attempt to put in convincing order, as his own life drew to a close, his thoughts about the meaning of a literary career and the significance, or insignificance, of the English poets whose inheritance was his. Roughly a hundred years later, Matthew Arnold wrote a little-known essay on Johnson in which he put forward a possible use that contemporary readers, especially younger ones, could make of the *Lives*.[2] Arnold's essay was an introduction to a volume that consisted of the six most substantial lives—in his opinion, Milton, Dryden, Addison, Pope, Swift, and Gray—and is opposed, in principle, to Lonsdale's magnificent edition. Arnold's idea was that in reprinting the six lives without encumbering notes and commentary, the selection would provide what he called an admirable "*point de repère*, or fixed centre" for the student of English literature. The lives of these six important authors, as told by a great man, would, Arnold hoped, lead students to acquaint themselves with some of the leading and representative works of each. Except for Milton, Arnold had less than the highest opinion of the authors as poets, especially Swift and Addison. He saluted the Restoration and eighteenth century as the great age when English prose became a natural, viable, and adequate vehicle for thought, as it had not been in the earlier seventeenth century and before. ("Inconvenient" and "obsolete" are words he uses to character-ize the prose of such seventeenth-century writers as Milton and George Chapman.) Although Arnold was relatively uninterested (as was Johnson, often) in the facts and dates of biography, and although he disagreed with Johnson's high valuation of Dryden and Pope, as well as with his dismissal of Milton's *Lycidas* and his thorough downgrading of Thomas Gray (except for "Elegy in a Country Churchyard"), Arnold believed his selection from the *Lives* would give a "compendious story" of an important age in English literature, and would itself be "a piece of English literature of the first class." Like his much-abused "touchstones"—great passages from Homer, Dante, Shakespeare, and Milton that would, as we recalled them, save us from overvaluing some contemporary lines from a lesser poet—Johnson's *Lives* provided a similar fixed center from which the life of literature could be contemplated.

T. S. Eliot, who never missed an opportunity to snipe at Arnold, nevertheless also used Johnson's *Lives*, specifically the "Life of Cowley," as a "fixed centre" when he closed his introduction to *The Sacred Wood* with a note that began thus:

> I may commend as a model to critics who desire to correct some of the poetical vagaries of the present age, the following passage from a writer who cannot be accused of flaccid leniency, and the justice of whose criticism must be acknowledged even by those who feel a strong partiality toward the school of poets criticized.

There follow two paragraphs from the "Life of Cowley" in which, having convicted the Metaphysical "school" of far-fetched conceitedness, Johnson turns on himself and says something in favor of the poets he's been criticizing: "Yet to write on their plan, it was at least necessary to read and think." Years later in his rich and lengthy essay "Johnson as Critic and Poet," Eliot addressed himself to the problem of Johnson's "ear" for poetry, or his lack of it, by noting that readers of the *Lives* remember most strongly the strictures against the Metaphysicals (including Donne) and against *Lycidas*, "of which the diction is harsh, the rhymes uncertain, and the numbers displeasing." Even more surprising than these strictures against poetry we take to be canonical was Johnson's silence about Shakespeare (in the "Preface to Shakespeare") as a writer of verse whose diction and movement—to apply the terms Arnold used in "The Study of Poetry—were exemplary. But rather than deploring Johnson's ear, Eliot explains it historically by implying that, as it were, Johnson was unable to read Eliot's "Tradition and the Individual Talent," in which is set down the "obvious fact" that "art never improves, but that the material of art is never quite the same." On the contrary, Johnson felt no need for the "renewal" of literature, as Eliot did in renewing his own verse by way of seventeenth century English poets and nineteenth century French symbolists. For, Eliot wrote, "the age in which Johnson lived, was not old enough to feel the need for such renewal: it had just arrived at its own maturity. Johnson could think of the literature of his age as having attained the standard from which literature of the past could be judged."

At about the time Eliot's essay appeared, F. R. Leavis also criticized Johnson's ear as a critic of poetry, but in a less far-seeing way.[3] While admiring of Johnson's greatness as a writer of prose and verse, Leavis dwelt on the limitations revealed in his criticism of Shakespeare's poetry, his inability to appreciate "the Shakespearean creativeness," "the exploratory-creative use of words upon experience" that "we" (Leavis and other enlightened modern readers) find in the verse of Shakespeare's tragedies, or—in another example Leavis adduces as beyond Johnson's appreciative power—in the fourth book of Pope's *Dunciad*. For Johnson, Shakespearean "complexity" was not to be marveled at, but rather explained as (in language from the "Preface to Shakespeare") "the writer becoming entangled with an unwieldy sentiment, which he cannot well express, and will not reject." So that, for example, Johnson felt it incumbent upon him to unpack Hamlet's famous "To be or not to be" soliloquy by translating it into clear, discursive prose.[4] At first glance Leavis's point seems final; but Eliot in his discussion of the same Johnsonian "limitation" manages to make something more positive out of it. If Johnson lacks the historical sense, is unable to understand "archaic" rhythm and diction such as is found in the Metaphysicals and in Shakespeare's poetry, then it was, Eliot writes, "not through lack of sensibility but through specialization of sensibility." He enlarges on this:

> If the eighteenth century had admired the poetry of earlier times in
> the way in which we can admire it, the result would have been chaos:
> there would have been no eighteenth century as we know it. That
> age would not have had the conviction necessary for perfecting the
> kind of poetry that it did perfect. The deafness of Johnson's ear to

some kinds of melody was the necessary condition for his sharpness of sensibility to verbal beauty of another kind.

This seems to me on Eliot's part a wonderfully capacious and generous use of the historical sense that, more than any other twentieth-century critic, he helped bring into awareness.

Unlike Arnold, who sponsored a pared-down "essential" *Lives of the Poets*, Eliot insisted that they be read entire if Johnson's achievement were to be appreciated. (Eliot also insisted the same thing with respect to Shakespeare, Ben Jonson, George Herbert, and Baudelaire.) I read through the Lives in order—they are arranged by date of the author's death—turning frequently but not invariably to Lonsdale's commentary. Doubtless I flagged, blurred, and failed to take in some of the less memorable Johnsonian sentences, and I skipped the occasional Latin epitaph which, in the case of the forgotten seventeenth-century poet George Stepney, takes up half of the two-page life. Occasionally I marked, then typed out, utterances that made me smile, like the beginning of the "Life of Otway": "Of Thomas Otway, one of the first names in the English drama, little is known; nor is there any part of that little which his biographer can take pleasure in relating." Lonsdale calls this "Johnson's most sombre opening to a literary biography," but I should have called it not devoid of mischief. By way of making a point against the over-explicit long-windedness of Cowley's imagery in his twelve-book poem *Davideis*, Johnson quotes Cowley's description of the angel Gabriel:

> He took for skin a cloud most soft and bright,
> That e'er the midday sun pierc'd through with light,
> Upon his cheeks a lively blush he spread,
> Wash'd from the morning beauties deepest red;
> An harmless flattering meteor shone for hair,
> And fell adown his shoulders with loose care;
> He cuts out a silk mantle from the skies,
> Where the most sprightly azure pleas'd the eyes;

This he with starry vapours sprinkles all,
Took in their prime ere they grow ripe and fall,
Of a new rainbow, ere it fret or fade,
The choicest piece cut out, a scarfe is made.

Johnson comments:

> This is a just specimen of Cowley's imagery: what might in general
> expressions be great and forcible, he weakens and makes ridicu-
> lous by branching it into small parts. That Gabriel was invested
> with the softest or brightest colours of the sky, we might have
> been told, and been dismissed to improve the idea in our different
> proportions of conception; but Cowley could not let us go till he
> had related where Gabriel got first his skin, and then his mantle,
> then his lace, and then his scarfe, and related it in the terms of the
> mercer and taylor.

Excellent! Of Sprat, the historian of the Royal Society and a less than
impressive poet: "He considered Cowley as a model, and supposed that
as he was imitated, perfection was approached." So much for Sprat.
Although Edmund Waller's "petty compositions" are less hyperbolical
than the "amorous verses" of some other poets, still

> Waller is not always at the last gasp; he does not die of a frown, nor
> live upon a smile. There is however too much love, and too many
> trifles. Little things are made too important; and the Empire of
> Beauty is represented as exerting its influence further than can be
> allowed by the multiplicity of human passions, and the variety of
> human wants.

Here is the Johnsonian proportion and sanity. I raised my eyebrows
when told that one of Waller's sons, Benjamin, was "disinherited, and
sent to New Jersey, as wanting common understanding." I pictured poor
Benjamin Waller as exiled to somewhere in the vicinity of Newark, per-
haps Bayonne, until Lonsdale assured me that Johnson was speaking of
Jersey, a colony in the West Indies. The brief "Life of William King"
is concluded by Johnson's noting that "if his verse was easy and his im-
ages familiar, he attained what he desired." Well and good, then Johnson

qualifies: "His purpose is to be merry; but perhaps, to enjoy his mirth, it may be sometimes necessary to think well of his opinion." A sentence that has thought and thought well about its own opinion.

I quote these examples of satisfying sentences, representative of many more, not for any larger significance they have in *Lives* overall, but because they are the other, humorous, side of Johnson's enterprise. As to the larger significances, Paul Fussell three decades ago named it in language that hasn't been improved on, placing the *Lives* within the tradition of a number of great eighteenth-century works of English prose and finding it, preeminently, "concerned with the nature, and more importantly, with the limits of human experience." Fussell sees the "Life of Savage," in its mordant and sympathetic account of that poet's ills and depredations, as giving an overall tone to the book whose "subject is the pathos of hope and the irony of all human and especially literary careers." Johnson scholar Greg Clingham has spoken of the writer's distinctive combination of criticism and biography as discovering "in human limitations and the historical realm a dignity and grace."[5] In other words, *Lives of the Poets* is the final investigation of matters Johnson has been exploring in various forms throughout his career: in the periodical essays from the *Rambler;* in the prefaces to the Dictionary and to Shakespeare; in *Rasselas;* and in "The Vanity of Human Wishes" and the poem to Dr. Levet.

But it is finally at the level of style—of the sentence, the paragraph— where we engage with Johnson most fully and unmistakably. Lonsdale speaks well in his introduction when he says that whatever Johnson's critical limitations and idiosyncrasies, his "energy and trenchancy" are always evident, particularly in passages from the *Lives*—"in which his prose evokes, and even competes with, the qualities of the poetry he is describing." This may be true of any great critic, but Johnson's trenchancy—usually informed by irony—is often such as to obviate the necessity of saying anything further about the literary work under consideration. Any reader of the *Lives* will encounter passages that aptly illustrate this critical power, and in limiting myself to three examples I'm aware of ignoring much. The first is from the "Life of Dryden," when Johnson, surveying the plays, has this to say about *The Conquest of Granada,* Dryden's over-the-top two-part heroic drama of 1672:

The two parts of the *Conquest of Granada* are written with a seeming determination to glut the public with dramatick wonders; to exhibit in its highest elevation a theatrical meteor of incredible love and impossible valour, and to leave no room for a wilder flight to the extravagance of posterity. . . . Yet the scenes are, for the most part, delightful; they exhibit a kind of illustrious depravity, and majestick madness: such as, if it is sometimes despised, is often reverenced, and in which the ridiculous is mingled with the astonishing.

Johnson's two-mindedness about Dryden's spectacle is nicely concentrated in the oxymoron, "illustrious depravity." How is any future critic of the play to top that, and why should he or she try?

From the paragraphs about Pope's *Essay on Man*, the following sequence suggests Johnson's less than fully admiring attitude toward the poem, "certainly not the happiest of Pope's performances." But as one paragraph turns into the next, we see the perspective moving from denigration to a somewhat reluctant admiration:

Having exalted himself into the chair of wisdom, he tells us much that every man knows, and much that he does not know himself; that we see but little, and that the order of the universe is beyond our comprehension; an opinion not very uncommon; and that there is a chain of subordinate beings *from infinite to nothing,* of which himself and his readers are equally ignorant. But he gives us one comfort, which, without his help, he supposes unattainable, in the position *that though we are fools, yet God is wise.*

This Essay affords an egregious instance of the predominance of genius, the dazzling splendour of imagery, and the seductive powers of eloquence. Never were penury of knowledge and vulgarity of sentiment so happily disguised. The reader feels his mind full, though he learns nothing; and when he meets it in its new array, no longer knows the talk of his mother and his nurse.

Such is the power of the "new array" in which Pope garbs his commonplaces that genius, dazzle, and seductive eloquence are the results.

The third and final example is one of Johnson's most quoted pronouncements. The "Life of Gray" was originally to have concluded the whole series, but George, Lord Lyttelton was added subsequently, thus ending things on an anticlimax. Johnson was severe about the body of Gray's poetry, particularly the Odes, and especially "The Bard," whose "puerilities" and "obsolete mythology" Johnson condemned ("I do not see that 'The Bard' promotes any truth, moral or political"). Near the end of the life, he sums up his distaste for Gray's Odes, which he says

> are marked by glittering accumulations of ungraceful ornaments; they strike, rather than please; the images are magnified by affectation; the language is laboured into harshness. The mind of the writer seems to work with unnatural violence. *Double, double, toil and trouble.* He has a kind of strutting dignity, and is tall by walking on tiptoe. His art and his struggle are too visible, and there is too little appearance of ease and nature.

Then follow two short paragraphs somewhat modifying the censure, after which Johnson abruptly directs attention to Gray's most famous poem, almost catching us by surprise:

> In the character of his *Elegy* I rejoice to concur with the common reader; for by the common sense of readers uncorrupted with literary prejudices, after all the refinements of subtilty and the dogmatism of learning, must be finally decided all claim to poetical honours. The *Church-yard* abounds with images which find a mirrour in every mind, and with sentiments to which every bosom returns an echo.

He singles out four stanzas for special praise, then writes the great final sentence: "Had Gray written often thus, it had been vain to blame, and useless to praise him." This deference to the "common reader" is so graceful and assured that we almost forget to ask whether there weren't at that time a number of such readers whose bosoms returned an echo to the Odes of Gray. In the two pages of commentary Lonsdale devotes to that final paragraph, he aptly quotes Lawrence Lipking, who wrote about its final sentence, "Johnson resigns his authority—and also asserts it, by merging the public judgment into his own."[6] Lipking adds, with an understandable flourish, that "his whole career had led up to this moment." If so, Johnson knew—once more and most memorably—exactly what should be said.

NOTES

1. Samuel Johnson, *The Lives of the Poets,* with an introduction and notes by Roger Lonsdale, 4 vols. (Oxford: Clarendon Press, 2006).

2. Matthew Arnold, "Johnson's Lives," in *Essays in Criticism,* Third Series (Boston: Ball, 1910).

3. Eliot's essay may be found in *On Poetry and Poets* (New York: Farrar, Straus, 1959); Leavis's "Johnson and Augustanism" is in *The Common Pursuit* (New York: George W. Stewart, 1952).

4. Johnson's note begins, "Of this celebrated soliloquy, which bursting from a man distracted with contrariety of desires, and overwhelmed with the magnitude of his own purposes, is connected rather in the speaker's mind, than on his tongue, I shall endeavour to discover the train, and to show how one sentiment produces another."

5. Paul Fussell's *Samuel Johnson and the Life of Writing* (New York: W. W. Norton, 1971) is still the best introduction to Johnson's work. Greg Clingham's words are in his *Johnson, Writing, and Memory* (New York: Cambridge University Press, 2002), 98.

6. Lipking's excellent chapter on *Lives of the Poets* may be found in his *Samuel Johnson: The Life of an Author* (Cambridge, MA: Harvard University Press, 1998), 259–94.

Possibilities for Wordsworth

*I*n 1950, when the centenary of Wordsworth's death was celebrated at Princeton, one of the speakers, Lionel Trilling, stated what he took to be a perception current at the time that Wordsworth was "not an intellectual possibility, not attractive." "Intellectual possibility" seems an odd phrase to use about a poet, as if it were somehow a primary determinant of whether that poet could be read with pleasure. Much of Trilling's essay "Wordsworth and the Iron Time" was devoted to comparing Wordsworth's "quietism" with the *Pirke Aboth* (a book of Jewish wisdom-sayings Trilling had been impressed by as a young man); but there was little by way of demonstrating convincingly that, as Trilling himself believed, Wordsworth was still very much alive as a poet. The editor of a 2003 volume of essays on Wordsworth,[1] Stephen Gill—himself a biographer and editor of the poet—assured us that all this has changed; that since 1950 the wave of biographies, scholarly editions, and shifts in intellectual concern (the "linguistic turn" of theory; the return to history, politics, and society that has situated Wordsworth's poems anew) have combined to make him what Gill calls "a fully 'intellectually possible' figure." Whether this also means that, other than by the scholars and critics in the academy who edit and write about him, Wordsworth is read with eagerness and passion is another story. When Matthew Arnold wrote his "Memorial Verses" upon Wordsworth's death in 1850, the unanswerable question Arnold asked, now that the poet had gone, was "But who, ah! who, will make us feel?" For Arnold, Wordsworth's ministration to our feelings was paramount and overwhelming:

> He found us when the age had bound
> Our souls in its benumbing round;

Reprinted by permission from the *Hudson Review* 59, no. 2 (Summer 2006): 309–16. Copyright 2006 by The Hudson Review, Inc.

He spoke, and loosed our heart in tears.
He laid us as we lay at birth
On the cool flowery lap of earth,
Smiles broke from us and we had ease;
The hills were round us, and the breeze
Went o'er the sunlit fields again;
Our foreheads felt the wind and rain.
Our youth return'd; for there was shed
On spirits that had long been dead,
Spirits dried up and closely furl'd,
The freshness of the early world.

Such a power was, at least for Arnold, to be described in terms that had nothing to do with "intellectual possibility." Yet Arnold preempted the "feeling" vocabulary so fully that its terms are unlikely to help readers coming to the poems a century and a half later.

To my knowledge no one believed that what we were all waiting for, in order to stimulate fresh interest in Wordsworth's poetry, was a new biography. Mary Moorman's meticulous two-volume one of 1957 has all the facts one is likely to require; and Stephen Gill's shorter, more critically acute one of 1989 is an excellent treatment in under 500 pages. But biographies have to keep coming, evidently, even of a figure like Wordsworth who—unlike his friend Coleridge and his younger contemporaries Keats, Shelley, and Byron—seems a particularly uninviting subject to read about at length. Juliet Barker, who has previously produced a massive book about the Brontë family, now gives us a biography of Wordsworth originally published in England in 2000.[2] The American version is streamlined, 548 instead of 961 pages; 160 of the pruned pages consisted of notes. Evidently Ecco Press decided American readers wouldn't want or need those notes, so it's impossible to check the source of anything Barker says or quotes—a curious way for a biography to present itself. But the major problem, one that surfaced here and there in the Brontë book, is that although the English blurbs insist how substantial, accessible, and readable is Barker's work, she has some crucial flaws: an absence of literary taste, and an inability to listen to her own sentences.

As a recipient of an Oxford doctorate in medieval history (she is an authority on medieval tournaments), there is no reason why Barker should be versed in English poetry, and this lack of familiarity is confirmed early on when she describes Wordsworth's relation to eighteenth-century poet-predecessors: "His favorites were from what is known as the 'graveyard school,' poets such as Gray, Chatterton, Collins, Beattie, Young and Thomson, whose work was driven by an affectation of melancholy and musings on the grave." Such a "school" would surely contain Robert Blair, author of "The Grave" (unmentioned by Barker), but just as surely not Thomson or Beattie or Chatterton. Are Gray's "Elegy in a Country Churchyard" and Collins's gloomy musings driven by an "affectation" of melancholy, or could it be the real thing? Barker's "accessible" writing style is in fact a consistently vulgarized one: when Wordsworth is introduced to his future wife, Mary Hutchinson, "he was instantly bowled over," and when his sister Dorothy met Coleridge she was "quite simply, bowled over" by him. We hear that Wordsworth "had fallen head over heels in love with" Annette Vallon, on whom he would father a child. We hear also of Coleridge's "sexual hang-ups" and how, apropos of his wife Sarah, "he slapped her down for being narrow-minded." Barker describes Richardson's *Clarissa* as "an overpoweringly dull exposition . . . in seven ponderous volumes." In a rare burst of mischievous play she calls Wordsworth's early poem "An Evening Walk. An Epistle; in Verse, Addressed to a Young Lady, from the Lakes of the North of England" one of the "snappy titles so beloved by eighteenth-century poets." In Wordsworth's great preface to the second edition of *Lyrical Ballads* (1800) she detects only "an aura of elitism and exclusion" and speaks of the writing as "verbose and otiose."

Her favorite adjective to describe Wordsworth poems she admires is "wonderful," as with the Westminster Bridge sonnet ("his wonderful hymn to a still and silent London"), or his poem about St. Paul's, "Press'd with conflicting thoughts of love and fear" ("a wonderful meditative poem"), or "Composed upon an Evening of Extraordinary Splendor and Beauty" ("a wonderful evocation of a sunset"). She calls "Ode: Intimations of Immortality" "quite simply, the greatest William ever wrote." Maybe so, but surely not quite simply. If you want to find out all the details of Wordsworth's finances or how his brother John's ship *The Earl of Abergavenny* sank with her captain aboard, Barker provides them unsparingly and is relentless in tracking every move in Wordsworth's itinerary year by year. And in case you wanted inside information on Coleridge's many health problems, the following is a memorable consequence of the rheumatic fever he suffered in 1800:

> When he was eventually carried home in a chaise, he retired once more to his bed, this time with a swollen testicle which, astonishingly, responded to the application of three leeches and a home made poultice of grated bread mixed up with a strong solution of lead.

This recipe may come in handy in time of need.

No English poet invites parody and satire among his admirers as does Wordsworth. Lewis Carroll's send-up of "Resolution and Independence" and "We Are Seven" (in *Through the Looking-Glass*) is unsurpassable; Max Beerbohm's drawing of a black-frocked old-ladyish clergyman-like gentleman questioning a little girl ("William Wordsworth in the Lake District at Cross Purposes") is similarly priceless; and the reworking by J. K. Stephen of Wordsworth's sonnet "Thoughts of a Briton on the Subjugation of Switzerland" ("Two voices are there; one is of the sea") can never be quoted enough, especially its first eight and a half lines:

> Two voices are there: one is of the deep;
> It learns the storm-cloud's thunderous melody,
> Now roars, now murmurs with the changing sea,
> Now bird-like pipes, now closes soft in sleep:
> And one is of an old half-witted sheep
> Which bleats articulate monotony,
> And indicates that two and one are three,
> That grass is green, lakes damp, and mountains steep:
> And, Wordsworth, both are thine . . .

F. W. Bateson, who opened his still lively *Wordsworth: A Reinterpretation* (1954) by quoting Stephen's sonnet, went on to entertain the possibility that the two voices weren't always separate in Wordsworth; thus the sheeplike one couldn't be extirpated by winnowing out the good poems from the bad, as

Arnold did in his selection in 1879. Bateson's notion is a plausible one if we think of two of his greatest poems by common consent, "Resolution and Independence" and the "Immortality Ode," in both of which passages of great power are juxtaposed with others deficient in such power.

Neither "Resolution" nor the Ode receives anything like critical treatment in the *Cambridge Companion,* as if there were a consensus about each that left no more to say. In fact the book's essays are not mainly concerned with providing new, revisionary readings of Wordsworth's poems. Two main issues appear to have dominated recent Wordsworth criticism: first, the argument as to whether the final, authorized version of the poems should be adhered to, or whether the poems as they were originally published should take precedence. Stephen Gill has led the "originists" when he edited the Oxford Major Works volume in which the poems are arranged, chronologically in their original versions, except for *The Prelude,* which concludes the volume in its version of 1805, never published in Wordsworth's lifetime.[3] The other issue among Wordsworth critics is their sympathy toward or distaste for new historicist revisionism, as most notably practiced by Marjorie Levinson, whose infamous (to my mind) readings of "Tintern Abbey" and "Michael" in terms of what is absent from them (contemporary history, politics, concern for the laboring poor) have generated forceful counterstatements.[4] This way of reading Wordsworth by looking at what the finished poem has "suppressed" or evaded or sublimated presumably gives the critic license to avoid dealing with the poem the poet in fact actually wrote, with all its actualities of diction and rhythm.

None of the contributors to the *Companion* practices such new historicist kidnappings of poems; yet for all their good sense, their commitment to seeing Wordsworth in relation to larger thematic units—Romanticism, gender and domesticity, the natural world, America—results in slighting matters of poetic technique. For example, what is to my mind a still unanswered question, unasked by contributors to the volume, is how Wordsworth, after publishing in 1793 poems in pentameter couplets ("An Evening Walk," "Descriptive Sketches") and in Spenserian stanzas (the Salisbury Plain poem that later became "The Female Vagrant" and finally "Guilt and Sorrow"), suddenly, in about 1797, began composing blank verse that is dazzling in its extraordinary invention. Consider lines from "A Night Piece" (1797), in which a musing traveler is suddenly startled by a natural phenomenon:

> . . . he looks up—the clouds are split
> Asunder,—and above his head he sees
> The clear Moon, and the glory of the heavens.
> There, in a black-blue vault she sails along,
> Followed by multitudes of stars, that, small
> And sharp, and bright, along the dark abyss
> Drive as she drives: how fast they wheel away,
> Yet vanish not!—the wind is in the tree,
> But they are silent;—still they roll along
> Immeasurably distant; and the vault,
> Built round by those white clouds, enormous clouds,
> Still deepens its unfathomable depth.

Or consider the following from "The Old Cumberland Beggar," composed at about the same time:

> He travels on, a solitary Man;
> His age has no companion. On the ground
> His eyes are turned, and, as he moves along,
> *They* move along the ground; and, evermore,
> Instead of common and habitual sight
> Of fields with rural works, of hill and dale,
> And the blue sky, one little span of earth
> Is all his prospect. Thus, from day to day,
> Bow-bent, his eyes for ever on the ground,
> He plies his weary journey; seeing still,
> And seldom knowing that he sees, some straw,
> Some scattered leaf, or marks which, in one track,
> The nails of cart or chariot-wheel have left
> Impressed on the white road,—in the same line,
> At distance still the same.

Both these sequences—and others could be adduced, notably from "Tintern Abbey"—exhibit the most delicate subtlety in their handling of blank verse rhythms. (I quote from Wordsworth's final 1849–50 edition of his poems.) The "ingenious critic" quoted by Samuel Johnson who said that Milton's blank verse was *"verse only to the eye"* is refuted by these lines of Wordsworth whose appeal and challenge to the ear is central. The varying of pauses within individual lines, the surprising extensions from one line to the next, the inclusion of full stops in places other than at line ends, all contribute to the movement, the "drive" of the moon and stars of "A Night-Piece" and the "bow-bent" pace of the beggar's weary and prolonged journey.

Any reader of *The Prelude* knows how much Wordsworth owed to Milton, both technically and morally, but one can't account for the distinctiveness of blank verse such as quoted above by ascribing it to the study of Milton's practice. What may be called Wordsworth's dramatic syntax in them has no obvious eighteenth-century antecedents either; we know he read and admired Cowper, but nothing in *The Task* prepares us for Wordsworth's originality. Compared to it the unsubtlety of Coleridge's blank verse in his "Conversation poems" (even though "Frost at Midnight" has a fine ending) is evident. Moreover, the contemporaneous blank verse of "The Ruined Cottage" is, in its quiet, unobtrusive behavior quite distinct from the psychologically energized verse of "Tintern Abbey" and the 1798 "Two-Part *Prelude*" as it is now called. Meanwhile at the same time and with his other hand, Wordsworth was turning out poems as unaccountable for as "The Idiot Boy" and others that make up *Lyrical Ballads.* There is astonishing variety in the verse of end-of-the-century Wordsworth, to say nothing of the about-to-come Lucy poems and "Michael."

In the *Companion* Lucy Newlyn has a good essay treating *The Prelude* as a "deeply Protestant poem" in the dissenting tradition of confessional autobiography of Bunyan, the Quaker George Fox, and John Wesley. Coming fresh from a reading of the poem in its 1805 version, I was struck by something Newlyn doesn't consider: the great disparities in poetic quality between sequences in which the verse is active, alive, vibrant with passionate conviction, and other stretches—most notably in the later books—where one sympathizes with Macaulay who found the poem, for all its fine things, filled also with "dull, flat, prosaic twaddle." Some of the dullness, the flatness, comes when Wordsworth attempts to look back on the growth of his mind and find fit language to describe what happened. A couple of such retrospective accounts occur late in the poem (I quote from the 1850 *Prelude* Macaulay read). In the first he tells Coleridge what his poem has been about:

> This narrative, my Friend! hath chiefly told
> Of intellectual power, fostering love,
> Dispensing truth, and, over men and things,
> Where reason yet might hesitate, diffusing
> Prophetic sympathies of genial faith.
>
> (Book 12, 44–48)

Or he tells of how his imagination and taste were restored:

> Thus moderated, thus composed, I found
> Once more in Man an object of delight,
> Of pure imagination, and of love;
> And, as the horizon of my mind enlarged, . . .
> Knowledge was given accordingly; my trust
> Became more firm in feelings that had stood
> The test of such a trial; clearer far
> My sense of excellence—of right and wrong.
>
> (Book 13, 48–51, 55–58)

How quickly one's own imperfect mind glazes over in navigating such stuff (what Macaulay would have called "twaddle") as compared with one of the great "spots of time" moments that come thick and fast near the poem's beginning. For example, there is the remembered singing of the bird in the nave of Furness Abbey, which the young Wordsworth has just visited:

> Our steeds remounted and the summons given,
> With whip and spur we through the chauntry flew
> In uncouth race, and left the cross-legged knight,
> And the stone-abbot, and that single wren
> Which one day sang so sweetly in the nave
> Of the old church, that—though from recent showers
> The earth was comfortless, and touched by faint

Internal breezes, sobbings of the place
And respirations, from the roofless walls
The shuddering ivy dripped large drops—yet still
So sweetly 'mid the gloom the invisible bird
Sang to herself, that there I could have made
My dwelling place, and lived for ever there
To hear such music.

(Book 2, 115–28)

Here, in the language of Milton's note to the second edition of *Paradise Lost*, is a beautiful example of "the sense variously drawn out from one verse into another," and it has very little to do with the "intellectual power" or "sense of excellence—of right and wrong" Wordsworth claims later in the poem to have increasingly informed his mind.

"Wordsworth was about strange things," Christopher Ricks once wrote in his discussion of the odd genius manifested in another *Prelude* passage. If anything, both Barker's biography and the *Companion* essays, in the process of making him more available to us, make him look less strange, so that an essay or book which confronts the contradictions that gave Wordsworth's great poems their energy would be more than welcome, even at this late date in the critical tradition. It's therefore unfortunate that there is an egregious omission from the comprehensive list of books and articles mentioned by Keith Hanley in his closing essay, "Textual Issues and a Guide to Further Reading." The omission—and there is similarly no reference to it in any of the other essays—is a book published nearly a half-century ago, David Ferry's *The Limits of Mortality: An Essay on Wordsworth's Major Poems* (1959). This strongly argued, wholly original essay studies the way what Ferry calls "sacramental" and "mystical" attitudes toward nature were at war within the poet, and how Wordsworth's attempt to demonstrate "Love of Nature Leading to Love of Man" (as he titled the eighth book of *The Prelude*) was not at all the straightforward "progress" toward, in language quoted earlier, "prophetic sympathies of genial faith." Ferry argues rather that a central and continuing fact of Wordsworth's temperament was a hostility toward man and his works as representing a disastrous falling away from the nature that had fostered the young Wordsworth "by beauty and by fear," thus in some way making him unfit for the world and vice versa. "Not a great lover of man but almost a great despiser of him," Ferry says at one point.

Ferry's capsule characterization of Wordsworth's later poetry hasn't been bettered. Although he still wrote the occasional beautiful poem, mainly as it continued to pour out, his work exhibited "shocking debilitation":

> a flat and moralistic and not often very passionate adaptation of Christian and classical vocabularies; a tendency to increased garrulity; a soberly cheery optimism about the relations of man and nature, man and God, combined with a sort of peevishness against railroads and a zeal for capital punishment.

Given the force of Wordsworth's early "mystical" yearnings and combined with increasing pessimism about their possible fulfillment, he turned to "other interests and other attitudes" in which, alas, he couldn't fully participate. Ferry ends his book with two sentences that on first reading seem almost to be about some other poet than the one Arnold celebrated as the laureate of human feeling: "His genius was his enmity to man, which he mistook for love, and his mistake led him into confusions which he could not bear. But when he banished his confusions he banished his distinctive greatness as well." Rather than being an overstatement forgivable at the conclusion to a book, it seems to me profoundly true about Wordsworth as well as making that poet very much a possibility, intellectually and otherwise, for twenty-first-century readers.

NOTES

1. *The Cambridge Companion to Wordsworth*, ed. Stephen Gill (New York: Cambridge University Press, 2003).

2. *Wordsworth: A Life*, by Juliet Barker (New York: Ecco Press, 2005).

3. The distinguished textual scholar Jack Stillinger makes the case for the 1850 *Prelude* in *Multiple Authorship and the Myth of Solitary Genius* (New York: Oxford University Press, 1991). See also Zachary Leader's *Revision and Romantic Authorship* (Oxford: Clarendon Press, 1996).

4. Levinson's essay on "Tintern Abbey" is in her *Wordsworth's Great Period Poems* (New York: Cambridge University Press, 1986). Notable counterstatements are David Ferry's review of Levinson's book (*Studies in Romanticism* 24 [1991]) and Helen Vendler's "Two Assaults" (in *Wordsworth in Context*, ed. Pauline Fletcher and John Murphy [Lewisburg, PA: Bucknell University Press, 1992).

Anyone for Tennyson?

O ne of the favorite card games of my youth was *Authors*, a variant of *Fish* (or *Go Fish*). Its deck was composed of various English and American literary worthies, each of whom was represented by four titles, and the idea of the game was to amass more "books" of authors than your opponents. It was here I first encountered—if that is the correct word—Charles Dickens and William Makepeace Thackeray, Sir Walter Scott and James Fenimore Cooper, Washington Irving, Ralph Waldo Emerson, and Nathaniel Hawthorne. Nobody before 1800 was allowed in except Shakespeare; no woman managed to make the club except one (token?) Louisa May Alcott. Its most recent authors were Twain and Stevenson, but the one who captivated my imagination was stately, dark, magnificently bearded Alfred, Lord Tennyson (I simply assumed "Lord" was his middle name), author—so his four cards individually announced—of "The Charge of the Light Brigade," "The Brook," "Idylls of the King," and "Crossing the Bar." Although the Tennyson foursome counted no more than any other packet, I felt especially satisfied when I was in a position to snare it and could demand of my opponent, "Give me 'Crossing the Bar'" or (knowing the answer already) "Do you have 'Idylls of the King'?" Somehow Tennyson felt like money in the bank.

Yet it never occurred to me to read these or any other of his poems, and for some reason Tennyson, like the other English nineteenth-century poets, got left out of our grammar school English classes where we read James Russell Lowell, Oliver Wendell Holmes, John Greenleaf Whittier, and other fireside American Classics cordially detested by most members of the class. So it wasn't until college that I discovered *In Memoriam* (or parts of it), and not until graduate school that a real acquaintance with

Reprinted by permission from the *Hudson Review* 41, no. 3 (Autumn 1988). Copyright by The Hudson Review, Inc.

his work began under the gentle hand of Douglas Bush. Bush admired the poet, partly I think as a defiance of the New Criticism and of modernism generally. For in "The Metaphysical Poets" (1921), T. S. Eliot had pronounced Tennyson's epitaph with the cleverly turned "But Keats and Shelley died, and Tennyson and Browning ruminated." What could a poet do worse than ruminate? Even before that, in writing to Harriet Monroe about how poetry had to be as well-written as prose, Pound had forbidden any more "Tennysonianness of speech; nothing—nothing that you couldn't in some circumstance, in the stress of some emotion, actually say." And while Frost wasn't exactly a modernist, he had insisted that the Tennysonian track of "effects in assonation" was "the wrong track or at any rate . . . a short track," and that he, Frost, was headed down a new track ("the sound of sense"). Eventually, in *New Bearings in English Poetry* (1932), F. R. Leavis codified such insights into Tennyson's limitations by labeling him "literary and Alexandrian" and charging him with major responsibility for the nineteenth-century cult of the "poetical"—with the creation of a dream world and a general unhealthy escapism.

Suddenly, in 1936, Eliot published his essay *"In Memoriam,"* which began with the astonishing declaration that "Tennyson is a great poet, for reasons that are perfectly clear." Those reasons were that his work showed "abundance, variety, and complete competence," that he had the finest ear of any English poet since Milton, and that his masterpiece, *In Memoriam,* was a great poem—though because of the quality of its doubt rather than its faith (*"In Memoriam* is a poem of despair, but of despair of a religious kind"). So this "great master of metric as well as of melancholia" had, with a stroke, been rehabilitated, fittingly enough by the man who fifteen years previously helped effect his dislodgment from the high poetic throne. With Eliot's blessing one of the deans of New Criticism, Cleanth Brooks, set about to show why "Tears, Idle Tears" was a great lyric rather than, as Leavis had insisted in a chilly phrase, one that offered "emotion for its own sake without a justifying situation." From Brooks it was only a step to Hugh Kenner, who despite his Poundian disapproval of "Tennysonianness of speech" wrote an essay in which he put forth Tennyson as a symbolist precursor of *The Waste Land* and *Finnegans Wake.*[1]

During the past few decades, the level of Tennyson criticism has been raised mightily, mainly through the force of Christopher Ricks: first with his 1969 edition of the poems; then his 1972 critical biography. Now Ricks has brought out in three volumes a second edition of the poems, this one incorporating the Trinity College manuscripts from which scholars were forbidden to quote at the time of the earlier edition.[2] The new edition is only a couple of hundred pages longer than the earlier one, but will take up a bit more shelf space. The most astonishing thing about it—as with its predecessor—is that Ricks seems to have accomplished it all more or less single-handedly, with the help of a few libraries. (There are no acknowledgments of lucrative fellowships, devoted research assistants—the sort of thing that for American scholars usually goes with the territory.) The lifting of the restrictions on copying or quoting from the Trinity College manuscripts has made it possible for Ricks to record many MS variants, all of which he has not attempted to record (such an edition would be, he says, "enormously valuable but also enormous"). Ricks's good sense in using the Trinity material comes out nicely when he remarks, "The editor has tried to resist the temptation to find the Trinity MSS more interesting (than, say, the good old Harvard ones) simply because they used to be under interdiction." He has also brought up to date the critical commentary on individual poems, adding to or revising headnotes to individual poems in the light of recent scholarship. A single example: the note to "Ulysses" in the first edition ended by referring to a 1963 article summarizing various arguments about whether or not we were to find Tennyson's hero in that poem altogether noble. We are now directed to two further articles on the subject, to another article about the Homeric and Dantean backgrounds of "Ulysses," to a further one suggesting as a source Samuel Daniel's "Ulysses and the Siren," and finally to one in *Tennessee Studies in Literature* (not a publication everyone keeps up with) arguing that Byron is as much a source for the poem as Dante. So a stanza from *Childe Harold's Pilgrimage* is quoted and the reader is directed to an allusion to Byron—noted in Ricks's first edition—in Tennyson's line "I am a part of all that I have met."

Since Ricks has the subtlest ear for allusion and the best-stocked memory for English poetry of any critic alive, it is a privilege to watch him listening to and recording the operations of England's most literary poet. In case there are those who distrust "source hunting" in an editor, the following sentences from his preface show how sensitive he is to the uses and misuses of such activity:

> The footnotes cite many parallel passages. As in any annotated edition these illustrate a range of possible likenesses. At one end is conscious allusion to another poet; then unconscious reminiscence; then phrasing which is only an analogue and not a source. Some of the instances cited here are probably analogues, not sources, but they are cited because Tennyson's phrasing can be illuminated by the comparison.

He then notes Tennyson's own contempt for certain kinds of source-hunters like John Churton Collins: "They will not allow one to say 'Ring the bell' without finding that we have taken it from Sir P. Sidney, or even to use such a simple expression as the ocean 'roars,' without finding out the precise verse in Homer or Horace from which we have plagiarised it (fact)." Aware of the force of this grumble, Ricks's editorial procedure is a mixture of discretion and boldness. Publicity material on the back cover of these volumes speaks of the edition as "one of the great achievements of modern editorial scholarship." Never was the adjective "great" less idly used; to read and study Ricks's notes to "Mariana," "The Lady of Shalott," "Tithonus," and the rest (which I have barely begun to do) is to open up Tennyson in unexpected ways and to widen the scope of one's mind. It feels like what undergoing a liberal education must feel like—or so this liberally educated reader felt.

Tennyson once remarked casually at a London dinner table, "I don't think that since Shakespeare there has been such a master of the English language as I"; then, as the guests looked embarrassed, added, "To be sure, I've got nothing to say." Ricks's 1972 critical biography was really the first book to focus seriously on the "saying," especially on the way Tennyson's poems characteristically recede from their affirmations and make a business (and a pleasure) out of not concluding, even as they talk about the necessity for concluding—Tennysonian mellifluousness both shapes and distorts the "statements" made by the poems. Since Ricks's there have been several useful and unapologetic studies of the poetry, culminating, so it appears to me, in Herbert F. Tucker's remarkable account of it up through *Maud*.[3] Although it is probably a mistake to speak of any critical work on a poet as "definitive," one feels, upon finishing Tucker's dense and difficult book, that it will be some time before another one on Tennyson's major poems is needed.

Tucker shows how Tennyson's poetry both exhibits and helps call into being "the doom of romanticism." He extends and consolidates some of Ricks's notions about the un-concludingness of Tennysonian narratives, and also places the poet in larger contexts of history—literary, but also political and social history—exploring in particular and patient detail Tennyson's transformations of earlier nineteenth-century poets, especially Keats and Shelley. One of his aims—I would call it the book's central aim—is "to tell the story of the life of Tennyson's texts to midcareer, and thereby to practice specifically *literary* biography." Tucker wants to be, and admirably succeeds in being, both historical and critical, thus avoiding mere "context-setting"—the attempt to understand a poem by submitting it to some structure external to it—and mere "close reading" that would treat the poems as historically and biographically context-less.

He also wants to distinguish himself from the New Critical and "modernist" responses to Tennyson: some sentences from his extremely fertile introduction to Part I stake out the ambitiousness of his critical enterprise:

> The dissociation of sensibility; the movement to rewrite Romantic and Victorian literary history in the mode not of comprehension but of indictment; the symbolist aim to purify the dialect of the tribe; the imagist aim to effect a fusion of thought and feeling somewhere, anywhere, outside the field of a historical relevance: these were powerfully attractive, mutually supportive modernist myths. They allowed two generations of poets and critics to wink at Tennyson's authority among them—inescapable though it then was, and largely uncharted though it still is—by regarding the result of his path-breaking work in the integration of lyric impulse and public responsibility as, on balance, a road better not taken by poets in the modern world. The soil of history had defiled Tennyson's

gift; and more was the pity exquisitely savored by a succession of patronizing heirs, whom we in our decades succeed, and now and then patronize, in turn.

The elegant and witty authority of this writing characterizes Tucker's book throughout and makes reading it a pleasure, though of an exceptionally strenuous sort: there are no "easy" pages, and the analyses of particular poems are uniformly long, packed, and somewhat unremitting in tone—which is not to deny the pervasive and salutary ironic humor Tucker often brings to them.

The "doom of romanticism" of the book's title has among other references a direct one to the language with which *Maud* ends (Tucker's book also ends with a most searching reading of that difficult poem, on which I may finally be getting a handle):

> It is better to fight for the good than to rail at the ill;
> I have felt with my native land, I am one with my kind,
> I embrace the purpose of God, and the doom assigned.

This is the hero's desperate attempt to come to terms with his own madness; but Tucker sees Tennyson's poetic career as "a series of just such submissions to an inevitable doom." The stylistic efforts of the poems are ingenious responses to a central conviction of powerlessness:

> When there is everything to be endured and nothing to be done [the phrase is Matthew Arnold's], endurance will be a leading virtue; the index of a speaker's strength will be the deepening stasis of a mood; and action will take the strictly subordinate place it takes in Tennyson's poetry.

Although in such poems as "The Gardener's Daughter" or "Enoch Arden" Tennyson showed that he could tell a "proper story" and artfully exploit an audience's taste for "moving" narration, his deeper bent was in another direction:

> Something about the stories he tells best, in their climactic emphasis on inhibitions or their diffuse sense of breakdown, scandalizes the assumption behind critical metaphors of narrative "development"

and "progression." Something opposes the thrust of narrative and deflects the poetry in an allegorical direction that has made readers since Walter Bagehot suspect that, whatever a Tennyson poem is ostensibly about, its real subject lies elsewhere.

Tennyson's imagination "was reluctant to believe in the efficacy of human action," and such reluctance is a feature (as both Ricks and Tucker have shown) of some of his most beautiful poems; from the early "Song" ["A spirit haunts the year's last hours"], to "Mariana," "The Lady of Shalott," "The Lotos-Eaters," "Ulysses," "Tithonus," all the way to "Crossing the Bar." In that final utterance (or so Tennyson asked that it stand in his work), the departing passenger would have no "moaning of the bar" when he puts out to sea,

> But such a tide as moving seems asleep,
> > Too full for sound and foam,
> When that which drew from out the boundless deep
> > Turns again home.

Death is the ultimate denier of human action's efficacy, but Tennyson could write a poem in which a subtle inward action is achieved. Henry James, while not speaking of "Crossing the Bar," shrewdly defined that action as follows: "When he wishes to represent movement, the phrase always seems to me to pause and slowly pivot upon itself, or at most to move backward"—as in the above stanza where "that which drew" eventually "Turns again home."

If it does not sound like a putdown under the guise of a pat, I shall venture to call *Tennyson and the Doom of Romanticism* the best sort of lit crit high-tech operation. Tucker's scrupulosity about recording every allusion or indebtedness to his critical predecessors extends to slightly disfiguring his own text with parenthetical references to them—so a sentence may close with "(Armstrong 1982, 183; Peltason 1985a, 43)." He has read, assimilated, and made use of when appropriate just about every piece of writing on Tennyson over the last century and a half, and he has been especially assiduous in acknowledging his immediate forebears. It is by no means a book to read in an evening, and most readers—even ones fairly devoted to Tennyson—may be tempted to skip sections on, say, "Fatima" or "Dora." But the temptation should be resisted, since whether the poem in question is a favorite or not, familiar or not-so-familiar, if one reads it through, then reads Tucker's account of it, one inevitably comes away generously repaid. Whatever reservations he has about the contextlessness of New Critical readings, the readings in this book—I think especially of "Mariana," "Ulysses," "Morte D'Arthur," and *Maud*—are as close, as delicate, and as exhaustive as I have ever seen readings to be, and I *do* mean "ever."

"You know that any day I would as soon kill a pig as write a letter," wrote Tennyson in a letter to some "friends over the sea." That sentence is about the best opening I've seen recently, and suggests how formidably entertaining a correspondent he could have been and occasionally was.[4] This second volume of letters covers the first twenty of the Laureate years, and they do not fully reveal "the soul within" ("For words, like Nature, half reveal / And half conceal the soul within," *In Memoriam*, v). Still I was delighted with how he treated the birth of his two sons. After his and Emily's first child died stillborn, he wrote to a friend about his (Tennyson's) suffering, noting that he "refused to see the little body at first, fearing to find some pallid abortion which would have haunted me all my life—but he looked (if it be not absurd to call a newborn babe so) even majestic in his mysterious silence after all the turmoil of the night before." Then when a year or so later Hallam was born, he wrote joyously to Monckton Milnes about how "the little sensual wretch roaring day and night" was depriving his wife (though not himself?) of any sleep. When his second son, Lionel, was born, "a lusty young fellow," he notes how this infant "strikes the elder one with awe, sometimes into sympathetic tears, sometimes into a kind of mimic bleating, when he hears the younger one's inarticulate cooings." But at that moment he thinks again of the dead first child, "really the finest boy of the three," who "lay like a little warrior, having fought the fight and failed, with his hands clenched, and a frown on his brow." The vitality and energy of a poet spills out from these sentences.

Much of this second volume—as of the previous one—is taken up with letters and journal accounts about Tennyson, or with letters from his wife to various people describing the great man's comings and goings.

Clough called him, flatly, "an unmannerly simple big child of a man"; but Hawthorne was uncharacteristically overwhelmed by seeing him at the Manchester Arts Treasures Exhibition: "of middle-size, rather slouching, dressed entirely in black, and with nothing white about him except the collar of his shirt, which methought might have been clean the day before. . . . His face was very dark. . . . His eyes were black; but I know little of them, as they did not rest on me, nor on anything but the pictures. He seemed as if he did not see the crowd nor think on them, but as if he defended himself from them by ignoring them altogether." Perhaps this is how Hawthorne himself yearned to appear; at any rate, he says, "Gazing at him with all my eyes, I liked him well, and rejoiced more in him than in all the other wonders of the Exhibition." But there are also glimpses of the poet in a more, one might say, relaxed mood, as when he is visited in Farringford by an American preacher who, after dinner on a stormy evening, proceeds to his inn, accompanied by the Laureate who, while directing the guest, loses his bearings:

> Bidding me walk close behind him, we went forward through the mud, when suddenly I found myself precipitated six or seven feet downward. Sitting in the mud, I called on the poet to pause, but it was too late; he was speedily seated beside me. This was seeing the Laureate of England in a new light, or rather, hearing him under a novel darkness.

For Tennyson proceeded to make himself heard, improvising "an amusing run of witticisms" delivered in a deep bass voice which "came through the congenial darkness like mirthful thunder," and crying out (in what tone we can guess) "That this should have happened after dinner . . . do not mention this to the temperance folk." Doubtless the port had gone round, yes.

These letters take us into a different world, and why else do we read the letters of dead writers? In the "Afterword" to Herbert Tucker's book, he considers the bitter "generational disappointment" that post–World War I writers and readers felt with Tennyson ("Lawn Tennyson" in Stephen Dedalus's scornful *mot*) whose voice could evoke, as if it knew what it was talking about, "One far-off divine event, / To which the whole creation moves." But Tucker focuses on the largeness of expectation out of which that disappointment was bred:

> Here, for once, a poet ranked among the *acknowledged* legislators of mankind. The wholesale revulsion that set in against Victoria's laureate, and against the culture he represented in the popular mind, attests to the depth, breadth, and immediacy of the influence once wielded through Tennyson, for better or worse, by the art of poetry itself. With its thoroughgoing rejection of the "poetic"—that is, of Tennysonian melodiousness and rhetoric—postwar culture in effect bestowed on poetry, for the first and probably last time in modern experience, the immense compliment of taking it seriously.

Taking Tennyson seriously, and not solemnly, is what these scholarly and critical presentations of him help us to do.

NOTES

1. Brooks's essay, "The Motivation of Tennyson's Weeper," may be found in *The Well-Wrought Urn* (New York: Harcourt, Brace, 1947), 153–62. Leavis's animadversions on "Tears, Idle Tears" occur most recently in *The Living Principle* (New York: Oxford University Press, 1975), 75–79. At one point he warns us that "habitual indulgence of the kind represented by *Tears, idle tears* . . . would be, on grounds of emotional and spiritual hygiene, something to deplore." (I remember a similar warning about masturbation in a Boy Scout Handbook from my youth.) Kenner's essay, "Some Post-Symbolist Structures," is in *Literary Theory and Structure*, ed. Frank Brady, John Palmer, and Martin Price (New Haven, CT: Yale University Press, 1973), 379–93.

2. *The Poems of Tennyson*, in three volumes, ed. Christopher Ricks (Berkeley: University of California Press, 1987).

3. Herbert F. Tucker, *Tennyson and the Doom of Romanticism* (Cambridge, MA: Harvard University Press, 1988).

4. *The Letters of Alfred, Lord Tennyson*, vol. 2: 1851–1870, ed. Cecil Y. Lang and Edgar F. Shannon, Jr. (Cambridge, MA: Belknap Press of Harvard University Press, 1987).

Epistolary Tennyson

The Art of Suspension

*P*robably only Tennysonians know a group of his poems that may loosely be called verse epistles, and as less than a Tennysonian I discovered them myself fairly recently. The occasion was a small course I taught in Victorian writers where Tennyson was the first poet considered and where the students, bright enough ones, seemed to be having trouble with him. We worked hard with some of the poems of 1842, then with *In Memoriam* and parts of *Maud*, but whatever they made of "major" Tennyson, they didn't much appear to be enjoying him. So it seemed a good idea to suggest that along with poems in the grand style ("Ulysses," "Tithonus") and of psychological-moral debate (*In Memoriam*), there existed a more "social" Tennyson, conveyed in a poetic voice from whose register urbanity and humor were not excluded. Here the Norton Anthology (*The Victorian Age*) was of absolutely no help, since except for parts of *Maud* and a couple of the *Idylls*, post–*In Memoriam* Tennyson pretty much consisted of "Crossing the Bar." Fortunately I made use of Christopher Ricks's critical biography, in which he considers, trenchantly though briefly, some of the poet's epistles. I brought four or five of them into class, reading parts aloud so as to demonstrate a different Tennyson from what the students had experienced so far. However much or little they made of the examples, I was delighted with the discovery that, with Ricks's invaluable help, I had made.

The index to Ricks's edition of Tennyson lists thirty-five poems, almost all with "To" in their title, that qualify as one or another sort of epistle. Of these, this essay will concern itself with the following, listed in chronological order: "To J.S.," "To the Vicar of Shiplake," "The Daisy," "To the Rev. F. D. Maurice," "Prologue to General Hamley," "To

---

First published in *Victorian Poetry* 47 (Spring 2009)

E. FitzGerald," "To Ulysses," "To Mary Boyle," and "To the Marquis of Dufferin and Ava." Some decades ago, a critic offered the following definition of the verse epistle, which I have not seen bettered:

> that kind of poem, presented as a letter, which discusses serious matters of individual, social, or political conduct in an intimate or middle style. On its discursive level, such a work attempts to persuade a recipient—and, through him, its public readers—of the wisdom in a certain attitude or course of action.[1]

By this definition we may rule out certain epistles, such as "To Virgil," "To Dante," "To Princess Frederic on her Marriage," or "To the Queen," in which the figure addressed is one of the august dead, or so far above the poet socially that an intimate or middle style is inappropriate. By contrast, the poems listed above, plus a few others, represent the most engaging examples of Tennyson's "familiar" epistolary style.

W. H. Auden, in his essay on Tennyson, made the too-often-quoted remark that he was "undoubtedly the stupidest" of English poets.[2] It was a stupid remark, since truly stupid poets lack the sense of humor Tennyson held in esteem when he wrote to his wife-to-be in 1839, "I dare not tell how high I rate humour, which is generally most fruitful in the highest and most solemn human spirits."[3] He adduced Dante, Shakespeare, and Cervantes as among those "pregnant with this glorious power." His good friend, the architect James Knowles, detected "a great abundance of playfulness under the grimness of his exterior," and declared that his humor "was all-pervading and flavoured every day with salt. It was habitual with him."[4] As a splendid example of Tennyson's grim playfulness, Eric Griffiths quotes, from Sir Charles Tennyson's biography, a great confrontation between the poet, "stumping along in his cloak and sombrero," and two girls on the beach at Freshwater Bay, Isle of Wight. One of the girls says, "Look . . . There goes Tennyson," and the other exclaims, "What . . . did that old man write *Maud*?" (How well-read the young people were in those days!) In reply, "Tennyson, whose hearing was always extraordinarily acute, stopped, turned round to them and said, with indescribable grimness, Yes, THIS OLD MAN wrote *Maud*, then stumped along on his way without another word."[5] Only a humorist, admittedly a dark one, could have brought this off.

A lighter note was struck in the little poem he wrote to the rector, Drummond Rawnsley, the day after Rawnsley had united Tennyson and Emily Sellwood in marriage. Here, in its revised version, are the first three stanzas of "To the Vicar of Shiplake":

Vicar of that pleasant spot,
    Where it was my chance to marry,
Happy, happy be your lot
    In the Vicarage by the quarry:
You were he that knit the knot.

Sweetly, smoothly flow your life.
    Never parish feud perplex you,
Tithe unpaid, or party strife.
    All things please you, nothing vex you;
You have given me such a wife.

Have I seen in one so near
    Aught but sweetness aye prevailing?
Or, through more than half a year,
    Half the fraction of a failing?
Therefore bless you, Drummond dear.

A trifle, but it is worth noting that the poem preceding it in Ricks's edition ends its lengthy self by invoking "One God, one law, one element, / And one far-off divine event, / To which the whole creation moves." God's earthly representative in "Drummond dear," the Vicar of Shiplake, is charmingly saluted in what, a century later, would be called Light Verse. (I can imagine John Updike turning out something comparable.) How convenient that the vicarage was located nearby a quarry, so as to marry "marry" in rhyme. And to have the swing of "In the Vicarage by the quarry" straighten out into seven monosyllables, neatly finished with "knit the knot." Even the too-perfect homage to the bride's perfection in stanza three is nicely flavored by the play on "half" ("Half a year, / Half the fraction"). Robert Frost once called "style" in prose or verse "that which indicates how the writer takes himself . . . the way he carries himself toward his ideas and deeds."[6] The way Tennyson carried himself

toward his just-completed wedding—lightly, playfully, wittily—is reso-
nantly heard in "To the Vicar of Shiplake."

Nothing could be more distant from this bit of play than one of
Tennyson's earliest epistles, the 1832 "To J.S.," in which he seeks to console
James Spedding, in a matter not too easily consolatory, on the death of
his brother Edward. James Spedding disliked the usual Christian mode of
consolation, and Tennyson's address is filled with doubts about the value
of any words, however well-meant, to compass this event: so he backs
away from words ("I will not say, 'God's ordinance /Of Death is blown
in every wind'" or he protests his necessary inadequacy as a consoler ("In
truth, /How *should* I soothe you anyway"). The poem's voice is, to say the
least, uneasy (Ricks calls it "wooden and strained"), and Tennyson's effort
to avoid speaking in a too-reassuring tone results in a muting, almost,
of any tone whatsoever. Thus the great resource of the verse epistle—
a vigorous and various speaking voice—is what this early poem denies
itself. Still, the final stanza of "To J.S." is a moving one, even as it favors
motionlessness:

> Sleep till the end, true soul and sweet.
>   Nothing comes to thee new or strange,
> Sleep full of rest from head to feet;
>   Lie still, dry dust, secure of change.

For all the possible ambiguity in "secure of change," Ricks is correct to
insist that "the whole feeling of these last lines is set against change, is
absolute for death."[7] And although it is not mentioned as an allusion
in Ricks's or other editions, the line "Nothing comes to thee new or
strange" reminds me of "Nothing ill come near thee," from the "Fear
no more the heat o'the sun" lament over the supposedly dead Fidele
/Imogen's body in *Cymbeline*. (After all, a copy of the play was placed
next to Tennyson in his casket.) Seamus Perry thinks that the ending
of "To J.S." offers a "rum kind of consolation"[8] in its directive to "Lie
still, dry dust, secure of change." But the reader mesmerized by the more
than earthly benediction of that final stanza is not likely to find anything
"rum" about it—or at least not until later reflection, when the music
of the poem has ceased.

It is somewhat of a stretch to use the label personal epistle to cover poems as far apart in their tone and movement as "To J.S." is from what W. W. Robson has called "the happy blend of dignity and informality"[9] found in poems like "The Daisy," "To the Rev. F. D. Maurice," and "To Mary Boyle." Tennyson said in his note to "The Daisy" that it was composed "in a metre which I invented, representing in some measure the grandest of metres, the Horatian Alcaic." In his "Milton" he would later produce, in what he claimed was as an imitation of not the Horatian but the Greek Alcaic meter, sixteen unrhymed lines, the first eight of which are as follows:

> O mighty-mouthed inventor of harmonies,
> O skilled to sing of Time or Eternity,
>> God-gifted organ-voice of England,
>>>> Milton, a name to resound for ages;
> Whose Titan angels, Gabriel, Abdiel,
> Starred from Jehovah's gorgeous armouries,
>> Tower, as the deep-domed empyrean
>>>> Rings to the roar of an angel onset—

Kingsley Amis, in a shrewd essay on Tennyson, calls "Milton" "a magnificent piece, deeply romantic and Romantic, unashamedly lyrical and stuffed with the luxuries of poetry."[10] He also says it makes "metrical sense" in English while employing an alien form. "Metrical sense" the poem does make, yet to these ears it feels somewhat muscle-bound, lacking the "freer and lighter movement" Tennyson attributed to the Greek Alcaic. In terms of English accentual-syllabic prosody, every fourth line of "Milton" can be heard as two dactyls and two trochees ("Milton, a name to resound for ages") or alternately, trochee, iamb, anapest, and iamb with a final unstressed syllable ("Rings to the roar of an angel onset").

Tennyson does something like it in the final line of each quatrain in "To Maurice," but the total effect is unlike the stiff formality of "To Milton." In "Maurice," dignity and informality are blended most skillfully; to produce the "courtesy" and "magnanimity" Ricks finds in the poem, qualities very much carried by the music of its verse and which contradict the discourteous, unmagnanimous behavior of Maurice's opponents at

Cambridge. (He had been ejected from his fellowship at Kings College for questioning the doctrine of eternal punishment; he was also Godfather to Hallam Tennyson.)

Come, when no graver cares employ,
Godfather, come and see your boy:
    Your presence will be sun in winter,
Making the little one leap for joy,

For, being of that honest few,
Who give the Fiend himself his due,
    Should eighty thousand college-councils
Thunder 'Anathema,' friend, at you;

Should all our churchmen foam in spite
At you, so careful of the right,
    Yet one lay-hearth would give you welcome
(Take it and come) to the Isle of Wight;

Where, far from noise and smoke of town,
I watch the twilight falling brown
    All round a careless-order'd garden
Close to the ridge of a noble down.

You'll have no scandal while you dine,
But honest talk and wholesome wine,
    And only hear the magpie gossip
Garrulous under a roof of pine:

For groves of pine on either hand,
To break the blast of winter, stand;
    And further on, the hoary Channel
Tumbles a billow on chalk and sand;

Where, if below the milky steep
Some ship of battle slowly creep,
    And on through zones of light and shadow
Glimmer away to the lonely deep,

We might discuss the Northern sin
Which made a selfish war begin;
    Dispute the claims, arrange the chances;
Emperor, Ottoman, which shall win:

Or whether war's avenging rod
Shall lash all Europe into blood;
    Till you should turn to dearer matters,
Dear to the man that is dear to God;

How best to help the slender store,
How mend the dwellings, of the poor;
    How gain in life, as life advances,
Valor and charity more and more.

Come, Maurice, come: the lawn as yet
Is hoar with rime or spongy-wet;
    But when the wreath of March has blossomed,
Crocus, anemone, violet,

Or later, pay one visit here,
For those are few we hold as dear;
    Nor pay but one, but come for many,
Many and many a happy year.

The sixteen quatrains are made up of four sentences, the shorter ones at
the beginning and end, the longest one stretching from the fifth through the
tenth stanza. Crucial to the poem's generous spirit is what Tennyson does
with the second half of each quatrain, adding a ninth unstressed syllable to
the octosyllabics in the third line, then following the prosody of the fourth
line in "Milton" but shortening it by a syllable. (Compare "Milton, a name
to resound for ages" with "Making the little one leap for joy".)

Horace and Ben Jonson are antecedents for Tennyson's manner here, as in

You'll have no scandal while you dine,
But honest talk and wholesome wine,
    And only hear the magpie gossip
Garrulous under a roof of pine:

In Hallam Tennyson's memoir of his father, Tennyson is reported to have said that he could not read Jonson's work, especially his comedies, but that he did like "It is not growing like a tree," the famous line from Jonson's Cary and Morison ode. At any rate the movement of the quatrain above is quite different from that of "Inviting a Friend to Supper," in which the virtues of rich Canary wine are promised the guest: "Of this we will sup free, but moderately . . . Nor shall our cups make any guilty men." The only scandal or gossip Maurice will hear as he is wined and dined is that of the magpie, but what *we* hear is the transit from "gossip" to "Garrulous," with its tumbling rhythm. Of course I've taken the tumbling from the stanza following:

> For groves of pine on either hand,
> To break the blast of winter stand,
>   And further on, the hoary Channel
> Tumbles a billow on chalk and sand;

Tennyson's closing lines to the quatrains are such "killers" that they override, for better or worse, any "ideas" the invitation may propose. John Bayley follows the demur of a nineteenth-century reviewer in finding too cozy the attempt to have timely conversation about the Crimean war in progress:

> Where, if below the milky steep
> Some ship of battle slowly creep,
>   And on through zones of light and shadow
> Glimmer away to the lonely deep,
>
> We might discuss the Northern sin
> Which made a selfish war begin;
>   Dispute the claims, arrange the chances;
> Emperor, Ottoman, which shall win:

Bayley finds this has "too neat a finish to it" that is "somehow inappropriate";[11] but my thoughts about appropriate or not get swept away instead by the tumbling dactyls of "Emperor, Ottoman," and the alliterative close of "which shall win."

No one, however, will disagree that the closing stanzas are perfect:

Come, Maurice, come: the lawn as yet
Is hoar with rime, or spongy-wet;
    But when the wreath of March has blossomed,
Crocus, anemone, violet,

Or later, pay one visit here,
For those are few we hold as dear;
    Nor pay but one, but come for many,
Many and many a happy year.

Along with the pleasing, purely sonic values of "Crocus, anemone, violet," it's an ending that doesn't end too quickly, the punctuation artfully varying from commas to colon to semi-colons as the conjunctive invitations and qualifications—Come . . . But . . . Or . . . For . . . Nor—provide exquisite timing for the invitation. Bayley thinks the poem "presents its picture in too full and humorous a light for the bard to muse and loiter with us in its composition." The objection may be answered by registering the lingering (another word Bayley uses) pace of those final quatrains. Like the linnet in Yeats's "A Prayer for My Daughter," they "have no business but dispensing round / Their magnanimities of sound."

John Bayley calls "The Daisy" the "most enchanting and open of all poems,"[12] a large claim that Ricks has gone some way toward substantiating as "one of the finest poetic evocations of gratitude."[13] Addressed to his wife, who has just borne their son Hallam, "The Daisy" is a retrospective look at the Tennysons' recent Italian journey. Too long for full quotation, the poem nicely embodies Tennyson's capacity for loitering and lingering, and is also notable for its humorous take on things, even in the midst of affirming marital love through the consecrations of memory. For the consecration is not solemn, and a playful wit surfaces memorably in a quatrain near the poem's middle, when after "golden hours" spent in Florence, the couple run into some bad weather in Lombardy:

But when we crost the Lombard plain
Remember what a plague of rain;
    Of rain at Reggio, rain at Parma;
At Lodi, rain, Piacenza, rain.

And stern and sad (so rare the smile
Of sunlight) looked the Lombard piles;
    Porch-pillars on the lion resting,
And sombre, old, colonnaded aisles.

(The plague-of-rain stanza has managed to run and rerun itself through my head so as to prolong an insomniac moment.) However much "The Daisy" expresses gratitude toward Emily Tennyson, the artful variety of rain in places visited on the way from Reggio to Milan, is a tour de force. "Light verse" is inadequate to summon up the performing mix, in the closing line of each stanza (iamb/iamb/anapest/iamb) that creates a graceful dance-step effect similar to—though not the same as—the closing lines of the "Maurice" quatrains. (Also crucial to the effect is the feminine ending in the third line of each stanza, giving the upcoming anapest something to answer to.) Never was traveler's discomfort more handsomely saluted: "In Lodi, rain, Piacenza, rain."

The magic word for it is perhaps timing, and one of the best timers in the next century, Elizabeth Bishop, once wrote an undergraduate essay about timing in the poetry of Hopkins. Bishop says about poetry considered as motion that it is "[t]he releasing, checking, timing, and repeating of the movement of the mind according to ordered systems."[4] She notes, as central to Hopkins's poetic timing, his use of "alliteration, repetition, and inside rhymes." The following sequence from "The Daisy" may suggest how central such timing is to Tennyson's operation as well. These four stanzas describe voyaging on flooded Lake Como, mention Vergil's alluding to the lake as "Larius," ("of thee, Larius, our greatest"), and identify a castle above the port of Varenna, once the haunt of the sixth century Queen Theodolind. One needs notes to recognize the players, but the play—the timing of the stanzas—is strongly felt, as in the earlier plague-of-rain one:

Remember how we came at last
To Como; shower and storm and blast
    Had blown the lake beyond his limit,
And all was flooded; and how we past

From Como, when the light was gray,
And in my head, for half the day,

> The rich Virgilian rustic measure
> Of Lari Maxume, all the way,
>
> Like ballad-burthen music, kept,
> As on the Lariano crept
>   To that fair port below the castle
> Of Queen Theodolind, where we slept;
>
> Or hardly slept, but watched awake
> A cypress in the moonlight shake,
>   The moonlight touching o'er a terrace
> One tall Agavé above the lake.

(An Agavé is a tropical plant.) Here Tennyson loiters grandly, unwilling to conclude even at the end of the third stanza where it looks to be time for sleeping, but not quite so: "Or hardly slept, but watched awake." Here also are the repetitions and alliterations Bishop speaks of, joining the words yet hesitating to conclude the journey too soon—to conclude with anything less than "One tall Agavé above the lake," with assonance and an inside rhyme.

"To the Rev. F. D. Maurice" and "The Daisy" were written in the mid 1850s, and thirty years later Tennyson returned to the epistolary form, now often as a dedicatory introduction to an enclosed longer poem. One of the best of these, and pretty much unnoticed even by specialists, is "Prologue to General Hamley," which prefaces "The Charge of the Heavy Brigade." Hamley was a Crimean veteran who deserved more credit than he had been given for his performance in the recent victory at Tel-el-Kebir in Egypt. Worth remarking in the Hamley prologue is its long suspension of a single sentence over thirty-two lines, something he achieved at about the same time in the better-known "To E. FitzGerald":

> Our birches yellowing and from each
>   The light leaf falling fast,
> While squirrels from our fiery beech
>   Were bearing off the mast,

You came, and looked and loved the view
　　Long-known and loved by me,
Green Sussex fading into blue
　　With one gray glimpse of sea;
And, gazing from this height alone,
　　We spoke of what had been
Most marvellous in the wars your own
　　Crimean eyes had seen;
And now—like old-world inns that take
　　Some warrior for a sign
That therewithin a guest may make
　　True cheer with honest wine—
Because you heard the lines I read
　　Nor uttered word of blame,
I dare without your leave to head
　　These rhymings with your name,
Who know you but as one of those
　　I fain would meet again,
Yet know you, as your England knows
　　That you and all your men
Were soldiers to her heart's desire,
　　When, in the vanished year,
You saw the league-long rampart-fire
　　Flare from Tel-el-Kebir
Through darkness, and the foe was driven,
　　And Wolseley overthrew
Arâbi, and the stars in heaven
　　Paled, and the glory grew.

The triumph of Hamley and Wolseley over the forces of Egypt's Pasha Arâbi fills us with less than exhilaration. Yet there is something compelling in the curve of the whole poem, as it moves from an intimate, rather Shelleyan opening (compare Shelley's late "To Jane: The Recollection") to the designedly stirring close which, like the stanzas quoted from "The Daisy", refuses to close ("When, in the vanished year, / You saw the league-long rampart-fire/Flare from Tel-el-Kebir/Through darkness"). It is as though the whole poem were constructed to lead up to the clinching rhyme of "Kebir" with "year," only to keep going "through darkness" and beyond. In *The Faber Popular Reciter*, Kingsley Amis calls poems "reciters" which, while touching no depth of complexity or inwardness, invite themselves to be read aloud with declamatory force. The Hamley prologue moves from quiet intimacy to a reciter-like ending; it would have been a good poem for Tennyson to read aloud to guests, and perhaps he did so.

We would expect that these epistles from the last decade of Tennyson's life should contain, centrally, an elegiac note. In the poem to Hamley, Tennyson compares himself to an "old-world inn" promising the guest "true cheer with honest wine," as he remembers Hamley's hospitality to a poem he once read to him. As in Jonson's "Inviting a Friend to Supper" mentioned earlier, the colloquy is between two men whose discourse, along with the food and wine, is blamelessly above the petty spites and frustrations of less pure discourse. Only the death of one party can put an end to such ideal communication, which is why the death of Edward FitzGerald, registered in the "epilogue" of "To E. FitzGerald" is so moving. In the prologue of this dedicatory poem (Tennyson is sending FitzGerald "Tiresias," an early poem not published until 1885), Tennyson marks the death of two of his and FitzGerald's friends, W. H. Brookfield and James Spedding ("Two voices heard on earth no more") and declares that "we old friends are still alive." He got the date of FitzGerald's birthday wrong, but, more sadly, did not foresee his dying before he could read Tennyson's poem. So in the lines he subsequently wrote to conclude the poem, "the tolling of his funeral bell" breaks in upon "the dreams of classic times, /And all the phantoms of the dream." FitzGerald's absence is compared to a residence (like the inn in the Hamley poem) now emptied and making Tennyson's rhymes

> That missed his living welcome, seem
> Like would-be guests an hour too late,
> Who down the highway moving on
> With easy laughter find the gate
> Is bolted, and the master gone.

That period after "gone" is the only one in the closing section of "To E. FitzGerald," and is a measure of Tennyson's recognition of finality:

> Gone into darkness, that full light
> > Of friendship! past, in sleep, away
> By night, into the deeper night!

Although the poem goes on for some lines more, declaring the "deeper night" to be in truth "a clearer day" than anything we know on earth, it doesn't quite declaim away the eternal putting-out of "that full light of friendship." "To E. FitzGerald" has had ample appreciation elsewhere for its stylistic and moral fineness, but the tonal shift from "the master gone" to "Gone into darkness" is particularly and finely touching.

His late epistles have something of the quality of a circus act about them, even as they confront, in a variety of tones, the facts of aging and oncoming death. In "To Ulysses" the Ulysses-figure is W. G. Palgrave, who had published a book of travel pieces titled *Ulysses*, and who was the brother of F. T. Palgrave, close friend of Tennyson and editor of *The Golden Treasury*. Tennyson had met W. G. Palgrave many times but the relationship seems not to have been a close one (Hallam Tennyson does not mention W. G. Palgrave in his memoir). This in no way deters Tennyson from putting on a truly high-wire performance, twelve quatrains in the *In Memoriam* stanza, spliced into a single sentence the first five quatrains of which contrast the recipient, living in South America, with the old poet who is enduring the English climate:

I

Ulysses, much-experienced man,
> Whose eyes have known this globe of ours,
> Her tribes of men, and trees, and flowers,
From Corrientes to Japan,

II

To you that bask below the Line,
> I soaking here in winter wet—
> The century's three strong eights have met
To drag me down to seventy-nine

III

In summer if I reach my day—
> To you, yet young, who breathe the balm

Of summer-winters by the palm
And orange grove of Paraguay,

IV

I tolerant of the colder time,
   Who love the winter woods, to trace
   On paler heavens the branching grace
Of leafless elm, or naked lime,

V

And see my cedar green, and there
   My giant ilex keeping leaf
   When frost is keen and days are brief—

On it proceeds, eventually ending in a host of names, the places Palgrave
had written about ("Hong-Kong, Karnac, and all the rest"), with noth-
ing "significant" accomplished except the turning of one more graceful
overture to another person. In a sense it is a superfluous poem, but it
is the sense that Frost evokes when, in the letter about "style" quoted
previously, he says about the writer, "The style is out of his superfluity.
It is the mind skating circles round itself as it moves forward." Somehow
writing a clever poem like this one to Palgrave ("the cleverest man I ever
met," Tennyson is quoted as having said of Palgrave), helped Tennyson
persist in going on living, skating circles of inventiveness around his mind
as it moved forward. Like FitzGerald, W. G. Palgrave died, says Tennyson's
note, "at Monte Video before seeing my poem." This was in September
1888, by which time "The century's three strong eights" had dragged
Tennyson down to age seventy-nine.

      Longevity of friendship was in no way a requirement for
Tennyson to turn out sumptuous verse to a friend. He did not meet
Mary Boyle until 1882 (she was an aunt of Hallam Tennyson's wife) but
wrote her perhaps his most vigorous and full-throated invitation to visit
Farringford. She has promised a visit, saying "I come with your spring
flowers," but has delayed the visit, and Tennyson warns her not to wait

until "Our vernal bloom from every vale and plain /And garden pass, /
And all the gold from each laburnum chain /Drop to the grass." As an
incentive he is sending her a "song of spring," an early poem "found
yesterday" (titled "The Progress of Spring") and written "half a hundred
years ago." Thus launched into considerations of youth and age, he gathers
himself and his recipient into the seven lovely quatrains that conclude the
poem, beginning with a recollected time

> ### XI
>
> When this bare dome had not begun to gleam
>   Through youthful curls,
> And you were then a lover's fairy dream,
>   His girl of girls;
>
> ### XII
>
> And you, that now are lonely, and with Grief
>   Sit face to face,
> Might find a flickering glimmer of relief
>   In change of place.
>
> ### XIII
>
> What use to brood? this life of mingled pains
>   And joys to me,
> Despite of every Faith and Creed, remains
>   The Mystery.
>
> ### XIV
>
> Let golden youth bewail the friend, the wife,
>   For ever gone.
> He dreams of that long walk through desert life
>   Without the one.
>
> ### XV
>
> The silver year should cease to mourn and sigh—
>   Not long to wait—
> So close are we, dear Mary, you and I
>   To that dim gate.

XVI

Take, read! and be the faults your Poet makes
    Or many or few,
He rests content, if his young music wakes
    A wish in you

XVII

To change our dark Queen-city, all her realm
    Of sound and smoke,
For his clear heaven, and these few lanes of elm
    And whispering oak.

No matter how hard "Faith" and "Creed" work, the only "clear heaven" is the one in this world—or rather, in the imagined world of the poem, where elm and whispering oak provide the true, if momentary, respite from the "dim gate" Tennyson and Mary Boyle are approaching.

In his fine essay on Tennyson, A. C. Bradley called "To Mary Boyle" "one of the most perfect things he ever wrote, and an example of a kind of verse in which no contemporary approached him."[15] This "kind" is, like most of the other epistles, felt through the variety and amplitude of voice-tones heard, never more so than here. Relatedly, it has to do with what Seamus Perry described astutely as "the involved relationship in Tennyson between eloquence and reticence, assertiveness and unspokenness."[16] Tennyson's eloquence is something taken for granted, but his reticence is not so easy to measure. In "Mary Boyle" it has everything to do with subtlety of timing: with the alternate pentameter/dimeter of each stanza; perhaps also, with the roman numeral given to each stanza imparting a little formality and distance to the warmly issued invitation.

But it is in "To the Marquis of Dufferin and Ava" that eloquence and reticence are most delicately balanced. Tennyson's elegiac tribute is both to his son Lionel, who died of fever while sailing home from India, and to Dufferin, the Governor-General of India who cared for Lionel in his illness. Here again the relative formality of the numbered stanzas may contribute to a slight checking of the impassioned outpouring that doesn't just pour out. The final six of its thirteen stanzas are part of a long sentence that sweeps through much of the poem's latter half. Lionel

Tennyson "might have chased and claspt Renown" if he had not, instead, caught jungle-fever:

> ### IX
>
> But ere he left your fatal shore,
>   And lay on that funereal boat,
>   Dying, "Unspeakable" he wrote
> "Their kindness," and he wrote no more;
>
> ### X
>
> And sacred is the latest word;
>   And now the Was, the Might-have-been,
>   And those lone rites I have not seen,
> And one drear sound I have not heard,
>
> ### XI
>
> Are dreams that scarce will let me be,
>   Not there to bid my boy farewell,
>   When That within the coffin fell,
> Fell—and flashed into the Red Sea,
>
> ### XII
>
> Beneath a hard Arabian moon
>   And alien stars. To question, why
>   The sons before the fathers die,
> Not mine! and I may meet him soon;
>
> ### XIII
>
> But while my life's late eve endures,
>   Nor settles into hueless gray,
>   My memories of his briefer day
> Will mix with love for you and yours.

Stanza nine has, rightly, attracted critical attention. Auden, in his essay, dismissed it without comment except to quote it as an example of being "unintentionally funny at a serious moment."[17] He thought Tennyson had produced a Stuffed Owl bit of maladroitness in his use of the word "Unspeakable" from Lionel's letter home. It is in fact a very un-Audenish moment in its cultivation of a somewhat twisted, just barely able to be articulated assertion. John Bayley corrected Auden by pointing out the "surprise effect" of "Unspeakable" as it "hovers between the colloquial exaggeration of social use . . . and a word that can mean exactly what it says."[18] Seamus Perry, also focusing on the stanza, quotes a relevant formulation from another critic: "In some ways Tennyson is a poet of deep inarticulateness, but he is an *emotional* intelligence of the highest order."[19] It is at any rate a very different intelligence from Auden's crisply knowing manner of expressing whatever he was believing at this or that moment in his career. Tennyson has no such facility, but—perhaps therefore—his emotional intelligence makes itself felt in the way the sentence-stanzas proceed with a hard won inevitability. I am thinking particularly of the timing, the painful rendering of the "dreams that scarce will let me be":

> Not there to bid my boy farewell,
> When That within the coffin fell,
> Fell—and flashed into the Red Sea,
>
> Beneath a hard Arabian moon
> And alien stars.

A poet less extraordinary and distinctive than Tennyson would surely have opted for a full stop after the lifeless "That" meets the Red Sea. Instead he goes on to place the flashing beneath moon and stars, finally coming to rest in the middle of a line and in so doing enacting one of his most affecting suspensions of death, brought to breathing life in the verse.

NOTES

1. Jay Arnold Levine, "The Status of the Verse Epistle before Pope," in *Studies in Philology* 58 (1962): 658–84.
2. W. H. Auden, "Tennyson," in *Forewords and Afterwords* (London: Faber, 1973), 221–32.
3. Hallam Tennyson, *Alfred, Lord Tennyson* (London: Macmillan, 1897), 1:168.
4. Quoted in Seamus Perry, *Tennyson* (Devon, UK: Northcote House, 2005), 15.

5. Eric Griffiths, "Tennyson's Breath," in *The Printed Voice of Victorian Poetry* (Oxford: Clarendon Press, 1989), 134.

6. Frost to Louis Untermeyer, 10 March 1924, in *Selected Letters of Robert Frost*, ed. Lawrance Thompson (New York: Henry Holt, 1965), 299.

7. Christopher Ricks, *Tennyson* (London: Macmillan, 1972), 98.

8. Seamus Perry, *Alfred Tennyson*, 38.

9. W. W. Robson, "The Present Value of Tennyson," in *Studies in Tennyson*, ed. Hallam Tennyson (London: Macmillan, 1981), 50.

10. Kingsley Amis, "On Tennyson," in *The Amis Collection* (London: Hutchinson, 1990), 184–92.

11. John Bayley, "Tennyson and the Idea of Decadence," in *Studies in Tennyson*, 194.

12. Ibid.

13. Ricks, 244.

14. Elizabeth Bishop, "Gerard Manley Hopkins: Notes on Timing in his Poetry" in *Poems, Plays and Letters* (New York: Library of America, 2008), 660–67.

15. A. C. Bradley, "The Reaction against Tennyson," in *A Miscellany* (London: Macmillan, 1910), 1–32.

16. Perry, 14.

17. Auden, 224.

18. Bayley, 204.

19. Perry is quoting James Richardson, *Vanishing Lives: Style and Self in Tennyson, D. G. Rossetti, Swinburne, and Yeats* (Charlottesville: University Press of Virginia, 1988), 90. W. David Shaw writes well about the stanza in *Alfred Lord Tennyson: The Poet in an Age of Theory* (New York: Twayne, 1996), 41.

Hardy's Poetry of Old Age

*T*homas Hardy's most distinctive volume of verse, *Sat-ires of Circumstances, Lyrics and Reveries,* was published in 1914 when the poet was seventy-four. Although it contains classic anthology pieces like "Channel Firing," and "The Convergence of the Twain," along with personal lyrics as fine as "In Death Divided" and "My Spirit Will Not Haunt the Mound," it is the sequence of poems provoked by the death of his wife Emma in 1912 that has most drawn the attention and admiration of critics—from Donald Davie and Irving Howe some decades ago, to current readers and teachers of Hardy's poems. *Poems of 1912–13,* most notably "The Going," "Rain on a Grave," "The Haunter," "The Voice," "After a Journey," and "At Castle Boterel"—two of which even made F. R. Leavis's severely restricted list of the dozen or so "major" poems Hardy wrote—contain what Leavis liked to call an "exploratory-creative" inclination and force that would never so dominate Hardy's lyrics afterwards.

Yet remember how much of an afterwards it was: four volumes fol-lowed *Satires of Circumstance,* making up the larger half of the *Complete Poems.* As with earlier collections, Hardy published poems that he had kept in his drawer for years, decades; still, even though we can't be fully definitive about it, the four last books include plenty of current work. Hardy was like Wordsworth in many ways, not the least in that he seems to have thought well of every poem he ever wrote and showed no shyness or hesitation about adding another to the pile, an enormous pile (919 in all, plus some uncollected ones in James Gibson's edition). My aim is to characterize some of Hardy's poems of old age, taking old age to cover the years from age seventy-five on when Hardy published them. It is an age that few of his poetic contemporaries and successors survived into

First published in *Literary Imagination* 6, no. 1 (2004): 78–93 and also kept on writing: Yeats died at seventy-four, Eliot got to seventy-six but had stopped writing poems; Stevens died at seventy-five; Frost and Pound made it into their eighties, and William Carlos Williams nearly did; Robert Graves reached ninety but had been senile for years. Hardy died short of his eighty-eighth birthday and the preface to his final, posthumous volume *Winter Words in Various Moods and Metres* contains a sentence that reads "So far as I am aware, I happen to be the only English poet who has brought out a new volume of his poems on his . . . birthday."

The Hardy scholar and critic Samuel Hynes, in an essay "How To Be an Old Poet," has addressed this fact or problem in relation to Hardy and Yeats. His way of distinguishing them is to compare Yeats to Lear, Hardy to Prospero, and he concludes that Hardy was "an old poet who was content to be entirely old, who was at ease with diminishment, even at ease with the prospect of approaching death, accepting silence, accepting forgottenness." "A philosophical old man," Hynes concludes, and in his opinion "a more disturbing model" than Yeats. "Life and poetry ran down together," Hynes writes, "and ended in silence—without continuance and without regret." Hynes also uses the word "modest" to describe Hardy's attitude, compared with Yeats's flamboyant, self-dramatizing defiance. But why should a modest stance on the part of Hardy disturb Hynes more than Yeats's turbulent declarations in "Why Should Not Old Men Be Mad?" or "The Wild Old Wicked Man"? And Prospero, after all, is scarcely modest in his invocations of cloud-capped towers and the great globe itself that will fade and leave not a rack behind. Perhaps Hardy as Old Poet is a little odder—more remote, even perverse—than Hynes quite suggests.

Reading Hardy's letters is, except for the complete specialist, a less than vivid experience, with some pretty thin gruel dished out. But the experienced reader, having ploughed through a number of unremarkable replies to various correspondents, begins to take some pleasure in the way, unfailingly, Hardy doesn't open up to the occasion. Thus when an American journalist sent him an article he had written, Hardy replied as follows:

> Dear Mr. De Casseres: I have read with interest your articles in this month's *International Review* and also some previous articles that you have sent. I am of course unable to criticize the former and the others do not require remark.

I am glad to hear that your hands are full of work, since your mind is, no doubt, full of ideas. Wishing you success believe me,

Yours very truly,

Thomas Hardy

No doubt De Casseres's mind was full of ideas, and surely it is beyond question that his essays didn't "require remark"—and if they did Hardy would of course have been unable to criticize them. (One imagines Hardy clearing his morning desk of letters to be replied to, before getting down to the requirements of a poem.) And it wasn't only intrusive American journalists who needed to be fended off. When Frederic Harrison wrote him a note of congratulation on his marriage to his second wife, Florence, Hardy assured him that for both of them the event was of "a sober color enough," and "that the union of two rather melancholy temperaments may result in cheerfulness, as the function of two negatives forms a positive, is our modest hope." In other words, things marital may be going to get better, though I'm not convinced that they did, at least beyond this "modest hope." What species of "modesty" is it that speaks this way about a significant life-event?

We might juxtapose the letter to De Casseres, which offers him the equivalent of nothing, with a poem from *Human Shows, Far Fantasies*, dated 9 October 1924, when the poet was eighty-four, titled "Nobody Comes":

> Tree-leaves labour up and down,
>   And through them the fainting light
>   Succumbs to the crawl of night.
> Outside in the road the telegraph wire
>   To the town from the darkening land
> Intones to travellers like a spectral lyre
>   Swept by a spectral hand.
>
> A car comes up, with lamps full-glare,
>   That flash upon a tree:
>   It has nothing to do with me,
> And whangs along in a world of its own,
>   Leaving a blacker air;

> And mute by the gate I stand again alone,
>> And nobody pulls up there.

The very beautiful, elegant evocation of the telegraph wire, wonderful means of communication, has nothing to do with any message it may bring Hardy the non-traveler, even as from the darkening land it "Intones to travelers like a spectral lyre /Swept by a spectral hand." Unheard melodies for Hardy are sweeter, no doubt about it, almost as sweet as unvisitors flashing by in the car, brightening for the briefest moment the darkening land. Any "normal" poet, especially one age eighty-four, might seize the occasion to lament his (increasing) isolation and loneliness; only Hardy could turn it into a small victory ("It has nothing to do with me") by dismissing the intruder with the excellent verb "whangs." The air now being blacker than it was before the momentary flash-up, the poet can celebrate his muteness (no message to communicate) with a doubling of isolation: "And mute by the gate I stand again alone, /And nobody pulls up there."

The most obvious way to contrast one of Hardy's late poems is to juxtapose it with one of Yeats's and note possible adjectives that could relevantly be used about the tone of each. Think of the third stanza of Yeats's "An Acre of Grass":

> Grant me an old man's frenzy.
> Myself must I remake
> Till I am Timon and Lear
> Or that William Blake
> Who beat upon the wall
> Till truth obeyed his call [...]

George Orwell was put off from this stanza by the histrionic posturing he detected in "Or that William Blake." Orwell wrote, "One seldom comes on six consecutive lines of his verse in which there is not an archaism or an affected turn of speech." It was the "that" in "Or that William Blake" which tonally offended Orwell. By contrast, "Mute at the gate I stand again alone, /And nobody pulls up there" seems resistant to any attempt to provide it with a specific personal inflection. J. O. Bailey finds, as I do not, that the lines suggest "an atmosphere of expectation, disappointment and loneliness." One might say instead that it is Voice with a capital V speaking, rather than a voice in any particular tone—affected, defiant, remorseful, bereft.

Although the Hardy-Yeats pairing or opposition was doubtless mentioned earlier in the century, it was Philip Larkin's two short reviews in the 1960s that memorably pointed up the effect of these two poets on a third—himself. Larkin's early volume *The North Ship* is full of Yeats, but in the preface he wrote to it later on he notes that, having come to Hardy after Yeats, he found himself with "the Celtic fever abated, and the patient sleeping soundly." In his radio talk, "The Poetry of Hardy," Larkin said that he took up Hardy "with the sense of relief that I didn't have to try and jack myself up to a concept of poetry that lay outside my life—this is perhaps what I felt Yeats was trying to make me do." And in the often-referred-to "Wanted: Good Hardy Critic," Larkin asks that this as yet unmaterialized figure pay attention to "the presence of pain in Hardy's novels." Larkin called that pain a "positive" rather than "negative" quality and handsomely named it as "the continual imaginative celebration of what is both the truest and the most important element in life, most important in the sense of most necessary to spiritual development." Certainly it was most important to Larkin's own spiritual and poetic development; one sees why the other kind of "positive"—Yeats's affirmations, for example, at the end of "A Dialogue of Self and Soul" ("We must dance and we must sing, / We are blest by everything, / Everything we look upon is blest") would have had no charms for the later poet of deprivation who didn't want to be jacked up into affirmation.

Larkin refers here to Hardy's novels, and in fact he never says much about the poems beyond asserting that he would not wish the *Complete Poems* a single page shorter and that it represented the best body of verse produced in the twentieth century. Presumably the concept of poetry that Hardy embraced, and that lay inside rather than outside Larkin's experience, had everything to do with its commitment to the sadness of life; it spoke to the younger poet who was wont to celebrate "Threadbare perspectives, seasonal decrease" ("Triple-Time"), for whom "Life is slow dying" ("Nothing to Be Said") and who titled a poem "Home Is So Sad."

He would go on to beat Hardy in the Sadness Sweepstakes, partly because the older poet was much more reticent about performing his grief than was Larkin.

In "Wanted: Good Hardy Critic" Larkin, with reference to *Tess of the d'Urbervilles*, said he had become more aware of an undercurrent of sensual cruelty in Hardy: "For all his gentleness he had a strong awareness of, and even relish for, both the macabre and the cruel." Larkin allows that there is an "ancient tradition" of such awareness, but seems slightly embarrassed to put Hardy in it. Sensual or not, the element of cruelty Larkin detected in *Tess* is there in certain poems of Hardy's that twist life into grotesque shapes too perfectly awful to be quite true. Two poems from his final volume, *Winter Words*, may suggest what I mean: neither of them wins a place in anyone's favorite anthology of Hardy's lyrics, yet they catch a reader's attention (they certainly caught this reader's attention), especially as a relief from yet another poem looking back guiltily on the death and subsequent absence of Emma Hardy.

The first of these is "Henley Regatta":

> She looks from the window: still it pours down direly,
> And the avenue drips. She cannot go, she fears;
> And the Regatta will be spoilt entirely;
>   And she sheds half-crazed tears.
>
> Regatta Day and rain come on together
> Again, years after. Gutters trickle loud;
> But Nancy cares not. She knows nought of weather,
>   Or of the Henley crowd:
>
> She's a Regatta quite her own. Inanely
> She laughs in the asylum as she floats
> Within a water-tub, which she calls 'Henley,'
>   Her little paper boats.

From half-crazed to wholly so, all in twelve lines. I have no idea when "Henley Regatta" was written; it bears resemblance to the group of "Satires of Circumstance" Hardy liked to conjure up in prose and verse. But its cruelty, I should hazard, is of a piece with its absolutely airtight, bullet-proof construction. The anonymous speaker shelters himself from any responsibility for what happened; after all, he merely knows everything and hands across to us a couple of juxtaposed items that make up all we need to know about the life of "Nancy." The triumph of the third stanza's opening line—"She's a Regatta quite her own," with its punch lines to come; the flaunting, callous off-rhyming of "Inanely" with "Henley"; the refusal overall to provide any specification or understanding of where this little bit of life has come from and why it is served up to us—if this doesn't amount to a kind of moral cruelty, it may at least strike us as opportunistic and manipulative, making sure, as Eliot said about Pound's canto, that hell is for the other people. One of Hardy's great poems, "The Convergence of the Twain," celebrated the consummation that jarred two hemispheres in a grand style of performance that designedly excluded expressions of the poet's sympathy and pity for victims of the Titanic disaster. Hardy succeeded there partly because he found an original language for a happening of inexpressible disaster. "Henley Regatta" does things on a very small scale: its perfect, too-perfect execution of this hapless woman leaves us wondering about the quality of Hardy's poetic sympathy, a rather shocking diminishment of Wordsworth's poet as "the rock and defence for human nature . . . carrying everywhere with him relationship and love."

Hardy's relation to pets—to birds and animals—has been remarked on, and he made public testimony to his concern about their humane treatment. "The Blinded Bird" is a touching poem with a great last stanza, and there is also "The Caged Goldfinch" and "Last Words to a Dumb Friend" in which he mourns his dead cat ("Pet was never mourned like you,/Purrer of the spotless hue"). That poem is dated October 1904 and in it he declares "Never another pet for me!" Evidently he changed his mind, for when E. M. Forster visited him eighteen years later, Forster was taken on a little tour of the pet cemetery at Max Gate:

> T.H. showed me the graves of all his pets, all overgrown with ivy, their names on the head stones. Such a dolorous muddle. "This is Snowbell—she was run over by a train . . . this is Pella, the same thing happened to her . . . this is Kitkin, she was cut clean in two,

clean in two—" "How is it that so many of your cats have been run over, Mr. Hardy? Is the railway near?" "Not at all near, not at all near—I don't know how it is. But of course we have only buried here those pets whose bodies were recovered. Many were never seen again."

Forster added, "I could scarcely keep grave—it was so like a caricature of his own novels and poems." As little Father Time put it in *Jude the Obscure,* having put himself away—"Done because we are too menny."

It's of course unfair to select a single poem of Hardy's and use it to demonstrate something about the moral character of the poet. But is there not something akin to the carefully stacked deck of "Henley Re-gatta" to be seen in another poem from *Winter Words* that not surprisingly gets overlooked—although once you've read and registered it, you don't forget it. This is a dog poem, "The Mongrel":

In Havenpool Harbour the ebb was strong,
And a man with a dog drew near and hung;
And taxpaying day was coming along,
    So the mongrel had to be drowned.
The man threw a stick from the paved wharf-side
Into the midst of the ebbing tide,
And the dog jumped after with ardent pride
    To bring the stick aground.

But no: the steady suck of the flood
To seaward needed, to be withstood,
More than the strength of mongrelhood
    To fight its treacherous trend.
So, swimming for life with desperate will,
The struggler with all his natant skill
Kept buoyant in front of his master, still
    There standing to wait the end.

The loving eyes of the dog inclined
To the man he held as a god enshrined,
With no suspicion in his mind

That this had all been meant.
Till the effort not to drift from shore
Of his little legs grew slower and slower,
And, the tide still outing with brookless power,
    Outward the dog, too, went.

Just ere his sinking what does one see
Break on the face of that devotee?
A wakening to the treachery
    He had loved with love so blind?
The faith that had shone in that mongrel's eye
That his owner would save him by and by
Turned to much like a curse as he sank to die,
    And a loathing of mankind.

I've always been shocked by this poem, a feeling that has only increased upon becoming part-owner of a lovely corgi. But what are we shocked at? Surely not merely at the treacherous owner who, even though taxpaying day was coming along, should not have resorted to this dreadful solution, should he have? And of course we don't blame the dog. But what about the poet supervising all this—what about Hardy? What and where is he? One answer is that he is overwhelmingly present throughout, at the same time as being thoroughly absent: no opinions of an onlooker are given, just the facts, even though the poet knows exactly what the dog was thinking as he perished. The form is unyielding, with the anapestic lilt continuing throughout; the rhymes are strong except for a couple of slanty ones. All the stops are pulled out to make the terrible event terrible: in stanza three, for example, the dog's eyes are "loving" and his legs "little" as they fail him against the tide. Like "Henley Regatta," the poem is airtight, with no place for any attitude or feeling to qualify the relentless narrative from its beginning to its end. Is there a relation between the poet who wrote and (however long he may have kept it around) published this poem, and the doleful Hardy puttering about his pet cemetery, moaning dolorously about all the dead cats? Is "The Mongrel" an aberration or bit of excess from a poet whom Larkin trusted as the finest of guides to life in the twentieth century? At any rate it presents a Hardy rather different from the Prospero-like figure evoked by Samuel Hynes, all passion spent; different also from the modest, selfless accentor of life in its final stage. It is rather an aggressive, even a provocative performance from this greatly self-contained man; indeed "self" is so contained as barely to exist in the poem.

Where, in the late Hardy, does one most feel human fullness, the sense of a self realizing itself and also moving toward a larger perspective? I first encountered "The Missed Train," number 759 of the *Complete Poems*, in the odd but memorable selection John Crowe Ransom put together forty years ago. Ransom doesn't discuss the poem in his introduction and it is followed in his selection by an utterly different performance, the humorous "A Popular Personage at Home" about Hardy's beloved dog ("I live here: 'Wessex' is my name: / I am a dog known rather well: / I guard the house; but how that came / To be my whim I cannot tell"). The dog poem is dated 1924, and "The Missed Train" bears no date, but I want it to be very late Hardy and thus far no one has proved me wrong:

> How I was caught
> Hieing home, after days of allure,
> And forced to an inn—small, obscure—
> At the junction, gloom-fraught.
>
> How civil my face
> To get them to chamber me there—
> A roof I had scorned, scarce aware
> That it stood at the place.
>
> And how all the night
> I had dreams of the unwitting cause
> Of my lodgment. How lonely I was;
> How consoled by her sprite!
>
> Thus onetime to me . . .
> Dim wastes of dead years bar away
> Then from now. But such happenings to-day
> Fall to lovers, may be!
>
> Years, years as shoaled seas,
> Truly, stretch now between! Less and less

Shrink the visions then vast in me.—Yes,
  Then in me: Now in these.

In *Lives of the Modern Poets* I took a quick stab at the poem, pointing to how the "dead" language employed made for life. I would now add that this language makes for "quickening" by leaving out the transitions from one state of feeling to another.

Their absence may be pointed up by a contrast with their presence in the two finest *Poems of 1912–13*, "After a Journey" and "At Castle Boterel." In the former, Emma's "voiceless ghost" is pursued by Hardy at Pentargan Bay until, in the third stanza, he catches on to what the ghost has in mind:

I see what you are doing: you are leading me on
  To the spots we knew when we haunted here together,
The waterfall, above which the mist-bow shone
  At the then fair hour in the then fair weather,
And the cave just under, with a voice still so hollow
  That it seems to call out to me from forty years ago,
    When you were all aglow,
And not the thin ghost that I now frailly follow!

The exclamation that ends the stanza signals a vivid registering of the time back then ("When you were all aglow" is surely part of some thirties American popular song?) and its difference from present elusive ghostliness. Fullness of specification is Hardy's intent, and in "At Castle Boterel," the climactic poem of the sequence, the speaker remembers a brief but richly consequential moment of conversation between him and his beloved, as they climb the hill at Boscastle:

It filled but a minute. But was there ever
  A time of such quality, since or before,
In that hill's story? To one mind never,
  Though it has been climbed, foot-swift, foot-sore,
    By thousands more.

Primaeval rocks form the road's steep border,
  And much have they faced there, first and last,

> Of the transitory in Earth's long order;
>> But what they record in colour and cast
>>> Is—that we two passed.

Donald Davie has written well about this moment, calling it perhaps the fullest, most responsively personal testimony to be found in all of Hardy's poetry. In both these poems, one follows the winding, exploratory voice as it picks its way through intricately paced stanzas, engaging both the reader's ear and eye.

By contrast, the first three stanzas of "The Missed Train," are held together by the adverbial "how"—"How I was caught . . . How civil my face . . . And how all the night . . . How lonely I was; /How consoled by her sprite"—which moves from specifying in what manner or way, to an absolute exclamatory testimony. There follow two stanzas where we hear the remembering voice both wanting and not wanting to be heard, to be fathomed. Or so I take "Thus onetime to me" and its break-off ellipsis. . . . The remainder of the poem consists of five declarations that succeed one another, each making a large claim for discontinuity or continuity but not taking the time, as it were, to fill in the omissions:

> Dim wastes of dead years bar away
> Then from now. But such happenings to-day
>> Fall to lovers, may be!

> Years, years as shoaled seas,
> Truly, stretch now between! Less and less
> Shrink the visions then vast in me.—Yes,
>> Then in me: Now in these.

"The last three words seem to have no explicit reference," remarks F. B. Pinion in his commentary on Hardy's poems, as if Pinion wouldn't have minded a little more filling-in on Hardy's part. But the poem's unsettling originality is *not* to fill in, rather to move from an exclamatory assertion of the vast, waste distance from present to past, to an exclamatory assertion that the same happenings are still happening to lovers. And in conclusion there is the wonderful "Yes" from the poet who was so good at saying No, and the perfectly monosyllabic balance of that final line, somehow using language—the most ordinary language—to move beyond itself and suggest immensities. "The Missed Train" is still the best-kept secret among all of Hardy's poems, despite Ransom's anthologizing it.

The "Introductory Note" to Hardy's final volume, *Winter Words*, is a masterly example of fending off reviewers, whose imperceptiveness about his most recent one deserved only silence: "I did not suppose that the licensed tasters had wilfully misrepresented the book, and said nothing knowing well that they could not have read it." Also fended off are those who would look for a "harmonious philosophy" in the new book, or even a sympathetic reader who might be naive enough to suppose the author had put his whole heart and soul into these poems:

> This being probably my last appearance on the literary stage, I
> would say, more seriously, that though, alas, it would be idle to
> pretend that the publication of these poems can have much interest
> for me, the track having been adventured so many times before to-
> day, the pieces themselves have been prepared with reasonable care,
> if not quite with the zest of a young man new to print.

"Reasonable care" is surely the minimal claim any poet has made for the pains he took over his words. Earlier critics of Hardy's poetry like Leavis, Howe, Douglas Brown, and Davie, paid no attention to any poem from the volume, and it was not until 1975 when Harold Bloom, in his High Precursor mode of analysis, pronounced it a masterwork: "A few books of twentieth-century verse in English compare with *Winter Words* in greatness, but very few." He does not name these books, and though he allows that the collection is diverse, he immediately undiversifies it by finding its emergent theme to be—whisper the name—"The Return of the Dead," *Apophrades*. It turns out that Hardy is the Dark Father of Shelley, and most of the commentary in Bloom's three pages about *Winter Words* is devoted to Shelley the son whose long poem *Hellas* is "hovering" all through *Winter Words*. At one point in these pages, Bloom surprises us by actually quoting a stanza from one of Hardy's poems in the volume. But although he finds "nearly every poem in the book to have a poignancy unusual even in Hardy," he confesses that "He Never Expected Much," Hardy's reflection on his eighty-sixth birthday, is the one that moves him most. The stanza, however, is quoted only as a trigger to talk, in the rest of the paragraph, about Wordsworth, Shelley, High Romantic Idealism, Yeats, Shelley again, and Browning. As usual, Bloom, at least the Bloom of the last few decades, is of no help in reading a particular poem.

> *He Never Expected Much*
>> *[or]*
>> *A Consideration*
> *[A reflection] on My Eighty-Sixth Birthday*

Well, World, you have kept faith with me,
       Kept faith with me;
Upon the whole you have proved to be
       Much as you said you were.
Since as a child I used to lie
Upon the leaze and watch the sky,
Never, I own, expected I
       That life would all be fair.

'Twas then you said, and since have said,
       Times since have said,
In that mysterious voice you shed
       From clouds and hills around:
'Many have loved me desperately,
Many with smooth serenity,
While some have shown contempt of me
       Till they dropped underground.

'I do not promise overmuch,
       Child; overmuch;
Just neutral-tinted haps and such,'
       You said to minds like mine.
Wise warning for your credit's sake!
Which I for one failed not to take,
And hence could stem such strain and ache
       As each year might assign.

The help that Bloom fails to give us is amply provided by Anne Ferry in her useful pages on Hardy in *The Title to the Poem*. She devotes two packed paragraphs to "He Never Expected Much," showing that the tone of both title and poem "is intended to be heard as a representation of Hardy's own voice," yet finding also that autobiographical matter—what one might be tempted to reveal about oneself on one's eighty-sixth birthday—is "hedged with dramatic and personative devices" and by "shifts in grammatical perspective." So the dialogue is between an "I" and the "World," in which the first person speaker (the "He" of the title) puts in quotation marks the speech of that nonhuman messenger who uses language matching Hardy's in the title of this poem and borrows also from the titles of early anthology pieces, "Neutral Tones" and "Hap."

I admire the poem, but have wondered why, unlike Bloom, I have never found it to be an especially "poignant" utterance; that may partly have to do with the hedging strategies Ferry points out, but I think also has to do with the final four lines in which the strategies disappear and the I and He become one. And to the speaker's satisfaction, as he sums up the impact and result of what the world told him ever since he was a child:

> Wise warning for your credit's sake!
> Which I for one failed not to take,
> And hence could stem such strain and ache
>> As each year might assign.

It is to say, "I for one—and I don't know about the rest of you—took the world's advice to heart and thus stemmed the strain and ache of yearly receivings." Is it perhaps a little too self-congratulatory to be poignant? Compare it with Housman:

> I to my perils
>> Of cheat and charmer
>> Came clad in armour
> By stars benign.
> Hope lies to mortals
>> And most believe her,
>> But man's deceiver
> Was never mine.

The thoughts of others
    Were light and fleeting,
    Of lovers' meeting
Or luck or fame.
Mine were of trouble,
    And mine were steady;
    So I was ready
When trouble came.

If this sounds more loudly bragging than Hardy, it is also more play-ful and unresolved than "He Never Expected Much." Think, after all, if throughout your life you've steadily kept your thoughts on trouble—rather than on luck or love or fame; then, just as expected, trouble comes and . . . what? You are "ready." The usefulness and virtue of being ready for big trouble seem to be at least arguably more up in the air than does Hardy's rather flat and pious declaration that he was able to "stem such strain and ache /As each year might assign."

By contrast, let us take a concluding look at three poems, two of them late, one early, that avoid pious declaration of personal triumph by moving into a remote key, and stem life's strain and ache by removing any human presence from the commotion so as to focus on, listen to, something else. Hardy wrote many bird poems and placed two of his best, "A Bird-Scene at a Rural Dwelling" and "Proud Songsters," as the second poems in both *Human Shows, Far Phantasies* and *Winter Words*. But there is an earlier poem about birds that I like to think my own discovery, the triolet "Winter in Durnover Field," probably written around the turn of the century. (It is placed two poems before "The Darkling Thrush" in Hardy's *Poems of the Past and Present*.)

> *Scene.*—*A wide stretch of fallow ground recently sown with wheat, and frozen to iron hardness. Three large birds walking about thereon, and wistfully eyeing the surface. Wind keen from north-east: sky a dull grey.*

    (Triolet)

Rook.—   Throughout the field I find no grain;
    The cruel frost encrusts the cornland!
Starling.—   Aye: patient pecking now is vain
    Throughout the field, I find . . .

Rook.—	No grain!
Pigeon.—Nor will be, comrade, till it rain,
	Or genial thawings loose the lorn land
	Throughout the field.
Rook.—	I find no grain:
	The cruel frost encrusts the cornland!

    In teaching Hardy I begin invariably with this poem as a motto for the poet's work generally: the "pessimistic" point of view made enlivening through formal intricacy and wit of a darkling sort; naysaying turned into something like exhilaration. Kenneth Burke once defined man as "inventor of the negative," but here the birds are sufficiently inventive in that regard, and when Keats addressed the urn as "Cold Pastoral," he couldn't quite have anticipated the temperature of winter in Durnover Field. It's an urban, a sophisticated indeed mischievous pastoral. But then does it make any sense to say that Hardy wrote pastoral poems? Paul Alpers writes in *What Is Pastoral?*: "Almost any type of Hardy poem can be a pastoral but none need be," and if so the whole matter might best be left alone. But another statement from Alpers is helpful, as he writes, "In poems so concerned as Hardy's with questions of strength relative to world, pastoral expression is one manifestation of more general lyric characteristics, such as ironic reserve, diffident first-person presence, and openness to feeling and to sense impression."
These terms fit the atmosphere of "A Bird-Scene at a Rural Dwelling":

> When the inmate stirs, the birds retire discreetly
> From the window-ledge, whereon they whistled sweetly
>   And on the step of the door,
>   In the misty morning hoar;
>   But now the dweller is up they flee
>   To the crooked neighbouring codlin-tree;
> And when he comes fully forth they seek the garden,
> And call from the lofty costard, as pleading pardon
>   For shouting so near before
>   In their joy at being alive:—
> Meanwhile the hammering clock within goes five.

> I know a domicile of brown and green,
> Where for a hundred summers there have been
> Just such enactments, just such daybreaks seen.

How little Frost's poems seem like performances, declared Randall Jarrell, and could have with even more justice declared about this one of Hardy's. Fourteen lines, the first ten with an unusual rhyme pattern (line eight pairing with line three, otherwise couplets); then surprisingly a space and a single sentence of three lines introduced by the first person. Where does this "I" come from and what is the "domicile" he knows so intimately yet is not at pains to share with us further? (The actual house is the cottage in Upper Bockhampton where Hardy was born.) The voice in "Bird-Scene" is characterized by ironic reserve, is diffident as a first-person presence, but open to sense impression and to the feeling that the poem as a whole creates in its unemphatic "enactment." "Bird-Scene" doesn't really go anywhere, doesn't tell a good story (no satire of circumstance here), and folds in upon itself in a very private, quietly confident manner that is suddenly over, has had its say before we quite know exactly what has been said.

Not saying is of course the strategy of the final poem in the complete works, "He Resolves to Say No More."

> O my soul, keep the rest unknown!
> It is too like a sound of moan
> > When the charnel-eyed
> > Pale Horse has nighed:
> Yea, none shall gather what I hide!
>
> Why load men's minds with more to bear
> That bear already ails to spare?
> > From now alway
> > Till my last day
> What I discern I will not say.
>
> Let Time roll backward if it will;
> (Magians who drive the midnight quill
> > With brain aglow
> > Can see it so,)
> What I have learnt no man shall know.

And if my vision range beyond
The blinkered sight of souls in bond,
            —By truth made free—
        I'll let all be,
And show to no man what I see.

Here there's absolutely no distinction I can see between the "he" of the title and the "I" of the poem: the hedging strategies mentioned by Anne Ferry are absent. Or rather, the hedging—the dark and ultimate playfulness—consists in Hardy's asserting that if he is granted a vision he'll keep it to himself. The ingenuities of non-saying are patent: "none shall gather"; "I will not say"; "No man shall know." This is not Prospero speaking nor are his claims modest ones; the final stanza is especially mischievous, however dark the truth about the world Hardy saw was coming, perhaps had already come. If his vision is wider and more far-seeing than the rest of mankind's ("souls in bond"), if indeed it has been made free by truth (the truth shall make you free), then that is the be-all and end-all: "I'll let all be /And show to no man what I see." Hamlet rendered a similar ultimate in his words just before the duel with Laertes (Hardy may have had them in mind): "Since no man, of aught he leaves, knows aught, what is't to leave betimes? Let be." After all, for Hardy at the end of life, the important kind of seeing has taken place in some domicile where, for a hundred years "There have been /Just such enactments, just such daybreaks seen." But seen by no man, overseen only by pastoral memory.

This is where Hardy ended, but my end will be with a poem not Hardy's greatest but my particular favorite. "On One Who Lived and Died Where He Was Born" is Hardy's tribute to his father, but not only to his father, since it brings together so many qualities of the son: the poet, the old poet, the rhymer, the architect, the maker ("engineer" Davie called him) of exquisitely built stanzas. Like Yeats he is the seeker after unity of being even as he knows it's impossible, or in memory only, re-considered passion. Hardy's memory celebrates the virtues of staying put, of piety toward the sources of one's being, and celebrates them in the manner of the song-maker, in both words and music. There is surely more that I have left out, but it is all there in the poem:

When a night in November
Blew forth its bleared airs
An infant descended
    His birth-chamber stairs
    For the very first time,
    At the still, midnight chime;
All unapprehended
    His mission, his aim.
Thus first, one November,
An infant descended
    The stairs.

On a night in November
    Of weariful cares,
A frail aged figure
    Ascended those stairs
    For the very last time:
    All gone his life's prime,
All vanished his vigour,
    And fine, forceful frame:
Thus, last, one November
Ascended that figure
    Upstairs.

On those nights in November—
    Apart eighty years—
The babe and the bent one
    Who traversed those stairs
    From the early first time
    To the last feeble climb—
That fresh and that spent one—
    Were even the same:
Yea, who passed in November
As infant, as bent one,
    Those stairs.

Wise child of November!
    From birth to blanched hairs

Descending, ascending,
    Wealth-wantless, those stairs;
    Who saw quick in time
    As a vain pantomime
Life's tending, its ending,
    The worth of its fame.
Wise child of November,
Descending, ascending
    Those stairs!

Housman in His Letters

*I*n 1971 Henry Maas published an edition of A. E. Housman's letters consisting of 883 items out of the 1,500 he traced. He excluded "short notes dealing with appointments and minor matters of business," and he separated the ones on classical subjects from the main body of letters. In his preface, Maas put a damper on any readerly expectation of revelatory material to be found in the letters, saying that although they revealed nothing startling they "at least provide solid materials for the study of his life and character." In other words, they would be useful to scholars and biographers of Housman rather than providing pleasure and profit in themselves. The new edition takes a rather different approach in that Archie Burnett, who in 1997 brought out his definitive edition of Housman's poems, has not only located many more letters but has decided to print all 2,327 of them—three times as many as Maas gave us.[1] The ones on classical scholarship now appear with the others, in chronological order, and no item, however brief ("All right," for example), is excluded. Moreover, Burnett is absolutely forthcoming in his recommendation of Housman's character, finding him on the testimony of these letters to be an "even gentler, more amiable, more sociable, more generous, more painstaking, and altogether more complex person" than previous biographies had found him to be. He concludes his introduction by declaring boldly, "My admiration and my liking for him has increased." This reader, having navigated the two volumes, strongly assents to Burnett's testimony, although perhaps not the "gentler" part.

Burnett's editorial work is, as expected, consummate, most notably in the footnotes to each letter. The only imperfection caught by this imperfect reader was a missed allusion in Housman's reference to "the loquacious

First published in *Literary Imagination* 9, no. 3 (2007): 359–65 (as "The Letters of A. E. Housman")

clock of Trinity" (vol. II, p. 509). He is alluding to Wordsworth's *The Prelude*, Book III, in which the poet-to-be, residing at St. John's College next door, tells us, "Near me hung Trinity's loquacious clock / Who never let the quarters, night or day, / Slip by him unproclaimed, and told the hours / Twice over with a male and female voice." Housman is relieved that the clock has now (in 1935) been silenced between midnight and 7 a.m.

Anyone familiar with Housman's prose knows how sharp is the turn he gives to individual sentences. For example, "If unthinking critics could know how much one is ashamed to answer what they write, they would begin to be a little ashamed of writing it" (note the careful weighing of "begin" and "little"). Frequent encounters with sentences that have a kicker in them predispose us to look in each letter for some original twist of expression. We should not, in our appetite for the "devastating" response, turn Housman into a curmudgeon for all occasions; still, his pleasure in turning sentences in unexpected ways is patent. It may be brought out by contrasting him with his friend and contemporary, Thomas Hardy. Like Housman's, Hardy's letters are often, especially in his later years, very short indeed ("My thanks for your good wishes"), but it is sometimes harder to characterize their tone. Hardy's habit is to work toward an epistolary response that is, or seems, blandly unforthcoming, as when he tells an American journalist who had sent him some articles that they "do not require remark." Should we take this to be an artful dismissal of the journalist, or is Hardy merely stating a fact? Both possibilities are reasonable, and they suggest why, in their evenness of tone, his letters have not much appealed to readers who admire those of Keats, Hopkins, or D. H. Lawrence.

Consider, by contrast with Hardy, the following from a letter to an American, Seymour Adelman, who had inquired about *A Shropshire Lad* and sent Housman a map of Shropshire. Now he asks him about the possibility of reprinting Housman's send-up of mistranslation, "Fragment of a Greek Tragedy." Housman replies: "Your amiable desire to print a limited edition in facsimile is one which I should do everything in my power to thwart." After being lulled by that "amiable" a reader (and perhaps Mr. Adelman?) is jolted by the sentence's end, with its non-amiable "thwart." No chance of wondering about the tone here, and no doubt that Housman has taken pains to write a sentence with a true snap in it; the trap has been baited and sprung almost before we realize it. A related example of terse compactness that surprises can be seen and heard in the following about a classicist who represented what Housman called "the low ebb" of nineteenth-century classical scholarship: "His learning was small, and so was his modesty, but he had common sense, and some of his impudence was sprightly." A seeming upbeat at the end, but only if you are delighted by a scholar's "impudence." Sometimes you can feel him growing more limber as he goes along, as when he tells his sister, Katharine Symons, of their brother Laurence's lecture in Cambridge in 1934. Housman's tone toward Laurence is in general slightly on the condescending side, and the lecture, Burnett tells us, was probably about pacifism, a movement that did not warm AEH's heart:

> Laurence was here for two or three days and his lecture seems to have been lively and much appreciated by the rather contemptible audience. These "Summer Meetings" consist of people who should never be allowed to enter a University town, and on this occasion I am told that the majority were foreigners—who to be sure were probably the better educated part.

So the lecture (which AEH did not attend) was a success, just the thing to please a "contemptible audience" that shouldn't anyway have been allowed into Cambridge. Then it gets worse (or does it?) when hearsay reports the foreigners were in a majority; but that those foreigners, who we're ready to believe have even less right to enter Cambridge than do the English, turn out to be "the better educated part" of the audience, therefore perhaps less "contemptible." It's another example of how reading Housman's sentences often means rereading them.

Housman is masterly at apologizing to someone and in the same breath making the apology anything but abject—in fact, making it a fresh occasion for humorous mischief. When Edmund Gosse published a life of Swinburne in 1917, Housman responded with a letter expressing his pleasure in the book, but also confessing surprise that Gosse found much to praise in Swinburne's *Poems and Ballads,* second series. He then made a number of corrections (Gosse was famous for his mistakes, as

Churton Collins showed in demolishing his *From Shakespeare to Pope*) that could be incorporated in a second edition. Gosse evidently took it amiss, and Housman responds to him a few days later:

My dear Gosse,

If you are going to indulge in depression of spirits because I manage to find half a dozen mistakes in 350 pages, you will cut yourself off from my valued corrections in the future. As for my finding "little to like," you know perfectly well that you write delightfully and that your taste and knowledge made you just the man for the work; and you do not need to hear it from me, especially when all the world is saying it. For my own part I always feel impertinent and embarrassed when I praise people: this is a defect of character, I know; and I suffer for it, like Cordelia. The chief fault of your book is one which I did not mention, that there is too little of it.

This is notable for its combination of a flattery I suspect Gosse felt flattered by (all the world is praising his Swinburne book) and a teasing suggestion that he should buck up or he will receive no more of Housman's "valued corrections." After all, Gosse had failed to value what the scholarly world recognized as Housman's brilliant editorial work. But the fine stroke here seems to me Housman's admission that his inability to praise is a defect of character, then adding that he suffers for it just like—who of all people—Cordelia! (Here the editor intrudes unnecessarily with a footnote telling us who Cordelia was and what she did or didn't say to her father.) For the fastidious Housman to ally himself with Shakespeare's noblest heroine is a piece of humor that is also serious. Gosse, like Lear, should have been more appreciative.

But the correspondence is not all super-sardonic performances within tightly compressed limits. Some of the most expansive and agreeable of the letters are ones he wrote to his stepmother Lucy describing the terrain and attractions of a foreign country, in this instance Zug and Lucerne lakes in Switzerland on the way to Milan:

The water is a strong opaque blue: the scenery, though it is not the best sort of scenery, must be quite the best of its sort: any number of cliffs falling straight to the water, pine trees and cottages adhering to them in impossible places, and narrow white waterfalls streaming all down them with a noise to be heard above the clatter of the train. After you quit the lake and draw near to the St. Gothard the country is still interesting and in some respects beautiful: the valleys are often surprisingly soft and pretty, full of smooth meadows and orchard trees and foaming streams of yellowish water; but many of the mountains would be the better for having their tops taken off them. Some of their tops actually were taken off, so far as I was concerned, by the clouds and mist, and I saw no snow.

Here the wit is at ease within an equable, carefully observed run of things. It looks easier to bring off than one might think, but as a character in Trollope reminds us, easy reading requires hard writing. To note that pine trees and cottages are "adhering to the cliffs in impossible places," and to register the "foaming streams of yellowish water" is to see with the poet's eye (think of the heartbreaking landscape of Housman's "Tell me not here, it needs not saying") and create something of real interest not just to a stepmother. When he reaches Milan, he compares the architecture of its cathedral with French and English examples, mentioning in particular Westminster, York, and Winchester. But previous to the extended comparison, he introduces us to Milan, "the least Italian town in Italy," with the following perfect epitaph: "It considers itself the intellectual capital of the country, and probably hopes to go to France when it dies." Note the careful qualification of "probably."

Four years later he visited Constantinople and wrote Lucy Housman that it was a comfort not to have her along, since "[i]t would have been 'poor doggie' every step of the way, and we should never have got a hundred yards from the hotel." He then expatiates on the creatures

> who all have something the matter with them. They are extremely meek and inoffensive: Turkey is a country where dogs and women are kept in their proper place, and consequently are quite unlike the pampered and obstreperous animals we know under those names in England.

The Turkish dog at night "grows melodious":

He does not bark over his quarrels so much as English dogs do, and when he does bark it is sometimes rather like the quacking of a soprano duck; but he wails: whether he is winning or losing seems to make no difference, so dejected are his spirits. . . . One night in the dark I trod on a dog lying exactly in the middle of the road; he squealed in a bitterly reproachful tone for a certain time; when he had finished, the next dog barked in an expostulatory manner for the same period, and then the incident was closed.

Here is the felt obligation, nicely carried out, to make one's observations entertaining. It is worth remarking, however, that after identifying dogs and women as objects of sensible Turkish care, he has nothing more to say about the latter.

Housman continued throughout his life to be serious about travel, taking regular holidays mainly in France and Italy. Some of his remarks thrown off about what he has seen in the art and architecture line reveal him to have been a discerning looker. (By contrast he had no ear for music, and was quite as willing to have people set his poems to it as he was not to have them reprinted in anthologies.) He describes in some detail to his stepmother the Byzantine wonders of St. Mark's, Venice, which he calls, carefully, "the most beautiful, not the grandest, building in the world." A brief, packed observation disposes of two of Ruskin's admired Venetian painters, "the lurid and theatrical Tintoret, whom I avoid, and Paul Veronese, whom one soon sees enough of." On the other hand, he singles out for praise the paintings of Giovanni Bellini and of his pupil Cima da Conegliano, and the "very interesting series" of Carpaccio paintings in San Giorgio dei Schiavone. This tallies with my own memories of some Venetian pictures, as does the following judgment of a Brittany artifact: "Carnac is almost as unimpressive as Stonehenge." When I confronted the stones of Carnac, I did not dare hazard the comparison, but certainly had nothing to say about them.

In his introduction Archie Burnett takes up the charge that Housman was a misogynist and says that it needs to be "heavily qualified," adducing warm letters to his sister Kate, to his godmother Elizabeth Wise, and to wives of various colleagues. This doesn't seem to me to qualify very heavily the fact that not only was Housman's social life entirely male-oriented, but he resisted anything that threatened to make changes in the present order. When the novelist Lucy Thicknesse sent him a copy of her husband's *The Rights and Wrongs of Women*, a pro-women's suffrage argument, Housman wrote to her "My blood boils" and ascribed it to the absurdity of the book to hand:

> "She cannot serve on any Jury"; and yet she bravely lives on. "She cannot serve in the army or navy"—oh cruel, cruel!—"except"—this adds insult to injury—"as a nurse." . . . I have been making marginal additions. "She cannot be ordained a Priest or Deacon": add *nor become a Freemason.* "She cannot be a member of the Royal Society": add *nor of the Amateur Boxing Association.* In short, your unhappy sex seem to have nothing to look forward to, excepting contracting a valid marriage as soon as they are 12 years old; and that must soon pall.

Was Lucy Thicknesse appalled by such insensitivity? Burnett, in his valuable "List of Recipients" identifying Housman's main correspondents, quotes her as telling Grant Richards, Housman's publisher, after the poet's death that "of the long talks I had with him, I chiefly remember the delicious humour of his descriptions of things and people." So it's possible that she was more amused than her husband may have been at Housman's mockery of *The Rights and Wrongs of Women*.

It would of course be heavy-handed to point out the number of Housman's light verse poems in which members of the female sex come to grief, but we remember the Salvation Army's Lieutenant-Colonel Mary-Jane who "tumbled off the platform in the station/And was cut in little pieces by the train." There follows one of Housman's most inspired rhymes: "Mary-Jane, the train is through ye,/Hallelujah! Hallelujah!" Or there is Morbid Matilda, an overeducated girl who drank a pebble in her tea, which she thinks may have been a pearl, then cried "'Don't call me Cleopatra,'/And jumped into the sea;/And with her latest gasp/Said 'Keep away the asp.'" Not one of his best efforts, certainly not up to the perfection of Amelia's treatment of her mother:

> Amelia mixed the mustard,
> She mixed it good and thick;

She put it in the custard
    And made her mother sick;
And showing satisfaction
    By many a loud huzza
"Observe" said she "the action
    Of mustard on mamma."

Housman's successor in the line of gleeful violence, often directed at children or women, seems to have been Edward Gorey.

But perhaps the purest and to me most amusing instance of Housman's mischievous gift for creating the ludicrous comes in response to William Rothenstein's sending him a book of poems by Darwin's granddaughter, Frances Cornford. Housman sends back his improvement of some lines from Cornford's poem "To a Fat Lady Seen from the Train":

O why do you walk through the field in boots
    Missing so much and so much?
O fat white woman whom nobody shoots
Why do you walk through the field in boots
When the grass is soft as the breath of coots
    And shivering-sweet to the touch?

The note informs us, in case we weren't familiar with Cornford's immortal verse, that her line-ending rhymes were "gloves," "loves," and "doves," which Housman replaced by "boots," "shoots," and "coots." The result was one of the surely great apostrophes to be found in English poetry: "O fat white woman whom nobody shoots" bestows on the lady an immortality finer, we may agree, than anything to be gained by serving on any jury or joining the Amateur Boxing Association. Housman loved such "emendations," especially when a newspaper reported an address of his as "On the Application of Thought to Sexual Criticism," "sexual" of course having replaced "textual."

"It looks to me as if the state of mankind always had been and always would be a state of just tolerable discomfort," he wrote to Gilbert Murray in 1900, when he had already published one of his very best poems, "On Wenlock Edge . . ." in which English yeoman and Roman soldier are made one in their troubled thoughts. He also put those troubles into

"I to my perils of cheat and charmer," which ends with "So I was ready / When trouble came." Can one ever be "ready" when the real trouble comes? Certainly Housman may have wondered about this in the final two years of his life, when his heart was failing, his nights often sleepless and followed by "the perpetual recurrence of discomfort" upon arising in the morning. "My life is bearable, but I do not want it to continue, and I wish it had ended a year and a half ago. The great and real troubles of my early manhood did not render those days so permanently unsatisfactory as these," he wrote candidly in 1934, a year and a half before he died. Not even perpetual recurrence of his unfailing routine on each December 31 of "eating any amount of oysters up to 4 doz. and drinking all the stout required to wash them down" could assuage things for long. But the mischief, the malice, the mockery never lost their bite, as when an American wrote him saying that he had spent much time in Cambridge but had never attempted to see Housman. The thank-you note in reply began, "Dear Mr Abeel, My heart always warms to people who do not come to see me, especially Americans, to whom it seems to be more of an effort."

In his affecting memoir of Housman, *A Buried Life*, Percy Withers, the recipient of some of Housman's best letters, aptly characterized his style in writing and speech as one of "fastidious precision." But it went along with a personality that in its great constraint and—in Withers's experience—a kind of "taciturnity" was one that could be deeply unsettling and disturbing. Archie Burnett in his identificatory note calls Withers's memoir "sympathetic but somewhat baffled," which seems to me a just response to Housman's intractability. The vein of terrific mockery informing so many of these letters and of Housman's critical prose has in English letters nothing comparable except for Swift (to whom Edmund Wilson compared him decades ago), who, like Housman, was anything but a well-rounded human being. It is a rare occasion when an utterance comes straight from the heart with no surrounding protection of tone. In this collection it occurs most piercingly in a short letter to A. W. Pollard, announcing the death, in 1923, of their roommate at St. John's, Oxford, Moses Jackson, the lost love of Housman's life. "I had a letter from him on New Year's Day, which ended by saying 'goodbye.' Now I can die myself. I could not have borne to leave him behind me in a world where

ESSAYS ON OLDER POETS

anything might happen to him." It is one of the letters Burnett prints that is absent from Henry Mass's previous collection, and its presence is but one more reason to be grateful for this superbly conducted enterprise.

NOTES

1. *The Letters of A. E. Housman,* vols. 1 and 2, ed. Archie Burnett (Oxford: Oxford University Press, 2007).

T W O

Reviewing Twentieth - Century Poets

"Reviewing" has a double sense here: first, that with one exception, these treatments of sixteen American and English poets were prompted by invitations to review a biography, a collected letters, or some other large compilation of the poet's work, frequently its incorporation in the Library of America. In gathering them together, I hope they provide a larger reviewing of two generations of poets who flourished in the last century's first fifty years. Most of the items are recent, from the last ten years, and put in proximity may simulate, explicitly or implicitly, a conversation among the poets. At any rate they are occasions to make comparisons: Frost as against Stevens; Jarrell criticizing Auden; Lowell in his poems and letters about so many contemporaries and predecessors.

I have divided the section chronologically into two parts: the first consists of poets from Yeats to Hart Crane, who were born in the nineteenth century and form the "modernist" generation, no matter how ill the word fits Robinson or Frost; the second comprises the "middle" generation and ranges from Auden and Empson to Larkin and Wilbur, all of them born between 1906 and 1928. I have tried to avoid repetition, although certain formulations and prejudices will be seen to recur.

The Modernist Generation

Our Secret Discipline: Yeats and Lyric Form, by Helen Vendler

*A*fter many critical and biographical treatments of W. B. Yeats appeared some decades past, it seemed that interpretation had done its work, and scholars turned to editing Yeats's letters, his poems, and, most usefully, draft versions of those poems. What neither the critics nor the scholars gave, as we can see from Helen Vendler's splendid new book, is an exhaustive account of Yeats's lyric styles as they variously revealed themselves in fifty years of verse forms. In their "bizarre variety," Vendler writes, they challenge us to understand the poet's commitment to form as "the necessary and skilled embodiment of the poet's moral urgency." In her preface she reveals that fifty years ago, as a graduate student at Harvard, she planned to write her dissertation on Yeats's poetry, then upon reflection decided that, at age twenty-two, she didn't know enough to write about a poet who kept going until age seventy-three. Instead she wrote a dissertation, which became her first published book, on Yeats's later plays. So it is satisfying and fitting that after producing substantial works about some of her favorite poets—Stevens, Herbert,

---

First published in the *Boston Globe*, February 17, 2008 (as "The Anatomy of Yeats's Inventions")

Keats, Shakespeare—as well as collections of essays (three of them during the past ten years), she should return to her first love in a book whose value may exceed that of anything she has hitherto produced.

Vendler is the ideal close reader and listener to undertake the very large task of coming to terms with Yeats's poetry. Over the years that poetry has been written about by a good many close readers—William Empson and Yvor Winters, Hugh Kenner and Donald Davie, to name four prominent ones—but it is surprising how relatively little they considered matters of verse technique. The great merit of Vendler's approach is that she never rests content with merely identifying and describing formal choices on Yeats's part (ottava rima, blank verse, heroic quatrains) but goes on to consider how such forms are employed in the service of moral and human content.

Rather than moving chronologically through the work, from Yeats's early lyrics to "Cuchulain Comforted" and "The Black Tower," she proceeds in a more indirect and ambitious manner, dividing poems up among various rhythmic and stanzaic categories. There are overlaps among the poems considered: for example, "The Second Coming" appears both in her chapter on Yeats's blank verse and as what she calls, in the section on sonnets, an "extended" sonnet made up by writing two octaves followed by a sestet. Her opening chapter selects three poems from different stages of Yeats's career, each of which is relatively clear in speech and does not depend for its comprehension on any esoteric knowledge, as do many of the visionary ones. "An Irish Airman Foresees His Death," "Easter 1916," and "After Long Silence" are poems that any reader of Yeats would agree show him at his finest and need no special pleading or "keys" to unlock their beauties. With "After Long Silence" Vendler has recourse, as she does at other places in the book, to Yeats's manuscripts, by way of helping us to follow "the poet's creative thinking as it motivates the evolution of the poem." As for "Easter 1916," which Harold Bloom once found was, in its clarity, uncharacteristic of Yeats, Vendler finely brings out its complicated clarity and also the ingenuity of its number symbolism, which a student pointed out to her: that the date of the Easter rebellion, April 24, 1916, is encoded in the structure of those four stanzas (April is the fourth month), with their alternate line groupings of sixteen, twenty-four, sixteen, twenty-four. "Easter 1916" returns in the chapter titled "The National-ist Measure," about poems in trimeter quatrains. Vendler emphasizes the "nervous" rapidity of the poem's trimeter by rewriting it—an exercise she often practices as a heuristic device—in pentameters whose "stately breadth" is inappropriate for the "lively" and "quick" step of the poem as Yeats wrote it. She is intrepid and only occasionally over-ingenious, not only in rewriting poems in order to establish the rightness of Yeats's choice, but in breaking them up by italicizing words so as to bring out how they cultivate "magical, non-rational, non-etymological relations" among them-selves. In this regard she gives an especially salient treatment of the early, and wonderful, "The Song of Wandering Aengus" ("I went out to the hazel wood, / Because a fire was in my head").

Her decision, announced in the preface, to write a book "taxonomically focused on Yeats's lyric style" is scrupulously borne out in her appendices to some chapters that further classify and enumerate poems—such as the ones in trimeter quatrains, which she lists in chronological order while providing notes on their special features. She is fond of drawing diagrams so as further to highlight poetic taxonomies. At times her commentary can be overwhelming, as it was for me in a long chapter on Yeats's ballads and another one on his "Supernatural Songs," poems of his with which I have the most difficulty. But the book rises to full majesty in a chapter ("The Renaissance Aura") on Yeats's poems in ottava rima, the rhymed pentameter stanzas of which (abababcc) imitate "lofty song." (One of Vendler's students called it Yeats's "senatorial" form.) The song can be heard thrillingly in "Sailing to Byzantium," "The Statues," "The Circus Animals' Desertion," and—most grandly and compellingly—in "Among School Children," a "philosophical poem for everyone" as she calls it. Summing up the ottava rima form, she writes that its "Renaissance as-sociations" are "brought forcibly into modernity by Yeats's modifications of its traditional architectonics, its diction and its 'flow.' . . . [H]e has removed the genre from a chiefly descriptive or speculative function, and made it sympathetic to intellectual and emotional autobiography." For her, as for this reader, "Among School Children" and the fifteen other ottava rima poems are "the most accomplished chapter in the history of Yeats's styles."

As someone who has taught Yeats's poems for decades, I took this book personally and was shocked to see, even after repeated readings of them aloud, talking and writing about them, how much I had missed in the technical effects that lie at the very heart of Yeats's aesthetic and human accomplishment. Who can indeed, in Eliot's words, say where "technique" begins or where it ends? Readers who have assumed they were familiar, even intimate, with Yeats's body of lyric verse will read Vendler's pages and find their eyes have been opened, in Hart Crane's words, to "[n] ew thresholds, new anatomies."

Edwin Arlington Robinson: A Poet's Life, by Scott Donaldson

*A*ll too often these days, a new biography of a writer mainly provokes the question of why, given the number already in the field, a further one was needed. Scott Donaldson's biography of Edwin Arlington Robinson more than justifies itself as the first in forty years, and his thorough documentation and responsiveness to Robinson's poetry altogether displaces previous accounts of this fascinating, enigmatic literary character. Mr. Donaldson, a veteran professional with lives of Hemingway, Fitzgerald, and MacLeish to his credit, explains in his introduction why his life of Robinson is, in the overused phrase, a labor of love. He had begun gathering material in 1977 with Robinson in mind but was stymied by the "minuscule and idiosyncratic hand" in which the poet wrote his four thousand or so letters, nine-tenths of which had never been published. When Donaldson recently returned to the project, the letters had been deciphered and most of them annotated by the late Wallace Anderson, a Robinson scholar. So Donaldson went to work at the task of presenting "an exceptionally fine human being"; a great poet who was also "one of the most private persons who ever lived."

His opening chapter begins where it should, with Robinson's name, which over the years so many have gotten wrong (one of his Pulitzer Prize citations had his first name as "Edward") and that the poet himself in his own words hated "with a hatred that is positively pathological." "Edwin Ar-lington Rob-inson," he would intone, declaring that it sounded like "a tin bathtub bumping down an uncarpeted flight of stairs." It was, Robinson declared, no name for a poet; yet how humorously poetic is the apt comparison to the bumping bathtub and his delight in confessing to

First published in the *Times Literary Supplement*, March 23, 2007 (as "By the Hair")

"pathological" self-hatred. Miniver Cheevy, child of scorn, would have understood such feelings.

Donaldson rehearses the story of Robinson's growing up in Gardiner, Maine, the youngest of three brothers in a family that, mocking its own promise, disintegrated in a close-packed series of disasters: his father's illness and death; his brothers, Dean and Herman, falling prey respectively to drugs and alcohol; his unrequited love for Emma Shepherd, who married Herman, precipitating Robinson's estrangement from his brother. What comes through positively is the sustaining friendships EAR (as Donaldson calls him) received in a small town not all of whose members were oblivious of poetry—at least those who formed a group called the Gardiner Poetry Society to which the seventeen-year-old Robinson brought his wares for criticism and encouragement.

Robinson attended Harvard for two years in the early 1890s as a special student (other "specials" from that decade were Robert Frost and Wallace Stevens). His academic performance was unremarkable, but Harvard freed him from provincialism. He also visited a number of Boston's houses of prostitution, though seldom, if ever, engaging in sexual activity. One of his friends, Mowry Saben (himself a libertine) thought Robinson was bisexual and repressed, thus reluctant "to indulge himself in either direction." Frost's way of putting it after Robinson's death was that he was a "truly gallant Platonist" who remained a bachelor in his idealization of women. But as Donaldson points out, the romantic triangle figures in many Robinson poems and bears witness to his unhappy experience with Emma Shepherd. It is remarkable, however, that this reticent man (he disliked the word "shy") managed to make, keep, and keep up with so many friends, both male and female.

His first book of poems, *The Torrent and The Night Before* (1896), was privately printed and received some good reviews; a revised version, *The Children of the Night,* containing what would be some of his best poems, was reviewed by President Theodore Roosevelt after his son, Kermit, called his attention to it. Roosevelt procured a sinecure for Robinson at the U.S. Customs Service, and the poet later wrote Kermit that his father "fished me out of hell by the hair of the head." It was a hell characterized by loneliness, poverty, and heavy dependence on alcohol—the last remaining an important feature of his life. Beginning with the summer of 1911 and continuing through twenty-three further summers, Robinson was in residence at the MacDowell Colony in Peterborough, New Hampshire; there, regular work habits and agreeable socializing (a game of pool every evening) contributed to a relatively abstemious and productive life. With the coming of Prohibition, he resumed drinking as a protest.

The Man against the Sky (1916) contains the finest of his lyrics, and Donaldson is scrupulous in according full attention to what he sees as the major ones. Here he builds upon the excellent criticism those poems have received over the last sixty years, beginning with Yvor Winters and continuing through Irving Howe's seminal essay of 1970 and more recent efforts by poets such as James Dickey, Donald Hall, and (in particular) Robert Mezey. Donaldson's welcome practice is to quote in full, whenever possible, the poems he devotes attention to, then proceed with pointed commentary—especially pointed on such classics as "Luke Havergal," "For a Dead Lady," and "Eros Turannos." He agrees with all readers of the poet in finding the splendid "Isaac and Archibald" Robinson at his most engaging, and he provides a most sympathetic reading of the poem Robinson himself thought was perhaps the best he had ever written, "Mr. Flood's Party." He does his best by way of making a case for some of the longer—mostly late—poems for which Robinson in his lifetime won accolades. But Robinson's lasting power is not to be found in these longer efforts (the early "Captain Craig" is an exception) but in such lyrics, first singled out by Winters, as "The Gift of God," "Veteran Sirens," "The Poor Relation," "Hillcrest" "The Dark Hills," and "The Sheaves." All these poems are in tightly rhymed stanzas; like Frost, Robinson despised free verse ("I write badly enough as it is," he said).

In his posthumous tribute to Robinson, Frost called him, in a wonderful phrase, "a prince of heartachers." Donaldson finds this inadequate in that it doesn't suggest the compassion that accompanied such sadness. But Frost was distinguishing "heartachers" from "countless achers of another part" (bellyachers, presumably), and at any rate he stands with Frost as the first major American poets of the early twentieth century. Their humorous rivalry came through in Robinson's saying "I understand they teach Frost and me in the school now," then smiling and adding, "I don't know which one they teach first." When Winfield Townley Scott told this to Frost, Frost responded, whacking his thigh in delight, "*Did* he say that . . . Did he really say that?"

Robert Frost:
Collected Poems, Prose, and Plays

*I*t is entirely fitting that the first twentieth-century American poet to be published in the Library of America series is Robert Frost. These one thousand pages of his poetry and prose (there are three plays as well, but they don't matter) constitute the most varied, humanly satisfying, and technically interesting body of verse by any modern American poet, not excepting Wallace Stevens or T. S. Eliot. They also contain an invaluable body of theoretical and critical writing *about* the art of poetry. To have such riches available for the first time in a single, compact, affordable volume, is a testimony to how, in a world where reading and criticizing poetry counts less and less, intelligent editorial tribute has been paid to the poet who counts more and more.

Frost has been well served by the two critics who collaborated on making the selection. Richard Poirier, one of the founders of the Library of America, has written what is still the most ambitious and rewarding critical discussion of Frost's poetry (*Robert Frost: The Work of Knowing*, 1978); Mark Richardson, whose doctoral dissertation was an edition of Frost's prose, has uncovered many interesting out-of-the-way items and has, I suspect, been instrumental in writing the very useful series of notes to both prose and verse. But what these editors have done that most deserves our gratitude is their restoration of Frost's *Complete Poems* (1949) as the proper text for the volumes of verse he brought out from *A Boy's Will* (1913) through *Steeple Bush* (1947).

That such a seemingly conservative editorial decision nevertheless deserves remarking, is the result of a bad mistake made twenty-five years ago by Frost's publisher, Holt, Rinehart and Winston, when they decided to bring out a "comprehensive and authoritative" edition of the

---

First published in the *Boston Globe*, October 22, 1995 (as "First Frost")

poetry. Claiming to be "scrupulously edited for textual accuracy," the book that resulted was nothing of the sort, since its editor, Edward Connery Lathem, went about "improving" the poems by repunctuating them when he thought they demanded it. So hyphens and commas were added or subtracted as Lathem saw fit, and Frost's usually lightly punctuated verse was tampered with to make it fit what the editor saw as more correct grammatical practice. To take one simple though egregious example of such tampering: "Stopping by Woods on a Snowy Evening," a poem nobody in the world ever thought stood in need of editorial attention, was unwisely granted it when Lathem added two commas to its four stanzas. The first comma changed line two, "His house is in the village though" to "His house is in the village, though"; the second turned "The woods are lovely, dark and deep" into "The woods are lovely, dark, and deep." (Poirier has pointed out that in Frost's original line the woods were not just "lovely, dark, and deep" but "lovely, [i.e.] dark and deep." In both cases an easy, unemphatic presentation was made to sound prim and "correct," while rhythmic and tonal implications were disregarded, even reversed, by editorial fussing. So to get rid of Lathem's corrections and additions was in itself a first-rate decision.

Frost's last book of poetry, *In the Clearing*, published the year before he died and with a pretty high percentage of forgettable poems, is likewise restored to its pre-Lathemized state. But of more interest to students of the poet are eighty or so poems, most of them hitherto uncollected, many written when Frost was a young man, some of them published in magazines. They include "La Noche Triste," composed when he was sixteen, about Cortes's retreat from Tenochtitlan ("The Montezumas are no more, / Gone is their regal throne"), and the class hymn he wrote for his high school graduation. There is "Twilight," the title poem of a little booklet he had hand-printed to woo his classmate sweetheart and future wife, Elinor White; there is a morbid, even suicidal piece, called "Despair," written sometime in the 1890s ("I am like a dead diver after all's /Done, still held fast in the weeds' snare below"); and there is the touching poem he wrote after he sold his Derry farm and prepared to depart for England. "On the Sale of My Farm" ends with this delicate gesture of regret:

Only be it understood,
It shall be no trespassing
If I come again some spring
In the grey disguise of years,
Seeking ache of memory here.

There are also a number of satirical poems, friendly verse letters to friends, and an unfriendly one written but not sent to Ezra Pound. Frost's occasional penchant for the bawdy is strongly revealed here in "Pride of Ancestry" which begins on this promising note:

The Deacon's wife was a bit desirish
And liked her sex relations wild
So she lay with one of the shanty Irish
And he begot the Deacon's child.

I am sorry however to see no sign of the little poem he used to say in hopes of shocking pious believers: "Mary had a little lamb, / Its name was Jesus Christ. / God, not Joseph, was the ram, / But Joseph took it nice."

In the prose collected here we encounter repeatedly striking formulations about reading and writing; many of them—the more notable for being hot off the griddle—came when Frost, living in England, wrote home to American friends, using them as soundingboards for his poetic "theory." Selections of his letters edited by his biographer Lawrance Thompson and by his friend Louis Untermeyer have been unavailable for years: a pity, since Frost was a wonderfully humorous, if occasionally exasperating, letter writer. The new collection picks out central ones about the importance of sentence sounds and of imagining the speaking voice. Decades later, in a series of apothegms written for the *Atlantic Monthly* under the title "Poetry and School," Frost took a last crack at the notion of reading poetry without listening to it: "The eye reader is a barbarian. So also is the writer for the eye reader, who needn't care how badly he writes since he doesn't care how badly he is read." The "best reader" will be "one who will read, can read, no faster than he can hear the lines and sentences in his mind's eye as if read aloud. Frequenting poetry has slowed him down by its metric and measured pace." These apothegms conclude with the one everybody knows about how, for pleasure, he would as soon write free verse as play tennis with the net down.

Frost was of course, among other things, a teacher, even though his courses at Pinkerton Academy, the University of Michigan, and Amherst College were to say the least unconventional. "We go to college to be given one more chance to learn to read in case we haven't learned in High School"; once we have learned that, he believed, the rest would follow. (He once defined college as a place to hang around until you catch on, after which you might be well advised—as he did—to light out for some other territory.) Frost delighted in not saying the obvious things about how "English" was the department where you went to improve your "writing skills," as the current depressing parlance has it. No, he says, "We write in school chiefly because to try our hand at writing should make us better readers." (I tell students that when their parents nag them about their writing they should ask Mom and Dad about how parental reading of Shakespeare or Milton has been going recently.) "The chief reason for going to school is to get the impression fixed for life that there is a book side to everything," he writes; that impression, not at all easy to come by for most students, even at elite colleges and universities, is something rather different from improving writing skills so as to be effective in business or law later on.

But after all is said and done, it's the poems that matter, and the Library of America's volume gives us the opportunity of reading through a life of poetry, from "Into My Own," the first poem in *A Boy's Will*, to "In winter in the woods alone . . . ," the final, untitled one from *In the Clearing*. It's a poetic world large and difficult enough to get lost in; also one you can't exhaust, since there are always new poems that did not quite register before, or old ones that sound slightly different this time around. No one has ever spoken more convincingly and truly about Frost's world than Randall Jarrell did in his great essay "To the Laodiceans," when he insisted that Frost's poetry is like the world we know;

> the world with its animals and plants and, most of all, its people:
> people working, thinking about things, falling in love, taking naps;
> in these poems men are not only the glory and jest and riddle of
> the world, but also the habit of the world, its strange ordinariness,

its ordinary strangeness, and they too trudge down the ruts along which the planets move in their courses. Frost is that rare thing, a complete or representative poet. . . . When you know Frost's poems you know surprisingly well how the world seemed to one man, and what it was to seem that way.

The Notebooks of Robert Frost,
edited by Robert Faggen

*T*his is the first in a projected series of works by Robert Frost that will include editions of his poems, essays, and letters, published by the Belknap Press of Harvard University under the general editorship of Robert Faggen. Mr. Faggen, author of a book about Frost and science (*Robert Frost and the Challenge of Darwin*), has undertaken the truly heroic task of presenting Frost's notebooks which, forty-three years after the poet's death in 1963, have been used only sparingly by scholars. Spanning six decades, from the 1890s to the early 1960s, they consist physically of the homeliest of materials: dime-store spiral pads and school theme books that Frost, so Faggen tells us in a useful introduction, kept with him in his movings from place to place and his busy life of reading engagements for diverse audiences. The editorial challenge they present is due in part to their helter-skelter character. There is no clear chronological ordering: a single notebook may contain entries from widely different times in Frost's life, while the layout of individual pages seems almost wilfully capricious, with sentences going in various directions. Deciphering many of them is also a problem—the word illegible appears frequently in the editor's interpolations.[1]

But the deepest challenge they present, even to a reader familiar with Frost's poetry, lies in the way they simultaneously invite us to colloquy while fending us off. A 1917 letter of Frost's suggests a principle behind these notebook entries: "You get more credit for thinking if you restate formulas or cite cases which fall easily under formulae. But all the fun is outside, saying things that suggest formulae but won't formulate—that almost but don't quite formulate." In another letter quoted by Faggen, Frost informs his correspondent, "I have written to keep the curious

---

First published in the *Weekly Standard*, September 10, 2006

out of the secret places of my mind both in my verse and in my letters to such as you." The notebooks might be thought to reveal those secret places more than did his poems and letters; yet, in their combination of what the editor calls "candor and cryptic evasion," they offer no easy and direct road to what Frost the human being "really" believed about central matters.

One of the most charming and pertinent of the entries is this four-line ditty:

> Nothing ever so sincere
> That unless it's out of sheer
> Mischief and a little queer
> It won't prove a bore to hear.

A "sincere," mischief-lacking poem is a bore to hear because absent from it are the twists and turns, the changes of tone, the "special posture" of individual sentence sounds that Frost, in his insistence on "ear" rather than "eye" reading, makes central to the reading and writing of poetry. He is also committed to humor: "I am never more serious than when joking," was one of his repeated avowals.

The poem just quoted is an example of a Frostian "joke" that is serious as well. But in one of the many entries that address themselves to what a poem is, or is like, or should be like, we get the following:

> The poem must have as good a point as an anecdote or a joke. It
> is the more effective if it has something analogous to the practical
> joke—an action—a "put up job" such as being carried out as a
> serenade or valentine or requiem or memorial address.

Notable here is the insistence on poetry as an action, something carried out with purpose in mind (elsewhere he refers to a poem as a "deed"), a practical joke, "sheer / Mischief and a little queer." The reader is engaged in an analogous activity, as when, in one of the many entries directed at teaching, students are advised, "Don't tell the poem in other and worse English of your own to show you understand it. But say something of your own based on the poem (*not* an opinion of it though)." To respond adequately to the "put up job" of a poem, it is not enough to call it beautiful or say you don't like it; you need rather to do something to keep the ball in play.

Another word for this recommended activity, within the poem or in response to it, is one of Frost's favorite words—performance. He addresses the matter directly with this admonition: "Performance in poetry and in life is recognition and admission of the fact that things are not to be too well understood." "Are not to be," rather than "are not," underscoring the insistence that nothing be closed down too confidently, too quickly. Faggen reminds us in his introduction of the poet's respect for, indeed fascination with, uncertainty and chaos. This is the "confusion" that in his crucial essay, "The Figure a Poem Makes," he said the poem provided a "momentary stay against." Only a momentary one, mind you.

Lest one get the impression that the notebooks are wall-to-wall nuggets of detachable Frostian wisdoms, it should be said that much of the material is relatively, sometimes wholly impenetrable, even with the editor's best efforts at annotation. For example, the following entry:

Story of the Gaget Gimlet no Longer Manufactured.
    "   " Hiring the One-armed Teacher
    "   " The Woodpecker's Daughter.
Nothing Fatal but Death Stigma
Of an [?Albenes] Tatoo
Brat Buster
Do you read [?Serviss]

The items that precede and follow this one shed no light on it, nor does Faggen venture to comment. It is one of the occasions in which an attempted look into the composer's mind reveals nothing—which is to say that any reader is going to skim a lot, looking for a moment when something shines through. Some items are repeated so often as to testify to how fond Frost was of them, such as "All men are created free and equally funny"; or "I hate the poor don't you Yes and I hate the rich. I hate them both as such." In one item he questions and answers this condition of hatred: "Why do I hate them. Because they bother me so. I have to think of them when there are so many other things I want to think of."

At moments we get memorable glimpses into Frost the bad boy who prided himself on "running away" from colleges (Dartmouth, Harvard) and like an earlier Frank Sinatra did things his way. He never missed the chance to bait Archibald MacLeish, especially after MacLeish's verse play *J.B.* was published. He takes MacLeish's much-anthologized poem "Ars Poetica," whose final lines reverently intone "A poem should not mean/ But be," and corrects it, by moving the words around, to: "It should be mean." "You have to be attractive enough to get people within striking distance," he noted, and the strike could be lethal. At other times the operative word is sly, as in this piece of timeless advice: "Keep on writing to her after marriage with a view to marrying her later in life when her husband dies or fails her." Then there are purely humorous entries that make us think of Mark Twain, as when Frost defines a "regionalist" as "one who picked out a region (such as the abdomen fundament or elbow) and has a pain in it."

The editor rightly points out the predominance of epigrammatic meditations in the notebooks—Frost says in one of them that students "must be taught that the fun of being epigrammatic is the legitimate fun of literature." Although I haven't seen the comparison made, there are compelling similarities of temperament and serious wit between Frost and the great Renaissance poet Ben Jonson, whose first collection of poems was titled *Epigrams*. Jonson later published *Timber, Or, Discoveries* "made upon men and matter, as they have flowed out of his daily readings." Perhaps the finest moments in Frost's notebooks are ones, always coming out of the blue, in which his discovery is such as to strike us as truly never said before. Sometimes they are about matters one wouldn't have expected him especially to reflect on, like the following two on alcoholic intake. In one of them he shrewdly imagines his way into the kind of person who is prey to drink: "Drink is a medicine for the too strict by nature. No one needs it who has ever lost himself without it." We are not allowed merely to feel superior to these overstrict people, nor are we invited to dismiss the following expansion of it: "Getting drunk is the glorification of waste—pouring libation {to the God of Waste} not onto the fire but into yourself. It is squandering with complete submissiveness to the nature of things your time your wealth your faculties." Faggen comments on Frost's frequent preoccupation with "waste," including a resonant line from his poem "Pod of the Milkweed": "But waste was of the essence of the scheme." Perhaps there is something to be said even for squandering central human qualities—time, wealth, faculties—in the interests of a gesture as large-scaled as "complete submission to the nature of things." In such formulations as these, the clever epigrammatist moves into realms rather deeper and less to be taken in "fun." "Life is a punishment. All we can contribute to it is gracefulness in taking the punishment." Nothing to ponder there; it has to be swallowed straight.

The editor cautions us to be wary of the "seductive finality" of some of the entries, and this is best done by trying to see the aphorisms and epigrams in the light of others that qualify or even contradict the one in question. Frost notes that "The tone of plain statement is one tone and not to be despised. All the same it has been my great object in poetry to avoid the use of it." These notebooks testify to how hard he worked at not being easily understood: "I should like to be so subtle at this game," he wrote in the letter quoted at the beginning of this review, "as to seem to the casual person altogether obvious." For the game, which he played over sixty years, the following entry may stand as a motto: "I have made a life study out of what I can say."

NOTES

1. Since this was written, doubt has been cast on Faggen's editorial practice by two critics, James Sitar and William Logan, who accuse him of inaccurately transcribing many items in the notebooks. Since Faggen has spent years editing them, my sense is that he should be trusted, despite whatever mistakes there turn out to be.

Parts of a World: Wallace Stevens Remembered, an Oral Biography by Peter Brazeau

What was Wallace Stevens really like? What sort of man was this poet who served as vice president of the Hartford Accident and Indemnity Company while composing lines like

> Life is a bitter aspic. We are not
> At the centre of a diamond. At dawn,
> The paratroopers fall and as they fall
> They mow the lawn.

Thanks to *Parts of a World*, Peter Brazeau's exemplary and seemingly exhaustive oral biography of the Stevens who dealt with bond claims and wrote those lines, we now have at least 50 times as much material for a judgment as was previously available. Some of it is perhaps not what we were waiting for to help us put man and work together in the usual inspiring ways. Arthur Polley, a fellow member of the board of directors of the Hartford Live Stock Insurance Company, a "legal board without any great responsibility" owned by the Hartford Fire Insurance Company, confessed that he tried to read Stevens's poetry but found it "the biggest bunch of gobbledygook." He wonders whether since "Wallace was a helluva kidder" who "never cracked a smile, never," it might be that he had written "a lot of these things with his tongue in his cheek, and the country picked up on him and said he was a great poet—and probably he was—and he was having the biggest private laugh of anyone in the world."

Mr. Polley's remark is exactly the sort Stevens would have treasured; at least, it is in touch with the mixed bag of virtues he wanted to be

First published in the *New York Times Book Review*, November 20, 1983 (as "The Man Who Wore a Four-Piece Suit")

remembered for, presuming he cared about such things. Yeats wrote, "The intellect of man is forced to choose / Perfection of the life, or of the work." Stevens's answer was to say, not at all; like the Canon Aspirin's choice in "Notes Toward a Supreme Fiction," "it was not a choice / Between excluding things. It was not a choice / Between, but of . . . ." When, a few lines later in that same poem, someone—quite clearly the poet—eloquently declares, "I have not but I am and as I am, I am," we may hear the voice of the Lord, but to my ears it also sounds like Popeye the Sailor Man.

Stevens is described by an employee in a Hartford bookstore as "a great big fellow, six foot three or four, and weighed two hundred and fifty. But he didn't look fat, just a big man, tightly bound and fully packed." Bigger than Popeye and, in the words of the poet and critic Elder Olson, "a tough kid of the kind I like," he permitted himself no tragic Yeatsian choices between Life and Work. This "tough kid" once wrote in a copy of his book *Harmonium*, which he presented to his employee John O'Loughlin, "When you read this, you won't know what the hell it's all about." As O'Loughlin recalls with some admiration, "That was part of his humor." When Stevens moved to Hartford in 1916 at the age of thirty-six, the Hartford Accident and Indemnity Company had been in existence for less than three years. His field of expertise was surety law, and he would come, as Mr. Brazeau puts it, "to oversee the legal affairs of the growing bond department." He continued to do so until his death thirty-nine years later, and the consensus of his associates is that he was very good at it indeed. "He thought other poets who had chairs in universities and read to women's groups or men's groups were kept men," remarks a lawyer, Herbert Schoen.

"You just had the feeling that this fellow was different than the common herd," Robert DeVore, another associate, notes. DeVore had firsthand experience of this distinctness when he met Stevens at the train station in Philadelphia, before a meeting at an attorney's office about a broken contract. Upon arriving at the station, the "tall, austere, very dignified" Stevens announced that they must get to the office without delay, to which DeVore assented. He was then taken aback when Stevens suggested they first pick up some cinnamon buns at a place called Lahr's. Stevens explained that always, when in Philadelphia, he purchased buns at this establishment. So the two men proceeded to Lahr's, where a dozen buns were dispatched to Hartford, then another dozen purchased and carried away in a bag. When the group assembled in the attorney's conference room, the bag of buns was held out to its seven members and they were invited to partake. Politely, and to a man, they partook. As DeVore puts it, "We all reached in and got a handful of goo." DeVore describes Stevens as a "superintellect," yet two other interviews with his associates suggests flaws in, at least, his legal behavior. Said one of them, he was "too impatient" to be "a good bargainer," and his dealings with people were "very cold, very distant." This superintellect was hard to fathom, partly because Stevens was a serious joker whose sense of humor more than one person interviewed in "Parts of a World" was discomfited by. Leslie Tucker, a bookkeeper, says that when he would go off on a business trip, Stevens would advise him to "be sure to stay at the Y.M.C.A." Tucker remains uncertain whether his boss was kidding.

According to another associate, Anthony Sigmans, Stevens arranged a hotel reservation for them both in Boston by writing to the Statler and saying, "I would like a room overlooking the Common. I will have with me Sigmans, who could be assigned a room overlooking most anything." Sigmans took no offense, but it is not clear what the company's message girl thought when, entering Stevens's office with some checks for him to sign, she heard him say to his companion, without looking up, "This is that girl I was telling you about at lunch today." In fact, there had been no such talk about "that girl," which, depending on your sense of humor, makes the joke less gross or more heartless. Then there were the racial and ethnic "jokes" that are certainly heartless and probably gross, as when the man Stevens's daughter, Holly, was to marry (John Hanchak, disapproved of by Stevens) is referred to as the "Polack-Communist." "I have not but I am and as I am, I am": the first two chapters of this oral biography, dealing with Stevens the businessman, tell us much about an arrogant, fair-minded, lordly, whimsical, no-nonsense joker with a superintellect who (according to his "manservant," John Rogers) "always carried new, clean money." As for when the poetry got written, opinions differ. One acquaintance says Stevens jotted down poetry on his long walks home, and Stevens told another acquaintance, John Gruen—who set some of the poems to music—"You see, I actually bring my poetry to work and my secretary types them up for me. It's my way of being disloyal." One of Stevens's researchers observes, "One could never tell whether he was writing poetry; I never peeked over his shoulder—not by any means." And Mr. Gruen puts into words what any reader is still pleased to feel, even after reading through Brazeau's compilation—"There was something rather mysterious about his writing the poetry." Gruen also says, "He told me that he didn't know what his poetry meant at times, that he really had to think hard as to what he meant by that image or that phrase or that word, even."

There was also something mysterious about Stevens's life with his wife, Elsie, who remarked after her husband's death that his poetry was a "distraction that he found delight in, and which he kept entirely separate from his home life." On the evidence in this book, we see that other things were kept entirely separate from life at home, such as virtually all his relationships with other people. Guests were rarely entertained (William Carlos Williams visited once and was put up in a hotel, at Stevens's expense), and the casual visitor was discouraged. Anthony Sigmans once brought Stevens flowers when he was ill, and was instructed (presumably on behalf of Mrs. Stevens) please not to bring them again. When Sigmans drove him home from the office, Stevens would say, "Oh, there's Mrs. Stevens out in the yard. Don't drive up there. Let me out here, and I'll walk up." Apologizing for not inviting him inside the house, he explained, "Mrs. Stevens won't permit it." How much Stevens used his wife as an excuse for his own reclusiveness at home is still not clear. But by all accounts Elsie Stevens was, to say the least, difficult—"unbalanced," "a mousy little creature," "not very helpful to him," "off the beam," "a witch." On the other hand, one interviewee notes chillingly, "He treated his wife as if she were ash." It is perhaps unseemly to submit their relationship to further prying speculation, but one result was that Stevens loved all the more his socializing with business colleagues on the road, in Florida or New York, at a cold roast beef lunch at the Canoe Club in Hartford.

There were martinis with the roast beef, for alcohol was a crucial element in the socializing. We hear of a party with business associates at the Biltmore in New York, at which everyone drank lots of whisky and Stevens did a polka. John Rogers remarks on how much his boss liked "a good drink- up," and since, unsurprisingly, Mrs. Stevens disliked booze, the frolicking had to go on off the premises. Perhaps Stevens's home life consisted mainly of the pleasures taken in his paintings (James Johnson Sweeney calls his taste in art "a comfortable bourgeois taste") and in music, where he must have had a more than bourgeois taste, since Samuel French Morse remembers that he owned all the Schnabel Beethoven sonatas and Maggie Teyte's recording of Berlioz's song cycle, 'Nuits d'Été.' Mrs. Stevens was reputed to have been a very good cook, so there was also that to look forward to away from the office. In later years, she and her husband shared an interest in genealogy.

Altogether Brazeau's book is a mine of new phrases through which we try to fix for a moment this "very eccentric man," this "crafty, marvelous genius" (in John Brinnin's words). "He was a man who wore a four-piece suit," says William Cole. My own favorite is by Richard Wilbur, who describes him, on one occasion, as "behaving like the noblest sort of traveling salesman." Stevens was the man who, when a Trinity College professor called up to ask whether he could bring Archibald MacLeish (then head of the Library of Congress) out to see him, replied, "Well, I don't think you'd better. Tell him when he gets a reputation I'll be glad to see him." In his last days, terminally ill with cancer, he became a Roman Catholic, saying to the hospital chaplain, the Reverend Arthur Hanley, "I'd better get in the fold now." He was baptized just a few days before he died, remarking, "Now I'm in the fold." Perhaps he was, but I choose to remember him for another sort of celestial aspiring. Arlene Van Raalte, a Hartford neighbor who once made and then served him a really "nice" piece of pie, recalls, "I put it on [the table] and I said, 'Mr. Stevens, this is called Heavenly Pie.' He looked at it and said, 'Open up the gates!'"

Wallace Stevens:
Collected Poetry and Prose

Wallace Stevens is the second American poet of this century to be published in the Library of America, Robert Frost having appeared previously. So it is appropriate to quote Frost's response when asked, in an interview, if there were affinities between his work and Stevens's. No, Frost said, there weren't ("Oh gee, miles away"), and by way of illustration provided an anecdote: "Once [Stevens] said to me, 'You write on subjects.' And I said, 'You write on bric-a-brac. And when he sent me his next book he'd written 'S'more bric-a-brac' in it." On another occasion Frost referred to their relationship as "the prettiest kind of stand-off," a good way to describe the claims of subjects as against bric-a-brac.

Hitherto Stevens's writings were scattered here and there: the Library of America volume presents, in its one thousand pages, first the *Collected Poems* of 1954, with a few Stevens omitted from that volume restored to their original places. There follow twenty-nine late poems, previously available in *Opus Posthumous*, then a hundred pages of previously uncollected poems, beginning with his earliest, most conventional efforts written while he was a special student at Harvard and concluding with the lovely "As You Leave the Room." There are also three short plays; *The Necessary Angel*, his essays "on reality and the imagination"; and a large swatch of uncollected prose, ranging from editorials in the Harvard *Advocate* about how or whether Harvard Yard should be fenced, to various short speeches in response to awards he received late in life. A brief final section consists of entries from the notebooks, journals, and letters. Frank Kermode and Joan Richardson (Stevens's biographer) have edited the volume with bibliographical expertise; as with other volumes in the Library, the notes are not extensive, but notes to Stevens's poems seldom help much anyway.

First published in the *Boston Globe*, December 28, 1997 (as "His Way of Saying")

Perhaps a reviewer like me, who read the volume from one end to the other (not always with equal attentiveness), should be mistrusted if he agrees with Frost and finds plenty of bric-a-brac not only in Stevens's poems but in the plays and prose reflections as well. The plays—*Three Travelers Watch a Sunrise, Carlos among the Candles,* and *Bowl, Cat and Broomstick*—declare by their very titles that nothing very serious is going on in them. Nothing all that humorous either: at the beginning of *Three Travelers,* whose dramatis personae are "three Chinese, two Negroes and a girl," a character identified as "Second Chinese" says, "All you need, / To find poetry / Is to look for it with a lantern." The stage direction that follows is "The Chinese laugh," though I found it easy not to. As for the essays, they have their eloquent moments, especially in "The Noble Rider and the Sound of Words" when Stevens insists, by way of concluding, that poetry,"the expression of it, the sound of its words, helps us to live our lives." There is a deft discussion of Marianne Moore's poem "He Digesteth Harde Yron," which shows Stevens could be a good practical critic when he put his mind to it.

But all too often, as in the title of one of his poems, the pure good of theory animates these and the other "philosophical" essays from the uncollected prose. I put the word in quotation marks, since I presume Stevens's procedures would drive most professional philosophers to annoyance, even rage. His method typically, as in "A Collect of Philosophy," an essay about poetry and philosophy, is to assemble quotations from philosophers and theorists—Leibniz, Paul Weiss, Whitehead, Jean Wahl, Jean Paulhan—and hope that somehow by the end of the essay they will fall together into a coherence. That didn't happen for me; indeed many of the essays I understand very imperfectly—a failure attributable to their wooliness rather than profundity. Consider these sentences: "Another thing not intended is a poetic way of writing. If thinking in a poetic way is not the same thing as writing in a poetic way, so writing in a poetic way is not the same thing as having ideas that are inherently poetic conceptions. This is an accurate statement in the sense in which I mean it." (The last sentence is particularly quixotic.) Stevens reiterates his desire, in poetry, for "freshness and strangeness"; announces, in 1946, "This is a time for the highest poetry" (but why then, especially?); or (in "A Note on Poetry") addresses himself to the relation of freedom to form: "The essential thing in form is to be free in whatever form is used. A free form does not assure freedom. As a form, it is just one more form. So that it comes to this, I suppose, that I believe in freedom regardless of form." I suppose too, but want to ask—as so often with these essays—what exactly is the point? Where have you gotten us by these murky lucubrations? Frost's uncollected prose, in the Library volume, is full of fertile, humorous statements and questions about the writing of poetry; Stevens, by contrast, seems placed on a pedestal, going on and on, gravely, endlessly. When he steps down from the pedestal he can be affectionately, slyly humorous, as in the portrait of "John Crowe Ransom: Tennessean": "They say that there are more Ransoms in Tennessee than Tates in Kentucky. However that may be, the more there are of you, the more you possess and the more you are possessed."

But of course it is the poems that matter. Two earlier critics of them, Yvor Winters and Randall Jarrell, much admired the brilliance of Stevens's first book, *Harmonium*, but for different reasons felt that something had gone wrong in his later work. (Later, after Jarrell had read *Collected Poems*, with its great concluding section "The Rock," he rightly judged Stevens to have ended in triumph.) Over the last few decades, and especially because of the powerful efforts of Helen Vendler and Harold Bloom on his behalf, Stevens's reputation soared and shows no signs of declining. The long poems especially—*Notes toward a Supreme Fiction, Esthétique du Mal, The Auroras of Autumn*, even the (to me unreadable) *Ordinary Evening in New Haven*—have been canonized, as if it weren't a dubious and dangerous venture for a poet to essay, repeatedly, the long form. Reading through, yet once more, the poetic oeuvre, my response is thoroughly mixed. Is it my obtuseness or laziness that continues to find so many of the poems after *Harmonium* impenetrable, elusive to the point of incomprehension, their gorgeous structures of sound not put to the service of illuminating "subjects"—human beings—nor often marked by vital, complex ideas about life, death, and the rest of it?

In one of the letters included here, Stevens wrote to Alice Corbin Henderson, "My poems seem so simple and natural to me that I am never able to understand how they may seem otherwise to anyone else. . . .

Whatever can be expressed can be expressed clearly." Assuming this is not a piece of sublime disingenuousness, we may ask whether he was kidding himself. Indeed his own willingness, in letters to correspondents, to "explain" particular poems, what this or that line meant—explanations that bear seemingly little relationship to the lines and poems themselves—is of a piece with his notions about how simple and clear his poems were. Repeated readings of Stevens's poems don't necessarily lead to clarification of them—as, in my opinion, they do with those of Yeats, Eliot, Frost. The poems and lines that baffled me in 1954, when I was given a copy of the *Collected* for Christmas, are still baffling. Furthermore there is the fact, not enough commented on, that Stevens's poems seldom rhyme and that increasingly he settled into the comfortable, mechanical mold of unrhymed pentameter tercets. Nor did he attempt complicated, challenging stanza forms. How much does the great outpouring of poems from him in the 1940s and '50s have to do with the facility and fluidity coincident with not having to rhyme or bother much about stanza? It's not exactly (as in Frost's quip about free verse) playing tennis with the net down, but it may have encouraged garrulity and avuncularity in Stevens.

These reservations—which would be qualified though not erased if I listed thirty or forty of Stevens's poem that are superb, and irreplaceable—may be understood (and rejected) as emanating from a reader who thinks Frost's poetry, as well as his prose reflections, to be the most satisfying and life-changing of any produced by an American poet of the twentieth century. I note that neither Vendler nor Bloom—nor Kermode, who wrote an important early book on Stevens—has written at any length about Frost. It is at least possible that, although of course there is "room" for both geniuses, one's heart and head can't be fully committed, equally, to both. "The fact remains that we are always fundamentally interested in what a writer has to say. When we are sure of that, we pay attention to the way in which he says it," Stevens once wrote to William Carlos Williams. Yet there is no poet more than Stevens for whom "the way in which he says it" remains, first and last, our prime object of attention. Readers of his work, as it is displayed in this fine volume, may measure the percentage of profundity to bric-a-brac it contains, by way of judging how much, and how many of, the poems help us to live our lives.

Ezra Pound:
Poems and Translations

*H*ere is Ezra Pound's poetry exclusive of the *Cantos*, making him the third American poet from the last century to have Library of America status conferred on him. His predecessors in the series—Robert Frost and Wallace Stevens—had not only their poems presented in a single volume, but also substantial numbers of essays and letters. Pound's voluminous production allows for no such tidy packaging—none of his critical prose or letters is represented. The book also presents some major stumbling blocks to the general reader, since over half of it consists of Pound's renderings of the Japanese "Noh" drama; three Confucian volumes—*The Great Digest and Unwobbling Pivot, The Confucian Analects,* and *The Classic Anthology Defined by Confucius;* and translations of Sophocles' *Elektra* and *Women of Trachis.* It may be hazarded that only the professional scholar or serious Poundian will spend much time with these six hundred pages.

That word "Poundian" is telling, since we don't speak of Frostians or Stevensians (or even Elioticians) when describing readers and students of Pound's contemporaries. Indeed all Poundians are "serious" in ways different from admirers of these other poets, since Pound-lovers feel the need to make a case for their man, not only by way of acknowledging his political and social sins—the anti-Semitism, the broadcasts supporting Mussolini and condemning Allied war efforts—but also for the poetry he wrote. Unlike Frost or Stevens or Eliot, Pound left no indisputable selection of "great" poems that bears comparison with theirs. Randall Jarrell thought it surprising that a poet of his extraordinary talents should have written so few good poems all his own. Putting the *Cantos* aside, how

---

First published in the *Boston Globe,* March 28, 2004 (as "Ezra Pound: Poems and Translations")

many readers will stand up impenitently to confess their pleasure in reading and rereading even Pound's best work: such short poems as "Sestina: Altaforte," "Pierre Vidal Old," "Apparuit," "Portrait d'une Femme," "The Return," "Near Perigord," "The River-Merchant's Wife: A Letter," or the longer sequences *Homage to Sextus Propertius* and *Hugh Selwyn Mauberley?* If Pound is judged to be a classic, it may be a classic of the sort Eliot feared Ben Jonson might become, "to be read only by historians and antiquaries."

Richard Sieburth selected and edited this volume, providing a hefty 140 pages of chronology and notes. The Library's practice is not to have introductions to their books, which seems unfortunate in this case since the bewildering variety of Pound's contributions could usefully be prefaced by some setting in order. Reading through the chronology, however, is more than usually instructive; his long life—Pound died the day after his eighty-seventh birthday—exhibits an active engagement with many forms of human endeavor: poetry, music, history, economics, politics. Those interests were accompanied by a varied sexual career and a near-manic conviction of his diagnostic powers. Gertrude Stein famously characterized him as a village explainer, "good if you are a village, if not, not" (although Jarrell countered that Pound really couldn't explain anything). But it wasn't until illness and depression overtook him in his late years that the explainer expressed any doubts about his own practices. So his late apology for anti-Semitism (the "cheap, suburban prejudice" he fell for), and his calling the *Cantos* a "botch," are lonely instances of his being anything other than single-minded about things. Pound's literary criticism stimulates and entertains, but is fatally lacking in nuance, qualification, or ambivalence in its pronouncements. Milton was ruined by "asinine bigotry" and "beastly hebraism"; Wordsworth was "a dull sheep"; Byron's technique was "rotten"—such opinions struck off at age thirty never modified themselves. In fact, Pound didn't think much of English poetry on the whole—which might be judged a serious mistake.

No one except perhaps Hugh Kenner, whose pioneering book on Pound makes the strongest case for his centrality as a modernist poet and invaluable critic, can rise to the challenge presented in bulk by these poems and translations. Certainly not this reviewer, whose lack of Provençal, Chinese, Greek, Anglo-Saxon is so patent as perhaps to debar him from opening his mouth at all about Pound's contribution. Yet these lacks have not kept me from returning periodically to his work. My continuing interest in Pound was immeasurably helped along by Kenner and Donald Davie (though Davie had many reservations about the poetry), preeminent critics who devoted so central a part of their own work to elucidating and commenting on Pound's. The questions and problems he presents—as "creative" translator, blockbusting critic, and bossy energizer of other writers—involve one in the history and life of poetry in ways that a more "pure" poet like Wallace Steven does not. Which is not to say that I would trade "Sunday Morning" or "The River of Rivers in Connecticut" for anything in these pages of Pound.

Kenner noted fifty years ago that Pound's poetry up to *Hugh Selwyn Mauberley* "may be very largely regarded as a series of rhythmic definitions." Regardless of whether such definitions are "enough," they are everywhere in Pound, as in lines from "The Spring":

> Cydonian Spring with her attendant train,
> Maelids and water-girls,
> Stepping beneath a boisterous wind from Thrace,
> Throughout this sylvan place
> Spreads the bright tips,
> And every vine-stock is
> Clad in new brilliancies.

Breaking up what Pound called "the heave of the pentameter" is the task of such rhythms that may be heard in the "Chinese" poems from *Cathay* (1915). These, along with a number of ones in *Lustra* (1916) and others mentioned earlier, will survive as distinctive if minor achievements. I am not so sure about the bitter-and-angry Pound from the early sections of *Mauberley*: it is invigorating, particularly when one is young, to declaim (perhaps in the shower) those ringing castigations of perfidious England, World War I, modern civilization in which "We have the press for wafer; / Franchise for circumcision." But do the castigations come too easily? Yeats wrote that Pound had more "deliberate nobility" than any contemporary poet, but the nobility was constantly interrupted by its opposite—"Nervous obsession, nightmare, stammering confusion." The opposites may depend on each other, at least they did in Pound.

And yet, and yet . . . There is an anecdote in Kenner's book about T. S. Eliot in which Pound advises Eliot against chastising some current idiocy: "You let *me* throw the bricks through the front window. You go in at the back door and take out the swag." Although this new volume can't be construed as brick-throwing, it still provides a cautionary jolt to any reader tempted to write off Pound.

Ezra Pound: Poet: A Portrait of the Man and His Work, Volume 1, The Young Genius, 1885–1920, by A. David Moody

Why should we want to read a biography of Ezra Pound? If you asked the question about one of his poet-contemporaries, Robert Frost or Wallace Stevens, the answer is that reading their poems, "Mending Wall" or "Sunday Morning," say, makes us eager to know something about the man who wrote them. Both Frost and Stevens led essentially private lives in their early decades, Frost in the isolation of a New England farm, Stevens studying law in New York City. Neither would publish a book of poems until roughly age forty. Nothing could be further from such lives than Ezra Pound's, whose first thirty-five years, packed with incident, were lived very much on the public stage. They make up a story more compelling in its aggressive daring than many of the poetic experiments Pound engaged in during that time.

These years are the subject of Pound's latest biographer, A. David Moody, author of a first-rate critical study of T. S. Eliot. Volume 1 of Moody's projected two volumes takes Pound up to the moment when he is about to leave London. Between 1908, when he left America for Venice and published his first book of poems at age twenty-three, and 1920, when one of his central works, *Hugh Selwyn Mauberley*, appeared, he produced hundreds of poems and critical essays, while sponsoring such literary movements as Imagism and Vorticism. Moody's subtitle "The Young Genius" accurately names the way Pound saw himself as possessing what Moody calls "the authority of alienated superiority." He relished controversy on all sorts of fronts in hopes of winning over or reforming or enlightening a public and a literary culture that, he was convinced, did not understand him.

First published in the *Washington Times*, January 20, 2008

Pound has been the subject of more than one previous biography, Humphrey Carpenter's *A Serious Character* (1988) being the best of them. The main story Mr. Moody tells does not significantly differ from Carpenter's, and Moody has discovered no hitherto unknown facts that alter our sense of Pound. What he has done is to proceed, meticulously and sympathetically, through the ins and outs of Pound's day-to-day career, suspending the march of events only when a new volume of the poet's appears. Moody's decision to treat both life and work is admirable, although anyone except a Pound expert will experience difficulty in being asked to consider in careful detail so many examples of Pound's early efforts to find himself as a poet. Beginning with *A Lume Spento* (1908), the thin volumes proliferate: *A Quinzaine for This Yule, Personae, Exultations, Canzoni, Ripostes, Cathay, Lustra,* with many of the poems reappearing in successive books. This is not to mention his translations and imitations of Italian and Provençal poets, or the Japanese Noh plays. The biographer assiduously traces continuities among the poems, especially their arrangement within individual volumes; even so, many of the poems strike at least this reader as precious and unsubstantial. The ones that stand out from these early collections—"Sestina: Altaforte"; "Pierre Vidal Old"; "Apparuit"; "Portrait d'une Femme"; "The Return"—are relatively few. It is not until the "Chinese" poems in *Cathay* ("The River- Merchant's Wife: A Letter," "Lament for the Frontier Guard") and the comic squibs from *Lustra* that the lyric Pound and the satiric Pound reveal themselves expertly.

Still, these twelve years of Pound in London make for inspiriting reading, since it was a time in which what Moody calls his "generous energy about the work of creation" was most vividly apparent. He had been a student of philology at the University of Pennsylvania and at Hamilton College, but found that, with a few exceptions, the academic presentation of literature "allowed little scope for comparative evaluations, critical responses, or discussion of whether one text was more or less pleasing, instructive or life-enhancing than another." From the beginning Pound was interested in, as he put it in an early poetic fragment, "always the spirit within / Shaping the form without." His developing conviction was that the best poetry could liberate people—Americans, for example—from, in Moody's words, "the tyranny of mass emotions and received ideas." A quixotic conviction, we say, looking from a hundred years later at the still unliberated state of all those people who don't read Dante or Cavalcanti or Confucius. But it is indeed life-enhancing to observe Pound's struggles with his contemporaries—poets, editors, publishers—who could not see what he saw; and it is instructive to follow, as Moody so faithfully does, his relations with Yeats, with Ford Madox Ford, and with perhaps his most prominent "discovery," T. S. Eliot. Clearly the young Pound was in many ways an impossible person, yet, at least for his friends, also impossible not to be compelled by. One of those friends, William Carlos Williams, whom Pound met at the University of Pennsylvania where Williams was a medical student, later wrote in his *Autobiography* that, although he couldn't take him for a "steady diet" and was annoyed by his posturings, still Pound was "the livest, most intelligent and unexplainable thing I'd ever seen, and the most fun." The effort to explain this unexplainable person animates Moody's biographical quest.

Pound's "livest" self may be seen in the humorous affection of letters he wrote to his parents, resisting his mother's suggestion that he come home to America ("I do not wish to be mayor of Cincinnati nor of Dayton, Ohio"), and in the unceasing efforts he made on behalf of writers he admired. He helped out others financially although he himself had arrived in London with three pounds in his pocket and was dependent on his father's generosity and later the patronage of the American collector John Quinn. His attractiveness to women is borne out by the number with whom he formed alliances: one of them, Dorothy Shakespeare, became his wife and would stand by him in the bad days of his later confinement; another, the young violinist Olga Rudge, who would later bear him a child and be his companion, appears briefly at the end of this volume.

Some of the most useful parts of Moody's criticism of Pound's works are found in remarks about his essays, especially reviews of his contemporaries—Frost, Ford, Eliot, Wyndham Lewis—and about *Hugh Selwyn Mauberley*, in which Pound bids farewell to London. *Mauberley* has been the subject of some of the best previous criticism of Pound (by Hugh Kenner, Donald Davie, John Espey), and Moody's pages on it are a heroic attempt to sort out the complicated interplay between Pound the writer and his persona, Mauberley (also a poet), by way of ascertaining just who is speaking at this or that moment and in what tone. *Mauberley* is a poem dense with such ambiguity, and even Moody's careful and strenuous attempt to sort it out doesn't convince me that, in places, ambiguity is not confusion and incoherence. But on balance it figures as one of the most challenging longer poems of the modernist era, and no subsequent poet has remained oblivious of its challenge.

In the concluding volume to come, Mr. Moody will have to deal with a Pound whose obsessions and recklessly publicized beliefs, most notably the anti-Semitic one, make for a more distressing, if potentially tragic, figure. By contrast, the years in America and London as treated in this first volume so intelligently and fully, wear the aspect of the human comedy from which, beginning in 1920, Pound would withdraw to occupy himself with writing the *Cantos* and with the disastrous public events he attempted so unsuccessfully to rectify.

T. S. Eliot: *The Varieties of Metaphysical Poetry,*
edited by Ronald Schuchard

With the publication in 1924 of *Homage to John Dryden*—a small book consisting of his essays on Dryden, the Metaphysical Poets, and Andrew Marvell—T. S. Eliot's influence as a critic became immense. Probably the most influential of his ideas was the big one about what happened to English poetry in the seventeenth century. It was then, Eliot asserted in "The Metaphysical Poets," that a "dissociation of sensibility"—of thought from feeling—had set in, and the centuries to come would not recover from it. This dissociation, he claimed, was "aggravated" by two great poets, Milton and Dryden, who "performed certain poetic functions so magnificently well that the magnitude of the effect concealed the absence of others." By contrast, the metaphysical poets of earlier in the century "possessed a mechanism of sensibility that could devour any kind of experience," and in this they were the heirs of their Italian thirteenth-century predecessors—Dante, Guido Cavalcanti, and Cino. For Donne, "a thought . . . was an experience; it modified his sensibility." By contrast, poets from the eighteenth and nineteenth centuries too often thought and felt "by fits and starts"; like Shelley, they fell upon the thorns of life and bled, or like Tennyson and Browning, they "ruminated."

Eliot's own career as a poet was, at this time, particularly uncertain. He published "The Hollow Men" as the final poem in *Poems 1909–1925,* ending things not with a bang but a whimper. He abandoned, without completing it, his verse drama *Sweeney Agonistes.* He was seriously thinking about a conversion to Anglo-Catholicism, and he was about to launch once again his magazine *The Criterion* (it would be "European" in tone) under the patronage of Lady Rothermere and his employer, Faber and

---

First published in the *American Scholar* 63 (Autumn 1994): 302–6

Faber. When, having been nominated for the post by Middleton Murry, he was invited to deliver the Clark Lectures at Trinity College, Cambridge, in the winter of 1926, he took it as an opportunity to explore further and at length the "dissociation" theory. In his preface to the lectures, Eliot announced his intention to rewrite them into a much longer work to be titled "The School of Donne." This would include detailed examination of other poets (the lectures concentrate mainly on Donne, Crashaw, and Cowley) and would be part of a three-part work titled "The Disintegration of the Intellect," in which Elizabethan dramatists and seventeenth-century prose writers would also be considered. None of these projects materialized, and Eliot decided not to publish the Clark Lectures.

They have at last been published, along with the Turnbull Lectures, three talks Eliot gave at the Johns Hopkins University in 1933, when he was in America delivering the Norton Lectures at Harvard (*The Use of Poetry and the Use of Criticism*) and the Page-Barbour ones at the University of Virginia (*After Strange Gods*). The Clark and Turnbull lectures have been edited within an inch of their lives by Ronald Schuchard, whose introductions to each set are deft and highly informative. Mr. Schuchard's learning and detailed grasp of Eliot's writings are manifest, but the heavily footnoted text of the lectures themselves (the notes often taking up from a third to half the page) can be seriously distracting. To identify at length every name Eliot mentions seems in many cases unnecessary; surely anyone who picks up a volume as highly specialized as this one doesn't need to be filled in, say, on who John Henry Newman was and what important books he wrote. Best to read the lectures first with occasional glances at footnotes, then a second time without such glances.

Schuchard's introduction to the Clark Lectures (I shall confine myself to them, since the Turnbull ones repeat much of the Clark material) gives an excellent sense of the vibrant Cambridge milieu into which Eliot stepped. Among the fellows at Trinity in 1926 were J. G. Frazer (of *Golden Bough* fame), Alfred North Whitehead, Frances Cornford, G. E. Moore, and A. E. Housman (who attended every lecture and sat in the front row). Younger Cambridge dons from the English faculty, also in attendance, included I. A. Richards, E. M. W. Tillyard, Basil Willey, Mansfield Forbes, and F. R. Leavis. T. R. Henn, a don who was hostile to Eliot, found the lectures "recondite and inaudible"; it is not clear whether the audience—including many "ladies" with notebooks (women were then often mocked for attending too many lectures too assiduously)—agreed. Schuchard suggests that Eliot eventually decided against publishing them because he did not have the economic security or the time to write scholarly books: in the editor's words, "the exploratory essay was to remain his critical forte." Another way of putting it is that Eliot's style of pronouncement was ideally suited to the short flight in which the author advanced an "exploratory" large assertion and presented something in a new and striking way, after which the writer quickly moved somewhere else rather than staying and developing the argument (as a book-length effort would need to do).

By 1947, in his second essay on Milton, Eliot had pretty much given up on the "dissociation" theory, saying that he now felt he shouldn't have put the finger on Milton and Dryden as culprits, and that if a dissociation did take place its causes were too complex and profound to account for in literary-critical terms. Ten years later, in his stunning chapter "Dissociation of Sensibility" from *Romantic Image*, Frank Kermode demonstrated how vague and vulnerable to criticism Eliot's theory was in its details, but how important it was for modernist poets like Yeats. Pound, and Eliot to imagine a time somewhere back there in history when life was single rather than double, the intellect at the tips of the sense, thought and feeling as one. (Yeats's phrase for it was Unity of Being.)

Eliot's great good place, as far as poetry was concerned, was, like Pound's, thirteenth-century Italy where, as he puts it in the concluding Clark Lecture, "the human spirit reached a greater sum of *range, intensity, and completeness* than it has ever attained before or since." Metaphysical poetry—as distinguished from "philosophical" or "allegorical" or "narcotic" poetry—"gives the emotional equivalent of thought, a rarified, but perfectly definite world." With Dante and his circle, "the feelings are organised according to an organised view of the universe, so that there is given the feeling-equivalent for every detail in the system." The English metaphysical poets even before the presumed "dissociation" show something less than such unity; Donne may be a great poet, says Eliot, but he is a great poet of "chaos," and his poetry—unlike

Dante's—shows "the absence of order, the fraction of *thought* into innumerable *thoughts*."

Eliot loved to try out the memorable formulation, almost too neat to be true—such as this one: "The trecento had an exact statement of intellectual order; the seicento had an exact statement of intellectual disorder; Shelley and Swinburne had a vague statement of intellectual disorder." Or this one: "In Dante . . . you get a system of thought and feeling; every part of the system felt and thought in its place . . . for the thought and the emotion are reverse sides of the same thing. In Donne you get a sequence of thoughts which are felt; in Crashaw . . . you have a sequence of feelings which are thought." These heady formulations are open to all sorts of critical query and attack, as was the "dissociation" theory. Eliot seemed to acknowledge this in the final lecture when, after apologizing for the relatively thin treatment given to Laforgue and Corbière as nineteenth-century metaphysical poets, he adds that he should also have dealt with Baudelaire and should have traced the problem of Good and Evil through the century. Then, with a sigh, he concludes the paragraph:

> My theory of metaphysical poetry is, you will have seen, a heavy one for a mere man of letters to shoulder. It implies a theory of the history of belief, in which the thirteenth century, the seventeenth century, and the nineteenth century, all occupy their places in what I have called a process of disintegration.

A heavy theory indeed, especially for the man who praised Henry James for having a mind so fine that no idea could violate it. When, in one of the Turnbull Lectures, discussing a stanza of Donne's "The Relique," Eliot suddenly opines that it indicates "that something was beginning to go wrong with civilization about that time," you know his mind has been violated by an idea that sounds quite half-baked.

The way to read these lectures, as with all Eliot's criticism, is to put up with or tolerate the theory for the practical results it produces—for, that is, the insights about particular poems and poets and literary periods it generates. In these terms the lectures are full of marvelous things, especially about Donne, but also about Crashaw and Cowley. The absences one most regrets are Herbert and Marvell, who surface only briefly. Eliot had already published his essay on Marvell, and he would not write about Herbert until his pamphlet of 1962, by which time his criticism had grown rather bland. But there was nothing the least bland about his judgments in 1926, especially in comparing one writer with another. Such comparison was at the root of Eliot's brilliance as a literary critic; typically he didn't do "readings" of poems by going through them in detail, but worked instead by hit-and-run, juxtaposing lines from two poets with only the briefest critical commentary (sometimes no more than a sentence), then moving away from the scene and on to something else. Often the commentary is surprisingly humorous. By way of describing Donne's satires, Eliot mocks the Elizabethan John Marston, who, he says, "lays it on with a trowel." Quoting a couplet from Marston—"Avaunt! ye curs, howl in some cloudy mist, / Quake to behold a sharp-tongued satirist!"—he remarks, "I am much mistaken if any cur, listening to this sharp-fanged satirist, would do anything but curl up and go to sleep." Of some terribly "conceited" lines from Crashaw, he notes, "One cannot conceive the state of mind of a writer who could pen such monstrosities."

Sometimes one of his sentences breaks on you with the wonderful force of fresh intelligence and you feel that he is perhaps the smartest man in the world: "Cowley is an inferior Petrarch; that Petrarch whom Johnson [Samuel] treats with the respect only given to a subject one knows nothing about and does not wish to take the trouble of looking into." Yet Eliot when he deals with particular poems reminds us of no one so much as Johnson. Sometimes he will put a good poem and poet into perspective by invoking a more demanding one: of the first stanza of Marvell's "The Definition of Love": ("My Love is of a birth as rare / As 'tis for object strange and high; / It was begotten by Despaire / Upon Impossibility"), he says, "Compared to the twistings of the brain of Donne, this is mere parroting of anagrams." From the now forgotten metaphysical poet John Cleveland, Eliot produces an especially barbarous stanza and calls it "[a] stanza which, I admit, I have never taken the trouble to understand." How refreshing to hear this from a literary critic! Sometimes a burst of admiration wells up and interrupts the point being made: about the final stanza of Donne's "The Blossome" Eliot exclaims, "In these lines—and one would go to gaol for ten years if it would help to write as good lines as these!—there is a good deal of what is called cynicism."

A year after he delivered the Clark Lectures, Eliot sent a typescript of them to Mario Praz, who is acknowledged more than once in them. Praz responded with some criticism of Eliot's scholarship (probably depressing him, says Schuchard), but he made the following excellent comment:

> It will be a book of criticism which will read like fiction, perhaps, and so much better for it, if it does: history is, after all, as somebody said, always contemporary history, and in writing your book, you will be writing the history of your own mind. And your mind, I am afraid, interests me even more than Donne, Crashaw, and all the dead worthies.

That should have cheered up Eliot (if anything could), on the verge of being baptized into the Church of England. Since the mind of that dead worthy, T.S.E., is of nearly limitless interest, it is splendid to have these lectures in print.

Hart Crane:
Complete Poems and Selected Letters

With this volume, Hart Crane joins Robert Frost, Ezra Pound, and Wallace Stevens in the Library of America publications of twentieth-century poets. Crane can be easily fitted into their 800-page format since his total poetic output, including unpublished poems, amounts to only 150 pages; so the bulk of the volume is a very full selection of his letters, plus a few essays and reviews. Langdon Hammer, the editor, not only has written an excellent book on modernism in the works of Crane and his friend Allen Tate, but previously edited a handsome volume of Crane's letters with generous commentary. Now he provides a useful and extensive chronology as well as pertinent biographical and textual notes. One couldn't ask for a more compact and finished presentation of the poet who may be the most problematic of his contemporaries—Edwin Arlington Robinson, William Carlos Williams, Marianne Moore, and T. S. Eliot, along with the names mentioned above already enshrined in the Library of America.

In Mr. Hammer's earlier book, he says shrewdly that although since around 1960 Crane has been judged to be a major modern poet, the many books of criticism written about his poetry have always felt the need to reintroduce him. (Probably the best of these books, by Warner Berthoff in 1989, is titled *Hart Crane: A Re-Introduction.*) This need, I should guess, has everything to do with the difficult brilliance any reader meets in coming up against Crane's poems for the first time as well as subsequent times, since both as wholes and as particular sequences they are characteristically hard to grasp. Early on Crane knew what he was seeking in the poetry he wished to write. At the beginning of 1922, when he was twenty-two, living in Cleveland and working as a copywriter, he wrote Sherwood

First published in *Commonweal* 134, no. 7, April 6, 2007 (as "An American Voice")

Anderson, who had recently published *Winesburg, Ohio,* about the thrill of reading John Donne. Quoting lines from two of Donne's poems, he tells Anderson:

> What I want to get is just what is so beautifully done in this poem, an "interior" form, a form that is so thorough and intense as to dye the words themselves with a peculiarity of meaning, slightly different from the ordinary definition of them separate from the poem.

He adduces his poem "Black Tambourine" ("The interests of a black man in the cellar") as an instance of such interior form.

A few months later he sent Gorham Munson, one of his New York acquaintances to whom he wrote frequently, a "tentative beginning" to what would be his three-part poem "For the Marriage of Faustus and Helen":

> The mind has shown itself at times
> Too much the baked & twisted dough,
> Food for the accepted multitude.
> The mind is brushed by sparrow wings;
> Rebuffed by asphalt, numbers crowd
> The margins of the day, accent the curbs.
> Convoying diverse dawns on every corner
> To druggist, barber, and tobacconist.

Crane called "Faustus and Helen" a "metaphysical attempt," and in his book on the poetry, R. W. B. Lewis devoted forty pages to explicating it. But though Crane eventually revised the lines he sent Munson, their "peculiarity of meaning" resulting from the poet's "dyeing of the words" not only resists definitive paraphrase but resists it in part through a lack of the dramatic tone of meaning we expect to meet in lyrics by Hardy or Frost or Yeats. Crane's lines typically lack the "special posture" Frost thought a poem's lines should have; instead they present themselves more coolly as utterance detached from any particular speaker, any certifiably human presence. They are just *there,* not quite abiding our uncertainties of response. Warner Berthoff correctly calls "Faustus and Helen" Crane's most "problematic" poem, but it seems, at the same time, an extreme instance of what is generally the case and what is central to Crane's intractability.

Allen Tate, who wrote a prefatory note to Crane's first book, *White Buildings* (1926), noted that by contrast with the sometime opacity of his verse, Crane's letters were written "in a clear and always lucid prose." Reading through them in this volume enforces the rightness of Tate's judgment. Whether he is painstakingly and painfully trying to clear or improve the air between himself and his divorced parents, or defending himself to Yvor Winters after Winters's devastating review of his second book, *The Bridge*, Crane does so with scrupulousness, tact, and ironic humor. The only letters that make for really depressing reading are the ones of humiliation and apology, written during the ill-fated year in Mexico that preceded his suicide, to friends he had embarrassed or insulted by drunken behavior. Earlier his correspondence is full of the enthusiastic reading discoveries he made in his autodidact's course of study—of Ben Jonson, Dostoevsky, Wyndham Lewis, Frost ("a good, clean artist, however lean"), and many others. In these letters the sensibility that, in Tate's words, was "locked-in" as it encountered "ordinary forms of experience" feels exploratory and free, even urbane. Unlike so many poets, Crane remained free of the nastier competitive envies and jealousies; it is right to be impressed by his moral character.

The history of his reputation is an odd one, which consisted first in being taken up, sometimes with the highest praise, by poet-critics like Tate and Winters, whose later judgment that *The Bridge* was, however heroic, a failure, surely more than disconcerted Crane. Another severe essay, following on Tate and Winters, by R. P. Blackmur, treated him as employing "an extreme mode of free association" that made paraphrase of his work unhelpful. Decades later, Harold Bloom's heated attempt to reinstate him as, along with Stevens, the significant modern romantic poets in the post-Emersonian line (Bloom enthused over what he called Crane's "orphic quest") generated perhaps more heat than light, but helped send readers to the poet once again. Coupling Crane with Stevens is useful, not only because each is often obscure, their "logic of metaphor" (Crane's phrase) a challenge which at least this reader often falls short of meeting, but also because each wrote a poetry of splendid rhetoric. Yeats said memorably that we make poetry out of the quarrel with ourselves, but there is no quarrel in Crane's verse. Its sole "argument" is between the poet and eternity, as at the conclusion to "Voyages II": "Bequeath us to no earthly shore until / Is answered in the vortex of our grave / The sea's wide spindrift gaze toward paradise."

Robert Lowell, who wrote a poem about Crane ("Words for Hart Crane"), called "Voyages II" a "love poem with a great confusion of images that are emotionally clear" and of which paraphrase would give no impression whatsoever. So much of Crane that stays in the mind and ear consists of rhetorical three or four line sequences—or single lines that lodge themselves permanently. Here follows a small anthology of them:

> The apples, Bill, the apples!
>
> ("Sunday Morning Apples")

> Scatter these well-meant idioms
> Into the smoky spring that fills
> The suburbs, where they will be lost.
>
> ("Praise for an Urn")

> I heard wind flaking sapphire, like this summer,
> And willows could not hold more steady sound.
>
> ("Repose of Rivers")

> Distinctly praise the years, whose volatile
> Blamed bleeding hands extend and thresh the height
> The imagination spans beyond despair,
> Outpacing bargain, vocable and prayer.
>
> ("For the Marriage of Faustus and Helen")

> Beyond siroccos harvesting
> The solstice thunders, crept away,
> Like a cliff swinging or a sail
> Flung into April's inmost day—
>
> ("Voyages VI")

The Bridge is of course packed with such lines and sequences, so much so that, though like Winters and Tate I can perceive no overall pattern of unification of the fifteen poems, there are enough moments of original composition to more than make up for a larger meaning that might, if discovered, prove not so interesting. By common consent, the close of "The River" is Crane at his finest, its rhythm and rhyme combining in powerful quatrains embodying the Mississippi:

> Poised wholly on its dream, a mustard glow
> Tortured with history, its one will—flow!
> —The Passion spreads in wide tongues, choked and slow,
> Meeting the Gulf, hosannas silently below.

Whatever one's verdict about *The Bridge,* Tate's encomium to Crane twenty years after his death is there to ponder, under the stimulus of this new volume:

> By the time he was twenty-five . . . he had written a body of lyric poetry which for originality, distinction, and power, remains the great poetic achievement of his generation. If he is not our twentieth-century poet as hero, I do not know where else to look for him.

The Middle Generation

Young Betjeman; John Betjeman: New Fame, New Love; Betjeman: The Bonus of Laughter, by Bevis Hillier

Thick and fast come the biographies of English writers from the century past: Graham Greene, Isherwood, Spender, Anthony Powell, V. S. Pritchett among the most recent. Bevis Hillier published the first volume of his three-volume life of John Betjeman in 1988, taking the poet up through childhood conflicts with his father, schooling at Marlborough and Oxford (which he left without a degree), and marriage to Penelope Chetwode in 1933 at the age of twenty-seven and in the face of her disapproving parents. Although *Young Betjeman* ran to a (relatively) modest 477 pages, Mr. Hillier warned that there was a lot more to come by quoting an earlier biographer of Betjeman who announced that he was "not an admirer of the vacuum-cleaner school of biography" whose aim was to heap up fact, anecdote, and whatever else into an enormous pile. Hillier demurred, noting that he was not only a biographer but a "source" who had direct access to many of the people appearing in his chronicle, "advantages which no future biographer of Betjeman can have:

Reprinted by permission from the *Hudson Review* 58, no. 3 (Autumn 2005): 481–88 (as "Betjeman's Way"). Copyright 2005 by The Hudson Review, Inc.

friendship and long talks with him and his wife Penelope, and interviews with many of his friends and associates."

These words recur in the preface to the second volume and now once more in the concluding one. Both books run to over 700 pages, bringing the grand total to just short of 2,000. Since Betjeman authorized Hillier way back in 1976 to be his Boswell, this means that nearly thirty years of immersion in the great man's doings have gone into the enterprise. (Bevis Hillier meanwhile has published books on plastics, porcelain, and art deco.) It is surely natural to wonder whether the agreeable and gifted Betjeman needs quite such a "grand canvas"—Hillier's phrase—as these volumes make up; evidently American publishers don't think so, since none of the books has appeared here. Is Betjeman too quintessentially an English phenomenon to bear transmission across the water?

Hillier's application of the vacuum cleaner was evident in *Young Betjeman* when, discussing Betjeman's homosexual inclinations while at Oxford, he notes that report of a bedding between Auden and his subject is "probably" true. (Presumably they paid the "scout" five pounds to keep quiet, Auden later remarking that it wasn't worth the money.) In the midst of reminding us that single-sex love was common in English all-boy schools, Hillier provides further evidence of Betjeman's proclivities:

> John Bowle said that at Oxford John frequently slept with an Old Marlburian Balliol undergraduate of John's year, David Dent (who took a first in Jurisprudence, married in 1930 and died in 1933). Lionel Perry remembered that John "had a crush" on Hugh Gaitskell. "He would say to him, 'Hugh, may I stroke your bottom.' And Hugh would say, 'Oh, I suppose so, if you *must.*'"

Good fun, no doubt, and in case you never heard of David Dent (as you must have done of Hugh Gaitskell), his "first in Jurisprudence" is dutifully recorded along with his brief marital career. (Was his early death a consequence of missing his old Marlburian friend?) There is enough similar trivia to make us wonder about its worth; this reader trawled the 2000 pages with some delight, but also with impatience, at times annoyance.

Why am I being told all this? Would it all come clear if I'd been educated at Marlborough and Oxford?

In the present volume, Hillier gives 1961 as the year Betjeman began to transform himself "from Bright Young Thing and *enfant terrible*, into Grand Old Man." With the publication of his *Collected Poems* (1958), which sold astonishing numbers of copies (Tennyson and *A Shropshire Lad* were comparable sellers), and his verse autobiography *Summoned by Bells* (1960), a popular if not exactly a critical success, Betjeman—who also began to appear frequently on television—became a kind of household word. For those who did not admire his work, he was a portent of English philistinism and complacency. John Wain, who compared the blank verse of *Summoned by Bells* to writing jingles on Christmas cards, found the fact that for many people Betjeman was the only attractive contemporary poet to be "merely one more sign that the mass middle-brow public distrusts and fears poetry." Betjeman was knighted in 1969 and became poet laureate in 1972 after the death of C. Day Lewis. His first "official" effort, on the marriage of Princess Anne in 1973 ("Hundreds of birds in the air / And millions of leaves on the pavement"), raised the hearts of few readers. But perhaps even more significant than his identity as a poet was his increasing role as upholder of England's architectural heritage, threatened by planners and developers. His role in forming the Victorian Society, his unsuccessful campaigns to save such monuments as the Euston Arch and the Coal Exchange, and his successes on behalf of St. Pancras Railway Station, the Criterion Theatre, and the London "garden suburb" of Bedford Park, are thoroughly treated in some of the most interesting pages of Hillier's book. His various travelogues in Britain for BBC television, as guide to, seeker of, and commentator on the out-of-the-way, opened many English eyes to what they'd taken for granted or had been told they mustn't admire. Indeed Betjeman's celebrity became such as to invite parody and creative fantasy: the funniest example of this is a *Private Eye* bit involving Sir John and an antiques expert, Arthur Negus, discovering something in a house they're visiting:

John Betjeman: Oh gosh, look at this, I think we've come to the smallest room in the house. Shall we go in? *(Sound of door creaking open. Sudden screech of female occupant.)*

Arthur Negus: Oh, this is very interesting, John. Just look at these
                 old legs. They're varicosey, I think. Yes, they're by
                 Carlo Varicosi, who was actually in these parts—who
                 was very active in these parts—about 1780. I wonder
                 if there's a mark. Let's have a look at the bottom.
                 (A further squawk from occupant.)

In fact, Betjeman insisted that he didn't want to preserve everything, and was quite willing for starters to get rid of Shaftesbury Avenue and Charing Cross Road *in toto*. As an effective agent of preservation he also showed limitations; a colleague in the Victorian Society noted that he was "a great one for lost causes and new societies, but when they begin to gather momentum he loses interest." Assuming such was the case, it points up a similarity between his identity as a lover of overlooked churches and the way his poems celebrate lost people and objects: a person truly in the grip of nostalgia is unlikely to be fully effective as a campaigner and preserver.[1] He once said that all his poetry stemmed from Goldsmith's "The Deserted Village," a poem he'd taken to as a youth, and of course Goldsmith's village is "there" only in the poem's lament for its having irretrievably disappeared.

Hillier doesn't set up as a literary critic, nor does Betjeman's poetry invite devoted exegesis. His most influential admirer, Philip Larkin, in the introduction to the 1971 *Collected Poems* that pretty much introduced Betjeman to these shores, placed him in strong terms that need some qualification:

> The first thing to realise about Betjeman as a writer of verse is that he is a poet for whom the modern poetic revolution has simply not taken place. Insularity and regression rule here as there. For him there is no symbolism, no objective correlative, no T.S. Eliot or Ezra Pound, no reinvestment in myth or casting of language as gesture, no *Seven Types* or *Some Versions*, no works of criticism with titles such as *Communication as Discipline* or *Implicit and Explicit Image-Obliquity in Sir Lewis Morris*. He addresses himself to his art in the belief that poetry is an emotional business and that rhyme and metre are means of enhancing that emotion.

The swats at Eliot and Pound, the mockery of what Larkin once called the "myth-kitty," the sweepings away of High New Criticism as in

Empson and Blackmur, or a *Scrutiny*-like emphasis on discipline, are anti-modernist sentiments we know Larkin shared and proclaimed—remember his alliterative contempt cast at modernism by invoking as its saints, Pound, Picasso, and Parker (Charlie, that is). And the statement that for Betjeman poetry is an "emotional business," to which business rhyme and meter are an enhancement, is equally shared by Larkin. Leaving aside how much of an emotional business Pound and Eliot in their different ways thought poetry was (but say to yourself "Pull down thy vanity" and "Old men ought to be explorers"), consider the emotional climax to a poem of Betjeman's I suspect Larkin admired, "Devonshire Street W.1":

> The heavy mahogany door with its wrought-iron screen
> > Shuts. And the sound is rich, sympathetic, discreet.
> The sun still shines on this eighteenth-century scene
> > With Edwardian faience adornments—Devonshire Street.
>
> No hope. And the X-ray photographs under his arm
> > Confirm the message. His wife stands timidly by.
> The opposite brick-built house looks lofty and calm
> > Its chimneys steady against a mackerel sky.
>
> No hope. And the iron nob of this palisade
> > So cold to the touch, is luckier now than he
> "Oh merciless, hurrying Londoners! Why was I made
> > For the long and the painful deathbed coming to me?"
>
> She puts her fingers in his as, loving and silly,
> > At long-past Kensington dances she used to do
> "It's cheaper to take the tube to Piccadilly
> > And then we can catch a nineteen or a twenty-two."

Like many of Betjeman's poems, especially later ones, "Devonshire Street W.1" has death in it, and the sweetly poignant attempt on the part of the wife to cheer things up is designed to touch our hearts. As always in the Betjeman landscape, things are particularized so as to provide one familiar with London Transport a small satisfaction—buses numbered 19 and 22 *do* pass through Piccadilly Circus, which can be conveniently reached from Baker St. on the underground.

The question is how rhyme and meter can be said to "enhance" the emotion Betjeman is concerned with; certainly they highlight it, make it available in a way no reader's ear can miss. Whether or not the emotion is explored or just held out there to elicit a throb in the heart seems worth asking. Larkin too, as a poet, consistently uses rhyme and meter to enhance the "emotion" in his poems: his "Cut Grass," unlike "Devonshire Street W.1," contains no people but is like Betjeman's poem insofar as it is about time, vulnerability, evanescence:

> Cut grass lies frail:
> Brief is the breath
> Mown stalks exhale.
> Long, long the death
>
> It dies in the white hours
> Of young-leafed June
> With chestnut flowers,
> With hedges snowlike strewn,
>
> White lilac bowed,
> Lost lanes of Queen Anne's lace,
> And that high-builded cloud
> Moving at summer's pace.

In his great essay "The Study of Poetry," Matthew Arnold directed readers to look for "high poetic quality" in the rhythm and movement of a poem—although he never defined "movement" nor demonstrated how it emerges in a particular case. But an important way to distinguish Larkin's poem from Betjeman's (and I think the distinction holds true for their work in general) would contrast the complicated subtlety of movement in "Cut Grass" with the lilting music of "Devonshire Street W.1." Consider merely the unobvious and satisfying richness of the sentence made up by the first three lines of Larkin's poem, followed by the expansive pace of the second sentence that comprises the rest of the poem. Betjeman's immense popularity—a few decades back at least—surely had something to do with the easy availability of his poetic rhythm and movement, by contrast not just with Pound or Eliot but with Larkin himself.

This is not to contradict Larkin's estimate of Betjeman (it is one of Larkin's best pieces of critical appreciation), even if his prediction or hope that the second half of twentieth-century English poetry would derive from Betjeman, as the first half did from Eliot, failed to realize itself. Larkin's quotations in the essay do much to illustrate the variety in Betjeman's work and he focuses convincingly on "The Metropolitan Railway; Baker Street Station Buffet," a fine poem that moves through five stanzas of a young couple's day in London, in by train ("Early Electric") and out again "through Rayner's Lane / To autumn-scented Middlesex again." Then we are moved to the present state of things in the final stanza which, in Larkin's words, cuts to the "poignantly brutal":

> Cancer has killed him. Heart is killing her.
> The Trees are down. An Odeon flashes fire
> Where stood their villa by the murmuring fir . . .

(A current visitor to London will look in vain for an Odeon movie palace—*sic transit.*) Larkin's summoning up of the case for Betjeman deserves to be seriously entertained:

> Betjeman is serious: his subjects are serious, and the fact that his tone can be light or ambivalent should not deceive us into thinking he does not treat them seriously. His texture is subtle, a constant flickering between solemn and comic, self-mockery and self-expression.

After comparing him, to Betjeman's advantage, with W. M. Praed, then with Housman and Hopkins ("they penetrate deeper, but he makes a bigger hole"), Larkin sums up:

> He offers us, indeed, something we cannot find in any other writer—a gaiety, a sense of the ridiculous, an affection for human beings and how and where they live, a vivid and vivacious portrait of mid-twentieth-century English social life.

Like Larkin, Kingsley Amis was unwavering in his admiration for Betjeman and his work, including seven poems of his in the *New English Book of Light Verse* (1978). In that book Amis proffered a definition of light verse that seems to have been arrived at by immersion in Betjeman's work, calling it "a kind of realistic verse that is close to some of the interests of the novel: men and women among their fellows, seen as members of a group or class in a way that emphasizes manners, social forms, amusements, fashion (from millinery to philosophy), topicality, even gossip, all these treated in a bright, perspicuous style." Such a style animated not only Betjeman's verse but his valuable and thoroughly entertaining writing about the English countryside (he edited the Shell Guides and wrote the one to Cornwall himself), church architecture, and London railway stations—his *London Historic Railway Stations* (1972) is a fine picture book with excellent commentary.

But he was also a clown and a joker, the sort of creative spirit who, one sociable evening, put forth the claim that Sir Walter Scott was a great erotic novelist. When challenged, he proceeded to read aloud a passage from one of Scott's novels, interpolating into it some strongly off-color contemporary smut. He coauthored a television play in which developers succeed in improving the traffic patterns in Westminster by getting rid of its central monument: one developer remarks with some regret, "Pity about the Abbey." Generally he was less of a satirist than a comedian—he and Barrie Humphries, of Dame Edna Everage fame, became good friends—and Hillier's subtitle to his final volume, "The Bonus of Laughter," is a good one. But Betjeman the showman, as he grew older and Parkinson's disease took its hold, often revealed a man within—the obverse of that showman. More than once he wondered to one correspondent or another whether he wasn't really a "fraud," his great act merely an act, all too easy to see through. Auberon Waugh astutely compared him to Gilbert and Sullivan's jester from *The Yeoman of the Guard*, Jack Point. "It's the sound of a merry man moping mum / Whose soul was sad and whose glance was glum," sings Point in the opera's concluding song, after which he falls dead.

Of course Jack Point sighed wholly for the love of a lady, and John Betjeman's sexual yearnings were rather more distributed. His wife Penelope's conversion to Catholicism in 1948 must have stimulated his long-term relationship with Lady Elizabeth Cavendish, whom he met and fell in love with three years later (and who did not make herself available to Hillier). At the time of Penelope's conversion, Evelyn Waugh wrote a number of hectoring letters to Betjeman, insisting that he follow her out of the halfway house of Anglicanism. Betjeman refused, and blamed Waugh in part for the estrangement in his marriage. He was genuinely responsive to women (some of the poems testify to that) but on occasion in his late years sighed over a lost single-sex passion of Oxford days. The indefatigable diarist and friend, James Lees-Milne, writes of a visit to Betjeman's flat in Chelsea two years before he died. After drinks, Elizabeth Cavendish leaves for a meeting and the two men reminisce. Lees-Milne has recently seen Lady Caroline Blackwood, daughter of Basil, Marquess of Dufferin and Ava, who was killed in Burma in 1945 and to whose memory Betjeman wrote one of his most nakedly exposed poems ("Friend of my youth, you are dead!"). Betjeman tells Lees-Milne he met Lady Caroline once but never could see her again since she reminded him so much of her father, and goes on to recall his Oxford unrequited love for the boy ("Never received so much as a touch of a hand on the shoulder"). Lees-Milne recounts that "He then said that in after-life no loves ever reached the heights of schoolboy love" and proceeds to tell Betjeman about his own (Lees-Milne's) deep love for a lad at Eton who afterwards "never again had any truck with me, and turned exclusively to women. J's eyes filled with tears." One is uncertain just what to call such a moment. Touching? Pathetic? Ludicrous? Perhaps none of our business. John Gross once described Betjeman as "a serious, not to say an impassioned writer, who uses objects and landmarks to conjure up the eternal moment, the sudden stab of terror, intimate feelings and buried memories." I think we should take the moment Lees-Milne describes as similarly constituted.

His last years do not make for happy reading, as he became increasingly immobile, his face frozen into a mask by Parkinson's. One of the excellent photographs in Hillier's book shows him at a ceremony in St. Pancras station sitting in a wheelchair, expressionless, while behind him a locomotive has just been christened "The Sir John Betjeman." He died the next year and was given a most grand memorial service at Westminster Abbey (Pity about the Abbey), described by Hillier, as he describes everything, in full detail. In his journals, Anthony Powell called it "a tremendous affair, the Archbishop of Canterbury in charge; prince of Wales reading the Lesson." Powell went on to note:

One could not help indulging in rather banal reflections about the seedy unkempt (but never in the least unambitious) Betjeman of early days, snobbish objections to him at Oxford, Chetwode's opposition to the marriage, crowned at the last by all this boasted pomp and show. It was a remarkable feat.

NOTES

1. Betjeman's "amateur" credentials as a student of architecture contrasted with those of his frequent ally in preservation, Nikolaus Pevsner, whom Betjeman disliked, referring to him with full anti-Teutonic prejudice as Herr Doktor-Professor. Near the end of his life he asked Hillier, "Why is it that when you've read what Pevsner has to say about a building, *you never want to look at that building, ever again?*" An interesting book about the two men is Timothy Mowl, *Stylistic Cold Wars: Betjeman versus Pevsner* (London, 2000).

William Empson, Volume 1, *Among the Mandarins,*
by John Haffenden

*E*arlier this year the third and final volume of Bevis Hillier's 2,000-page work on John Betjeman appeared, and now John Haffenden weighs in with just short of 700 pages on the English critic and poet William Empson. You might think that so long a book would suffice for Empson; but wait, it's merely volume one, and takes its subject only up to age thirty-three (Empson died in his seventy-eighth year). Mr. Haffenden, who is Professor of English at the University of Sheffield where Empson taught for many years, is a practiced biographer, author of a life of John Berryman, and since Empson's death in 1984 he has been busy amassing material and bringing out volumes of Empson's essays that never found their way into print when Empson was alive. Haffenden has left no stone unturned in his quest to get down the facts, many of them bizarre, about the unruly genius he believes his subject to have been. It is a devoted and exhaustive enterprise that only the most curious reader will not be worn down by.

The central facts of Empson's earlier life as painstakingly recounted here reveal an individual who was intransigent in his relation to authority, careless about—indeed hostile to—anything that looked like prudent behavior, and eager to follow the flights and perchings (the latter never for long) of his extraordinary mind. His earlier years were spent at Yokefleet Hall in Yorkshire, the youngest child of four, and with a heritage that included literary and political distinction. He excelled in the impressive intellectual atmosphere of school at Winchester, then at Magdalen College in Cambridge, where he took a degree in the sciences. (His seriousness about science would permeate the poems he began to write and publish at Cambridge.) He went on to take a degree there in English, studying under the electrifying I. A. Richards, whose *Practical*

First published in the *Washington Times,* July 10, 2005

Criticism (1929) revealed how much difficulty students had in attending to the sense and feeling of poems. Empson wrote some essays for his tutor that investigated the complicated interactions of a poem's words—essays that would very soon become the substance of his first and most famous book, *Seven Types of Ambiguity* (1930). But by the time it was published, he had been expunged from his college's rolls, even banished from the precincts of Cambridge, because he was discovered to have kept a supply of condoms in his rooms, also to have entertained a young woman there. The punishment was severe and, so it seems to us, absurd; but it set the stage for an uprootedness that would characterize his life in the 1930s: two years teaching at a Japanese university; a three-year period of London literary activity, heavy drinking (a given then and later), and—witnesses agree—residence in conditions that might best be described as squalid. In 1935 he published his first book of poems and his second book of criticism, *Some Versions of Pastoral.* There followed two years of teaching in China under the most adverse conditions—the Sino-Japanese war, the absence of books, forced migrations from here to there. He left China in 1939, returning to England via the United States, and joined the Overseas Services of the BBC, for which he would work throughout the Second World War.

Haffenden's labors have been prodigious, including trips to the Far East to nose out the facts of Empson's teaching in Japan and China. As a consequence, he is reluctant to pass up detailing and quoting at length from all possible sources of information. In an important way, the biographer's urge to get everything into his account accords with the temperament and principles of his subject, who believed that anything, whether in literature or in life, was the better for its manifesting multiple possibilities of meaning and implication. A poem's ability to suggest various meanings was, to Empson's mind, an indication that it should be praised rather than disparaged for its plural significances. In a related manner, he became fascinated with the ambiguous possibilities of expression he discerned in representations of the Buddha, and wrote an essay about his findings. This penchant for ambiguity—for both/and rather than either/or—showed itself in sexual matters as well; in his attraction to both males and females, as Haffenden puts it, he "always left open the by-way of bisexuality." Undoubtedly the most outlandish instance of this hospitality to ambiguity occurred when, in Japan, he got drunk and made a pass at a taxi driver, later explaining that "the Japanese men and women look so alike that I made a mistake." As with so many of Empson's claims, one wonders how to take it: Mr. Haffenden says that it is made "with absurd implausibility." But Empson may have thought such implausibility made it the more worth claiming.

Seven Types of Ambiguity and *Some Versions of Pastoral* will continue to be read for something other than their objective presentation of judgments about literature to be agreed or disagreed with. The critic Barbara Hardy once called *Seven Types* a book that was "exciting about literature and exciting as literature. It was amused, amused by itself." In other words, Empson was always writing "literature," exploiting the kinds of complicated doubleness of sense and tone in the works he wrote about. Haffenden quotes a paragraph from his chapter on *Alice in Wonderland* in *Some Versions* and remarks that it is "apparently casual and freewheeling," words that apply equally to all of Empson's prose. And not to his prose only, since the difficult, often obscure poems he wrote in the late 1920s and '30s (after that he stopped writing poems) challenge our attempt to settle into any confident reading of them. One of the (relatively) easier ones, the well-known villanelle "Missing Dates," begins "Slowly the poison the whole bloodstream fills. / It is not the effort nor the failure tires. / The waste remains, the waste remains and kills." Haffenden calls it one of his greatest poems for its "sheer emotionalism." Yet on the recording Empson made of it, he reads the whole poem in a melodramatic, even ghoulish voice, as if he were some evil magician casting a spell. Could this be less an expression of sheer emotionalism than one more dark, if scintillating, joke? If we find greatness in some of the work of his contemporaries, such as Robert Lowell and Philip Larkin (to say nothing of predecessors like Frost, Eliot, Yeats), then perhaps a better word than greatness should be found for Empson's undeniably individual, yet queer and eccentric, verse.

Perhaps his most moving attempt to state the human condition in memorable words comes in the final stanza of one of his best poems, "This Last Pain." It may serve as an epitaph for Empson's inimitable procedure as a poet-critic, and for the troubled brilliance of his life as Haffenden has so fully presented it:

> Imagine, then, by miracle, with me,
> (Ambiguous gifts, as what gods give must be)
>   What could not possibly be there,
>   And learn a style from a despair.

Selected Letters of William Empson, edited by John Haffenden

*H*aving brought out the first hefty volume of his two-part biography of the English critic and poet, William Empson, John Haffenden has edited a generous selection of Empson's letters and done so with his usual painstaking thoroughness. This involves frequent inclusion of passages from letters and other writings by correspondents who provoked Empson into responding, usually at length and often repeatedly. No collection of letters by any writer I'm aware of comes even close to matching these fifty years' worth of continuing argument about literature, the criticism and teaching of which made up Empson's life. His criticism is to be found in such works as *Seven Types of Ambiguity* and *The Structure of Complex Words;* his teaching was done in Japan, in China, for many years at the University of Sheffield in England, and after retirement in brief stints at American universities.

This is not to say that the results are always edifying to the hardworking reader; maddening, rather, is the word that more than once comes to mind. Sometimes the exchanges are about topics and matters that have ceased to hold interest for us, such as questions of "feeling" and "sense" he discusses with his mentor, I. A. Richards. The result is impenetrable stuff like the following: "A feeble attempt at putting (x) for 'feeling $(=$ sense not in focus of consciousness) of x' and X?," it begins, and continues just as mysteriously. Or we find him, more than once, going on at length about Thomas Kyd's *The Spanish Tragedy,* a play that only English graduate students have read and probably only once: "The play is morally disgusting unless you recognise that it is based on indignation about these appallingly tricky royal marriages, their immense irrelevance to the

First published in the *Washington Times,* August 13, 2006

political results they entail (such as the Spanish rule over the Netherlands, always a sore), the nastiness of having to force the girls into accepting them (or even seeing the poor debauched frog having to pretend he would be able to poke the terrifying old Elizabeth)." What? Haffenden prints some sentences from Christopher Ricks's response to this letter, in which, after praising Empson's "splendid interpretation," Ricks admits he has no interest in the play "wh. just rests in my memory as bric-a-brac."

An English reviewer of the letters noted the prevalence of pugilistic metaphors in what Empson liked to call his "argufying" mode. One of his best-known poems is titled "Just a Smack at Auden," and there's no denying he actively sought out rough-and-tumble verbal encounters with other critics. In his introduction Haffenden points out Empson's fondness for "joke-phrases," odd, slangy turns of speech that impart to the argufying a colloquial, informal, and sometimes puzzling tone. One doesn't—and surely Empson's correspondents must often have felt this—know just how to take an obvious insult that is not quite obvious in its delivery. How, for example, did the American scholar Rosemond Tuve, a specialist in Renaissance and seventeenth-century literature, take the following compliment: "I think that your style has greatly improved in your last book but is still very bad, simply from failure of communication." *Simply?* He goes on to suggest that if Tuve would try to write more clearly she would find "your ideas are a great deal more muddled than you suppose." One Penelope Doob, who sent Empson an article she'd written on a Jacobean play, Thomas Middleton's *The Changeling*, is first thanked, then dismembered over five pages in which she is treated as another of those critics who have bought into the hated "Christian revival." (Empson regularly and obsessively referred to Christianity as "torture-worship.") But, he concedes near the beginning of his reply, perhaps he has been too hasty: "Maybe I wrong you in supposing that you actually do suffer from a loathsome mental disease, putting you into what you would describe as a state of Sin. It is more likely that you talk like this because it is a skill which you have earnestly acquired, and that you murder the play because you have been taught to consider all plays as dead already." Did Professor Doob wonder at that moment why she'd sent along the offprint?

Absent from this very large volume are any letters to parents, siblings, and family generally: a couple of short ones to his son Jacob are the exception proving the rule. Empson writes from Peiping in 1948 that his wife, Hetta, is due back from a jaunt to Mongolia. "She is very fond of Mongols," he says parenthetically, but adds—Hetta by this time having returned—that she "tired of meals consisting only of a sheep boiled without salt." Most other references to his wife explain that she is staying in London while he teaches at Sheffield, of which she's not fond. He seems to have had little need for unburdening himself to others in "sincere" confessions of any sort; instead he notes "the duty of sounding cheerful in letters." Sounding cheerful involved playing a role, and Mr. Haffenden described that role well in the first volume of his biography when he spoke of Empson's critical writing as produced by "a great entertainer lavishly broadcasting as many scintillating jokes as sparkling critical jewels." There are fine examples in this volume as when, upon the occasion of being knighted, he invites Christopher Ricks to what he calls a "boasting party." In his introduction Mr. Haffenden quotes John Gross, who, after he became editor of the *Times Literary Supplement* in 1974, called Empson for a contribution. He was answered by a sing-song voice that asked "Are you in the chair already?" Gross affirmed that he was, and Empson asked, "Does it swivel?"

In a suggestive definition of humor, Robert Frost called it "the most engaging cowardice" and said that it served him to keep "my enemies in play far out of gunshot." Empson's jousting with his "enemies" can be seen as a form of sociable aggression by which he kept himself, as it were, in trim. Although he did not engage directly with his early admirer but soon-to-be adverse critic, F. R. Leavis, he more than once spoke of the "lunatic self-righteousness of the Leavisites." But Empson's "play" more than once turns, over the course of a letter, into something unpleasant, verging on the lunatic, or at least the loony. He writes to the critic F. T. Prince, thanking him for his "courteous response" to an Empson letter, yet by the end telling Prince that "it is impossible to invent any convolution of your mind which would make your behaviour anything except dirty twopenny cheating." He was fond of using joke-phrases to demean his opponent: "I suspect all you mean is that he won't parrot the shibboleths of your vain bibble-babble" (this to Mark Roberts). Writing to his sometime pupil Philip Hobsbaum, he hopes that Hobsbaum "will not boast of being my pupil any longer without admitting that I think all your present opinions harmfully and disgustingly wrong." There are many more where those came from, and although he wrote that "No man likes being promoted to the class of Licensed Buffoon," he clearly promoted himself into that role, even as his style of buffoonery was apt to lurch out of control, at least by usual standards of civility. Perhaps the most vivid pages in these letters are taken up with an exchange between Empson and Ricks in which the former suggests that something written by the latter can be attributed to Ricks's "very unhealthy frame of mind." Ricks, who deeply admired Empson's work, responds with a devastatingly effective rebuke to the charge.

Haffenden reveals what I hadn't known before, that Empson was an admirer of Evelyn Waugh: this makes sense, since both Waugh and Empson were "impossible" persons who talked for victory and almost always won it. Empson was perhaps a great, surely a unique, literary critic; these letters reveal his enormous gifts as a writer along with an absolutely intransigent conviction of his own rightness and the invariable wrongness of the scholars and critics with whom he engaged.

Auden, by Richard Davenport-Hines

Speculating on the demise of literature, D. J. Enright has suggested that a branch of it may be killing the rest of the tree: "Biography, I mean, the great growth industry, the stealer of review space, greeted by a thousand pens, the crowder-out of bookshops." The sentiment is overstated, doubtless, but worth thinking about as one walks into the local shop and sees new biographies and novels on the front table, with poetry and criticism looking for space on a back shelf. At any rate, biographies keep coming thick and fast. Richard Davenport-Hines's new one of Auden is blurbed as necessary—"the first in nearly fifteen years,"—and definitive—"the first to take the full measure of the poet's achievements." One may wonder about this, even though there have been no biographies of Auden since Humphrey Carpenter published his excellent one in 1981 (it was preceded by a comparably good one by Charles Osborne). Exactly why Mr. Carpenter, a consummately professional practitioner in the biographical mode (J.R.R. Tolkien, Ezra Pound, and Benjamin Britten) needed to be updated is not clear; nor is it clear that the new book measures Auden's achievements in a strikingly new way.

To be fair to him, Mr. Davenport-Hines is aware of the redundancy of following a comprehensive treatment like Carpenter's with something on the same line, and in the acknowledgments he pays handsome tribute to his predecessor, whose "meticulous and even-handed" work freed Davenport-Hines "to write a biography that is more thematic, or selectively emphatic." Yet Auden scarcely needs more thematic treatment than he has already been accorded. In *Early Auden* (1981), Edward Mendelson exhaustively traced thematic patterns and ideas in the poetry up to 1939, when Auden left England for America; recently, Anthony Hecht has given us an excellent study of nearly 500 pages of Auden's major poems and

First published in the *Boston Globe*, February 25, 1996

plays up through the 1950's (*The Hidden Law*, 1993). So the current biographer has a problem: how, in 350 pages, can he rehearse the important events in Auden's life and also say something newly useful about the voluminous writings? Although Davenport-Hines is never less than readable, and though his intelligent inwardness with Auden's career is manifest, I think the problem remains.

One notes in his book what Humphrey Carpenter's carefully avoided: a protectiveness in the biographer's relation to his subject, along with a tendency to oversell Auden's poems—as if they stood in need of that. The oversell can be seen in how often the word "great" is used to characterize this or that work of Auden's. For example, the book's prologue calls Auden's attempts at integration and synthesis of various ideas and experiences a "great feature of [his] thought and work," as if a recurrent habit of mind is also greatly to be commended. We are referred to Auden's "great prose poem on the limitations of the artist," *The Sea and the Mirror*; while *New Year Letter*, written just after he came to New York is "the first great poetic expression of Auden's reversion to Christianity." "In Sickness and in Health," his poem of the same period, is a "great, gloomy epithalamium." Caliban's long speech in prose at the end of *The Sea and the Mirror* "introduces great, brave ideas that were essential to his poetry for the rest of his life," and "In Praise of Limestone" is judged to be, in a quotation from Stephen Spender, "one of the great poems of this century." There are also Auden's "great poems of the late 1960s," one of which ("Partition," about the India-Pakistan partition, and undeniably an expert poem) is inflated into "one of his great historical poems." *The Dyer's Hand* is Auden's "first great collection of critical essays" (were there more great ones to come?). The carelessness in such writing betrays a too-eager partisanship on the writer's part, with "great" being asked to do work that can only be done, if at all, through even-handed analysis.

In fact, it wouldn't hurt to have an occasional colder eye cast on Auden. Davenport-Hines is always on the lookout for those critics who spoke less than well of him. George Orwell, for example, who found that a line from "Spain" revealed a collaboration "between the gangster and the pansy," is accused of "sexually rubbishing" Auden, and Orwell's criticism of Auden's "left-wing thought" is termed by Davenport-Hines "a piece of Etonian bullying." Even more despicable, we are to feel, is F. R. Leavis, whose magazine *Scrutiny* took a negative line toward what it called Auden's "immaturity." Davenport-Hines speaks of Leavis's "mean and querulous spirit," informs us that he is "now a negligible figure," and charges that *Scrutiny* provided "police bullying" in its disapproval of homosexuality. It's true that Leavis's criticism of Auden's work was partial and wrong-headed, but *Scrutiny* had a poor record of appreciating interesting contemporary writers of whatever sexual persuasion (Evelyn Waugh, Wyndham Lewis, Robert Graves were three non-homosexual peers of Auden's whom *Scrutiny* wholly ignored). A later critic, Ian Hamilton, joins the hit list and is censured as "deeply unjust" for his account of why he was determined not to be impressed by Auden when Auden came to read at Oxford in the 1960s. It is painful to watch the biographer's vigilant put-downs of lively writers who happened to speak disrespectfully about the poet's work. And it is unnecessary, since Auden was a tough guy who managed to take very good care of his writerly career by intrepidly following whatever individual light he glimpsed at a particular moment.

Davenport-Hines is a good reporter on the year Auden spent in Germany after his graduation from Oxford in 1928, and he navigates us skillfully through the strange company of friends and influences the young poet put to one or another use. There is John Layard ("Loony Layard") and his biological theory of the psychoneuroses; or George Groddeck, psychologist with a water-therapy institute at Baden-Baden; or Homer Lane and his equation of sin with neurosis—and there are a host of other lovers, seers, and counselors. Auden managed to survive them, returning to England to publish *Poems* (1930) and its splendid successors, *Look, Stranger* (1936) and *Another Time* (1940). With Louis MacNeice he wrote the agreeable *Journey to Iceland*, containing his tour-de-force "Letter to Lord Bryon." Throughout his work in the 1930s Auden was always telling us—often contradicting himself in the process—what to do: he was the great know-it-all who got away with it because of his astonishingly witty invention in the use of English.

In the Iceland book, he recorded his horror at witnessing the gory debris of whales that were being torn to pieces by a steam-winch. Mr. Davenport-Hines takes this moment as the beginning, in Auden's work, of a new phase of ethical questing. He had wanted to settle his relations with other people, to scrutinize his influence on others, and to test his capacity for good and evil. He wanted, in short, to check that he did not do harm. The biographer sees this questing as a movement toward religion, and he traces this movement through the China sonnets from *Journey to a War* (the Auden-Isherwood collaboration of 1939) and the long poems that followed: *New Year Letter, The Sea and the Mirror,* and *For the Time Being.* Yet this is the Auden I have most trouble taking seriously, as opposed to solemnly, since to my ears the sonnets sound rhythmically inert and dishearteningly abstract (Davenport-Hines admires them); *New Year Letter,* for all its intermittent life, goes on much too long, and the two ambitious poems to follow reach for their profundity largely at the expense of wit.

Auden rediscovered wit only when, in the shorter poems from the late forties and fifties in *Nones and The Shield of Achilles,* he moderated his "religious" aims and brought back into his verse the speaking voice, now older, more proselike and self-deprecating, as it comes to life in a prosody even more dazzling than before. Some English admirers, the most notable of them being Philip Larkin, claimed it was really only thirties Auden that counts and that when he came to America he lost his subject and his peculiar genius. But readers who spend time looking at the poems from *Nones* up until his death will be rewarded by all sorts of things they had forgotten about or never noticed the first time round: "The Shield of Achilles," and "In Praise of Limestone," yes, but also the "house" poems from "Thanksgiving for a Habitat" (especially "The Cave of Making" dedicated to MacNeice), "Under Sirius," "Cattiva Tempo," "Fleet Visit," "The Chimeras," and "The Houseguest," the last of which Davenport-Hines rightly singles out for praise. Nor do you have to be an academic to revel in the brilliant light verse, found in "Academic Graffiti": "George Herbert / Once tried ordering sherbet / On Salisbury Plain: / He ordered in vain."

"The last of the great English eccentrics," Jarrell called him (the other one, Evelyn Waugh, called Auden "a public bore"), and Davenport-Hines's pages on the last decades are filled with plenty of corroborating details. There is the appalling mess of Auden's living quarters, his apartment bathroom where, under the impression that it was a basin of dirty fluid on the floor in keeping with the rest of the filth, Vera Stravinsky mistakenly flushed Chester Kallman's chocolate pudding down the toilet. Perhaps she did the wise thing. (Kallman, the man Auden fell in love with when he came to New York and remained close to until the end, comes off as disagreeably as ever in these pages.) Auden smoked, a friend calculated, fifteen thousand cigarettes a year, and also drank copiously, mixing, Mr. Davenport-Hines assures us, "lethally strong vodka martinis" to be drunk punctually at six-thirty p.m. (But how do you make a vodka martini that's not "lethally strong"?) The saddest pages in the book describe Auden's ill-fated return to England, where at the end of his life he spent an unhappy year at Oxford's Christ Church, his undergraduate college.

> He still loves life
> But O O O O how he wishes
> The Good Lord would take him

he wrote shortly before he died, and the final poem, "Lullaby," in his collected works ends, "Sleep, Big Baby, Sleep Your Fill." Along with Tennyson's "Crossing the Bar" and Yeats's "Under Ben Bulben," Auden's lullaby to himself takes its memorable place as famous last words.

Randall Jarrell on W. H. Auden,
edited by Stephen Burt,
with Hannah Brooks-Motl

*R*andall Jarrell had hoped to write his master's thesis in English on W. H. Auden's poetry but was deterred by his supervisor at Vanderbilt on the grounds that Auden was still alive, thus not a proper subject for scholarly treatment. It was 1937, and Jarrell changed his subject to A. E. Housman, who had conveniently died the preceding year. But he did publish, in the 1940s, two long essays on Auden's work, "Changes of Attitude and Rhetoric in Auden's Poetry" (1941) and "Freud to Paul: The Stages of Auden's Ideology" (1945), which together make up some seventy-five pages. Those pages constitute a substantial part of the six lectures he would deliver on Auden in the spring of 1952 at Princeton University, where Jarrell was in residence as a visiting writer. For decades these lectures have been reposing as part of the Jarrell archive in the Berg Collection of the New York Public Library. Now Stephen Burt, author of an intelligent book on the poet (*Randall Jarrell and His Age*), has performed the difficult task of editing them.

A difficult task, since the nine folders of Auden material from which Mr. Burt has put together this book present many textual problems too complicated to go into here, but requiring conjecture about exactly what should go where. Burt has coped manfully with the task, providing admirably full notes, identifying, amplifying, and correcting Jarrell's allusions and quotations. This does not mean that he has solved the problem of making the lectures add up to a progressive narrative with a beginning, middle, and end. Many of the parts are brilliant, as one comes to expect brilliance from Jarrell's witty and original formulations; the impression left by the lectures as a whole is somewhat more cloudy.

First published in the *Washington Times*, June 15, 2005

In his foreword to the book, Adam Gopnik speaks of "the long pieces that were extracted from these lectures" and says they make up an "almost comically detailed analysis of the transformations of Auden's rhetoric in the 1940's." Gopnik gets two things wrong, since the "long pieces"—"Changes of Attitude . . . " and "Freud to Paul"—were published well before the lectures. (There is an academic etiquette that says you shouldn't read aloud as lectures very much of what you have already put in print—Jarrell seems not to have worried about that.) And the changes for the worse in Auden's rhetoric, which Jarrell considers, were taking place well before the 1940s, were in fact to be heard prominently in such well-known poems as "Spain 1937" and "September 1, 1939." Jarrell had begun to read Auden in 1932 as an undergraduate, when he discovered *Paid on Both Sides,* Auden's first attempt at a drama (he called it a "charade"), and his groundbreaking first volume, *Poems* (1930). He admired in Auden what he would later call "the tough, magical effects" of these poems written in "an eccentric variety of ordinary English" that resulted in a difficult, often obscure, but compelling indirectness. (Jarrell's favorite early Auden poem was the untitled one beginning "Who will endure / Heat of day and winter danger, / Journey from one place to another.") Many of these poems, to adapt a phrase of Wallace Stevens's, resist the intelligence almost successfully, and Jarrell thought they were the better for such resistance, especially when contrasted with the rhetorical style Auden increasingly employed from the middle 1930s on.

As Auden became one of the most professional poets who ever lived, he became also a kind of symbolic figure who spoke, in Jarrell's eyes, too directly, too "professionally" to his audience. His poems from the mid-1930s on into the 1940s were characterized by "a slightly vulgar or crude or too-direct appeal, a sure-fireness, some variant of which Virgil Thomson [the music critic] calls the 'wow technique.'" Auden became, in Jarrell's words, "a master at moving an audience as he wished it to be moved," "a true and magical rhetorician." One of the most amusing and just demonstrations of such rhetoric, delivered in Jarrell's most extravagantly witty manner, concerns Auden's use of capitalized personified abstractions, as in, for example, "one thirteen-line menagerie from the volume *Another Time* (1940), in which capitalized abstractions such as I Will, I Know, I Am, I

Have Not, and I Am Loved peer pathetically out from behind their bars. Nearby, gobbling peanuts, throng the Brothered-One, the Not-Alone, the Just, the Happy-Go Lucky, the Filthy, hundreds of We's and They's and Their's and Ours's and Me's." The list continues, and Jarrell finally declares that "Reading *Another Time* is like attending an Elks' Convention of the Capital Letters." By contrast he found this practice largely absent in Auden's earlier poetry, where the poet "said he-knew-not-quite-what to an audience that couldn't quite make out what he meant." At this moment in the fourth lecture, Jarrell has just read aloud "Spain 1937," calling one of its phrases ("the poets exploding like bombs") "worthy of the Stalin prize." He might also have quoted Keats's remark about Wordsworth, "We hate poetry that has a palpable design on us." To Jarrell's tastes, Auden's designs, however much they shifted as he frequently changed his mind, had become all too palpable.

But his doubleness of feeling about the poet shows itself when, after convincingly demonstrating the faults in such a poem as "Spain 1937" he immediately calls them "the faults of one of the best of living poets," then proceeds to an account of Auden's many virtues, bringing them out in some of his most attractive and inimitable prose. Among the "many noticeable virtues" of that poetry are, he says, its intelligence, its extraordinary wideness of subject-matter, and its range of wit and humor. As for Auden's technical mastery, Jarrell writes, "If the work demands a comic sestina in the style of Henry James, using as its six rhyme words the names of six of the seven sleepers of Ephesus, Auden's eyes gleam, light up, sparkle, and he has it done by teatime." Finally, he has "an angelic or diabolical gift just for *being interesting.*" Summing up these virtues in a wonderful comparison, Jarrell supposes that Auden "would be, of all modern poets, the easiest for Pope or Byron to become accustomed to," an imaginative piece of literary history that is absolutely right.

My reservation about the overall shape of these lectures as the editor has put them together is that what Burt terms the "conjectural reconstructions" of the fourth and the sixth (and final) ones do not contribute to a satisfying progression overall. In the fourth one, the account of "Spain"'s faults, then of Auden's general virtues, is followed by a jump to the then-just-published *Nones* (1951), which Jarrell finds the best book Auden has published in years: "So many of these poems are poems written by someone who is past, who has gotten over almost everything," he justly characterizes the book. But then the final lecture goes back to Auden's beginnings, with remarks about the early longer poems, *Paid on Both Sides* and *The Orators*. Jarrell fails to convince me of the eminent virtues of either of these poems, nor of the ones with which he ends the final lecture—Auden's longer ventures from the 1940s, *For the Time Being* and *The Sea and the Mirror*—about which his remarks are too brief to carry the requisite weight. In fact the only thing one misses from these wholly engaging performances is something Jarrell usually did in his essays about contemporary poets—picking out the best poems and describing why they are so good. He didn't do this with Auden, but rather left the challenge in the hands of his listeners—now, happily, his readers.

Elizabeth Bishop: *Poems, Prose and Letters*

*E*lizabeth Bishop died in 1979 and immediately ascended to the heaven inhabited by dead poets—George Herbert, John Keats, and Emily Dickinson—whom everyone venerates. In a review of Alice Quinn's edition of Bishop's unfinished poems, William Logan put the following question apropos of Bishop's ascendancy: "Why has our age become so enamored of a poet who almost to the end of her life required a special taste?" Logan doesn't quite answer that question, though he does suggest what is probably undemonstrable—that readers "adore themselves for adoring her." Nor can I demonstrate that the poets listed above are indisputably ones whom everyone venerates; but they share a winning vulnerability to the assaults of life, a vulnerability that many sorts of readers find deeply appealing, indeed irresistible. By contrast, two poets who ascended to another part of heaven, John Donne and Robert Lowell, for all their dramatizing of vulnerability ("Batter my heart three-personed God"; "I hear my ill spirit sob in each blood cell"), beat—in Lowell's words from a letter to Bishop—the "big drum" so forcefully that they seem scarcely in need of our sympathetic concern. At any rate, it is undeniable that Bishop's reputation has been untouched by anything like adverse criticism, and it is no surprise that she is the first twentieth-century woman poet to be included in the Library of America.

With the exception of Robert Lowell, it would be difficult to find a poet who, with her first book, *North & South*, got off to a more smashing start. She had met Randall Jarrell in January 1947—he was spending a year as literary editor of *The Nation*—and he introduced her to Lowell, with whom she would have a rich, sometimes troubled friendship that lasted until Lowell's death. (Her beautiful poem "North Haven" is dedicated to his memory.) Both Lowell and Jarrell reviewed *North & South* briefly

First published in the *Hudson Review* 61, no. 2 (Summer 2008): 321–34 (as "Bishop's Time")

but trenchantly. Lowell called her poems, in the tripartite clusters of adjectives he was addicted to, "unrhetorical, cool, and beautifully thought out," also praising her "large, controlled and elaborate common-sense." Already, in her first book, she is "one of the best craftsmen alive." Jarrell said that all her poems had written under them, *"I have seen it,"* and called "Roosters" and "The Fish" "two of the most calmly beautiful, deeply sympathetic poems of our time." There would follow over the years, and as future volumes were published, accolades from poet-contemporaries such as James Merrill, John Ashbery, Anthony Hecht, and Richard Wilbur, as well as from younger ones like Frank Bidart, Robert Pinsky, Mark Strand, and (one of the coeditors of this volume along with Robert Giroux), Lloyd Schwartz. David Kalstone's 1989 book, published after his death, explored Bishop's relation to Marianne Moore and to Lowell; there have also been a biography by Brett Millier and a number of useful critical studies, Thomas Travisano's being the first comprehensive one.[1] Books and essays will continue to appear, with "readings" of individual poems proliferating until a weary reader returns gladly, once more, to the poems themselves.

Bishop's poems and translations make up about a third of the Library of America's thousand pages; the other two-thirds consists partly of stories, most of them set in the Nova Scotia landscape where Bishop spent part of her childhood. There are also essays and reminiscences, including a memoir ("Efforts of Affection") of Marianne Moore, and a very amusing piece titled "The U.S.A. School of Writing," about a correspondence school in New York City where Bishop worked for a short time after graduating from Vassar. Some "Literary Statements and Reviews" in this collection are mostly brief, and the volume ends with a selection of her letters, the most interesting of them to Lowell. But it is the poems that count and that will be considered here.

The four volumes of them she published during her life are evenly spaced out in roughly ten-year periods: *North & South* (1947); *A Cold Spring* (1955); *Questions of Travel* (1965); and *Geography III* (1976). *The Complete Poems* (1983) appeared after her death, and the volume of unfinished poems and fragments (*Edgar Allan Poe and the Juke-Box*, 2006), welcomed by some, was strenuously condemned by Helen Vendler on the grounds that, considering Bishop's scrupulousness about what she published, she could not have looked favorably on resurrecting into print such unpublished items. In their questioning, exploratory, nonauthoritarian way of proceeding, her poems are extremely hospitable to critics, who are unlikely to be "wrong" about some particular interpretive scheme to which they are inclined. Similarly, from my classroom experience with her poems I can say that students don't feel intimidated by them and are relatively unworried that they have missed something big. This is all to the good, insofar as it encourages them to give plenty of time to the poem's surface; it presents a problem when, in writing, a critic substitutes, for Bishop's patient procedures, his or her own probably less delicate and qualified effort. In other words, professional academic criticism may be tempted to say too much, go on for too long, in the attempt to reach language adequate to Bishop's effects.

An example of such straining can be seen in the following commentary on a crucial sequence from her much-admired "In the Waiting Room," the first poem in *Geography III.* In this poem the almost seven-year-old girl accompanies her aunt to the dentist, and while the aunt is in the dentist's chair, the little girl sits in the waiting room full of grown-up people. She reads an article in *National Geographic* and looks at its pictures of a volcano erupting, of a dead man, of babies, and of black, naked African women whose breasts are "horrifying." Suddenly a cry of pain comes from inside the dentist's office, precipitating in the little girl a sensation of identifying with the voice and of "falling off the round, turning world / into cold, blue-black space." Nothing stranger has ever, could ever happen to the child, who thinks

> Why should I be my aunt,
> or me, or anyone?
> What similarities—
> boots, hands, the family voice
> I felt in my throat, or even
> the *National Geographic*
> and those awful hanging breasts—
> held us all together

or made us all just one?
How—I didn't know any
word for it—how "unlikely" . . .

Here are some words from a three-page commentary on the poem by a practiced critic of modern poetry:

> A shocking experience of identification, as we have seen, creates a simultaneous loss of original identity, and this loss is never overcome. The inscrutable volcano, the inside of the child's mouth, the dentist's chamber, are all figures for the abyss the child has discovered, and as she peers into it she is full of questions, another and another—why? what? how?—until she is thrown back into the exclamatory "how 'unlikely,'" and it is clear that they will never be answered. But the transformation of question into exclamation does create a sense of recognition, even if it is the permanently strange that is recognized. We get only a "sidelong glance," not fulfillment or total recognition. Yet, for a moment, this glance does begin to organize the dualities toward some unutterable simplicity. The questions mediate between absolute difference and undifferentiation, between stillness and total flux, and in this way, however fleetingly, accommodate the self most.[2]

It cannot be said about these sentences of Bonnie Costello's that they fail to notice this or that about the poem's language, or misstate the dramatic situation of "In the Waiting Room." At the same time, they feel overburdened and heavy-handed—not helping a reader make a more successful entry into the poem. What might be accepted as useful clarifications and identifications of a poem by Yeats or Pound or Stevens seem beside the point when the language is as free of difficulties to be puzzled out or extravagances to be described as Bishop's in these particular lines. She loved George Herbert, but does not attempt his witty conceits and doublenesses. Admittedly the poems in the late *Geography III* are different, in their achievement of a phrasing that is natural and breathlike (she used these adjectives about Lowell's *Life Studies*), from the complicated, "surrealist" wit of early ones like "The Man-Moth," "The Weed," or "The Monument," which seem better candidates for explicative commentary. But for most readers, I think, the later poems represent the summit of

Bishop's poetic art, and they present a special and formidable challenge to the critic who aims at relevant notation.

When a precocious senior at Vassar, Bishop published (in *The Vassar Review*) a first-rate essay on the poet who, along with Herbert, ranked at the top of her "favorite" list. The essay on Gerard Manley Hopkins bears the subtitle "Notes on Timing in His Poetry," and its opening paragraph calls attention to what would be a central preoccupation in her own work. Since, she begins, poetry is motion, it is essential to consider "the releasing, checking, timing, and repeating of the movement of the mind according to ordered systems." For her, at least,

> an idea of *timing* in poetry helps to explain many of those aspects
> of poetry which are so inadequately expressed by most critics; why
> poets differ so much from each other; why using exactly the same me-
> ters and approximate vocabularies two poets produce such different
> effects; why some poetry seems at rest and other poetry in action.

Hopkins's poems need to be considered in such terms, and she mentions among other things, as central aspects of his technique, "abundant use of alliteration, repetition, and inside rhymes" as "characteristics which place firm seals upon his words, joining them, at the same time indicating the sound relationships in the same way that guide lines, or repeated forms might, in a drawing." Attention to such matters is crucial in responding properly to any poet, but seems especially so when Bishop's work is the subject.[3]

One of her most motion-filled poems is "Sandpiper" (in *Questions of Travel*), a detached (compared to "In the Waiting Room") contemplation of a bird on a beach. "Sandpiper" features the alliteration, repetition, and inside rhymes she speaks about in her Hopkins essay as central in creating the "timing" of a poem. Here are the first three stanzas of the five-stanza poem:

> The roaring alongside he takes for granted,
> and that every so often the world is bound to shake,
> He runs, he runs to the south, finical, awkward,
> in a state of controlled panic, a student of Blake.
>
> The beach hisses like fat. On his left, a sheet
> of interrupting water comes and goes

and glazes over his dark and brittle feet.
He runs, he runs straight through it, watching his toes.

—Watching, rather, the spaces of sand between them,
where (no detail too small) the Atlantic drains
rapidly backwards and downwards. As he runs,
he stares at the dragging grains.

The only allusion in these stanzas, indeed in the whole poem, is to the first line of Blake's "Auguries of Innocence" ("To see the world in a grain of sand"), since this is a Blakean sandpiper in its awkward but controlled panic. Robert Lowell once remarked sardonically that no one, except for St. Anthony or a catatonic, wants to see the world in a grain of sand, but this little sandpiper seems wholly committed to the project. A reader who listens to the poem and follows the curve of its developing voice will encounter pleasing surprises (Bishop thought that surprise was the *sine qua non* of any poem). The movement of its first line ("The roaring alongside he takes for granted") is extended in the thirteen-syllable second line, as the "r" sound builds up ("roaring," "granted," "every," "world"). We are given not just one "runs" but two, with its pause after the third line's first foot, both awkward and controlled. "Shake," "south," and "state" aren't exactly internal rhymes but perhaps close enough to count. The third line hiccups after "he runs," then pulls itself up (as the bird veers to the south) with the unobvious but perfect "finical," and with "awkward" pointing toward the "state of controlled panic" (that last word picking up "finical"). The stanza completes itself with the cool rhyming of "shake" and "Blake," and there will be more of the same in stanzas that follow.

Perceptions about a poem's "timing," such as the remarks above, do not make for sentences one takes great satisfaction in writing, or that a reader is likely to warm to. What they remind me of is how much more rewarding it is to deal with a Bishop poem in the classroom, by reading aloud, by rereading a line with a different emphasis on this word, that syllable. If this could be said about any poet, it seems especially to the point with someone who continually and subtly exploits the resources of voice, the natural or breathlike sounds of a Herbert, a Hopkins, a Frost. (It may also help explain why previous to this I have never attempted to write about Bishop's poetry.)

From Randall Jarrell on down, every critic has praised her for regarding, like the sandpiper, "no detail too small." Jarrell's italicized *I have seen it* was taken as conferring upon her an unambiguous compliment. Yet a passion for detail may have its possible overkill. The critic James Wood, writing about prose fiction, notes that while he relishes and consumes "detail," he also chokes on it. "Overaesthetic appreciation of detail" (Wood's words) in a post-Flaubertian world can stifle as well as stimulate. So it is possible to have mixed responses to the plethora of detail in certain Bishop poems; for example, the very first one in *North & South*, "The Map," which begins

> Land lies in water; it is shadowed green.
> Shadows, or are they shallows, at its edges
> showing the line of long sea-wedded ledges
> where weeds hang to the simple blue from green.
> Or does the land lean down to lift the sea from under,
> drawing it unperturbed around itself?
> Along the fine tan sandy shelf
> is the land tugging at the sea from under?

Very delicate, scrupulous, fastidious—yes, but there is a part of me that says, in responding to "Shadows, or are they shallows," oh, *you* decide, *I* really don't care. "Is the land tugging at the sea from under?" Well, it could be, poet, please let me know. She wrote in 1964 to her first biographer and critic, Anne Stevenson, that so far she had produced "what I feel is a rather 'precious' kind of poetry, although I am very much opposed to the precious." This is well said, and it shows that she was aware of possibly sounding just too, too . . . Another letter, to Lowell in 1960, wondered whether "I'm going to turn into solid cuteness in my poetry if I don't watch out—or if I do watch out." Again we see how clearly she was aware of her gift, also aware of its possible abuse, its manner becoming—as Jarrell said happened to Auden's in the 1930s—"bureaucratized," formulaic.

  With hindsight, and doubtless some simplification, it appears to me that the "surreal" mode on display in many of the poems from *North and South* was something Bishop needed to develop out of; that is, out of the highly worked fantasies of such impressively built poems as "The Monument" and "The Man-Moth" that can also be charged with the inclination toward preciousness, even cuteness. (The final directive of "The Monument," "Watch it closely," has always seemed to me a shade cute.) Jarrell was right to single out "Roosters" and "The Fish" as the two "deeply sympathetic" poems in which a more resonant, not at all fussy, voice takes command. It is a voice that will emerge again in the final section of "At the Fishhouses," as the narrator confronts the water ("Cold dark deep and absolutely clear, / the clear gray icy water") and imagines dipping her hand in and tasting it:

> If you tasted it, it would first taste bitter,
> then briny, then surely burn your tongue.
> It is like what we imagine knowledge to be:
> dark, salt, clear, moving, utterly free,
> drawn from the cold hard mouth
> of the world, derived from the rocky breasts
> forever, flowing and drawn, and since
> our knowledge is historical, flowing, and flown.

What is "seen" here is something far beyond the visual, as it is at the end of "The Armadillo"—the Bishop poem that meant so much to Lowell— when in the italicized final stanza, after observing the fire balloon and its effects on the small animals it disturbs, the anonymous voice speaks for everyone:

> *Too pretty, dreamlike mimicry!*
> *O falling fire and piercing cry*
> *and panic, and a weak mailed fist*
> *clenched ignorant against the sky!*

The too pretty, dreamlike mimicry at which the voice exclaims may well refer to the preceding un-italicized stanzas describing the emergence of the owls from their burned nest, the rabbit "with fixed ignited eyes" and the "glistening" armadillo himself, " a weak mailed fist" against the sky. At any rate it is a visionary moment (the overused word still seems appropriate) created by the narrator's rising to a pitch of statement, exclamatory in "The Armadillo" but correspondingly intense in "At the Fishhouses," moving the utterance out of or beyond any particular tone. To the extent that Bishop moves, and moves us beyond "tone," such apostrophes resist paraphrase by making interpretive efforts feel somehow beside the point, crude or callow. She wrote May Swenson in 1955, "I think myself that my best poems seem rather distant, and sometimes I wish I could be as objective about everything else as I seem to be in and about them. I don't think I'm very successful when I get personal,—rather, sound personal." Such depersonalizing occurs in these sequences from "At the Fishhouses" and "The Armadillo," but they would hardly be so effective—breathtaking, even—without the breathed, nuanced, varied tone and tones in the earlier parts of each poem.

Bishop once provided Anne Stevenson with a capsule account of her own temperament. She said she had never liked Emily Dickinson much, but after reading through the collected edition found many poems to admire "though not the oh-the-pain-of-it-all" ones. She admits to snobbery about "the humorless Martha-Graham kind of person who does like Emily Dickinson": "In fact I think snobbery governs a great deal of my taste. I have been very lucky in having had, most of my life, some witty friends—and I mean real wit, quickness, wild fancies, remarks that make one cry with laughing." Most of her friends, such as the aunt she liked best, her partner Lota de Macedo Soares, Marianne Moore, E. E. Cummings, were very "funny" people: "Perhaps I need such people to cheer me up." A moment in her poetry that seems to me quintessential "real wit," a truly wild and "funny" stroke, occurs in "Arrival at Santos," the first poem in *Questions of Travel* (although she had printed it previously in *A Cold Spring*). Its ten quatrains, with their rollicking, offbeat cadences and seemingly catch-as-can rhymes, present the speaker, about to debark into the port city of Santos, for customs inspection. She notes that despite this new environment, she will encounter familiar things, like a "flag,"

> And coins, I presume,
> and paper money; they remain to be seen.
> And gingerly now we climb down the ladder backward,
> myself and a fellow passenger named Miss Breen,
>
> descending into the midst of twenty-six freighters
> waiting to be loaded with green coffee beans.

Please, boy, do be more careful with that boat hook!
Watch out! Oh! It has caught Miss Breen's

skirt! There! Miss Breen is about seventy,
a retired police lieutenant, six feet tall,
with beautiful bright blue eyes and a kind expression.
Her home, when she is at home, is in Glens Fall

s, New York. There. We are settled.

An important, though not the only, reason why I find this sequence so satisfying—so satisfyingly *funny*, to use Bishop's word—is that I once heard James Merrill read the poem aloud. His wonderfully nuanced voice did an especially fine job with "Watch out! Oh! It has caught Miss Breen's // skirt!"—exclamations he delivered in a mock-horrified, somewhat campy mode that Bishop herself would surely have loved. Merrill would speak, in a tribute written just after she died, of her poems as "wryly radiant, more touching, more unaffectedly intelligent than any written in her lifetime." That phrase "wryly radiant" is as good as any I've found to catch the mixture of wit and wonder that was hers in so many of the poems. To be wryly radiant is to be something quite distinct from what Frost liked to call, with a condescending twist in his voice, "poetical." In a rather unbuttoned conversation she had with an interviewer in 1966, when she had begun to teach writing at the University of Washington, Bishop said she had told her class that the poems they'd handed in contained "a disproportionate number of *haikus*" and were "not very well written either," "more like the sort of thing one might jot down when one is feeling vaguely poetic." She mused upon the students in that class,

> with their trusting eyes and their clear complexions. Have you seen
> the expensive cars that some of them drive? . . . Most of them look
> quite well fed and rather well off. And what do they write about in
> their poems? *Suffering*, of all things!

She told the students they should come to Brazil and see what *real* suffering was like, then perhaps they wouldn't write so "poetically" about it.[4]

North & South has thirty poems; *A Cold Spring*, eighteen; *Questions of Travel*, twenty. The last book Bishop published in her lifetime, *Geography*

III, consisted of only ten poems. This is extraordinary, and becomes more so when, in the Library of America edition, we note roughly 150 pages of uncollected, unpublished poems and translations, some of which are perfectly good work that most poets would not have held back. *Geography III* has been widely admired and praised, and seven of its ten poems are among the best ones she ever wrote. "In the Waiting Room" has had more than its share of attention, and "Crusoe in England" is surely as original a creation as she produced. "The Moose" seems to me, even more affectingly, to contain the surprise Bishop felt essential to any good poetry, most beautifully in the sequence that moves from the bus passengers "Talking the way they talked / in the old featherbed," as sleep comes over them, only to be startled by the great animal, "Towering, antlerless, / high as a church, / homely as a house / (or, safe as houses)." As for her villanelle "One Art," Brad Leithauser wrote recently that, along with Dylan Thomas's "Do not go gentle into that good night," it figures as a poem "that might have taken the elaborate stanzaic arrangement even if the Italians hadn't invented it three hundred years ago." "The End of March," in its serious play, is also top-grade Bishop. My own two favorites—maybe not the two "best" ones—turn out to be "Poem" and "Five Flights Up," and I will say just a word about their superb endings by way of one more gesture at Bishop's originality.

"Poem," the most modest and accurate of all Bishop's titles perhaps, is about the small painting by an uncle ("About the size of an old-style dollar bill") passed down to her as a "minor family relic" of seventy years back. The course of "Poem" enacts the quickening of interest as the emerging Bishop-figure recognizes houses, elm trees, a church steeple, tiny cows, and two white geese. In fact it's not just a Nova Scotian landscape but one closer to home ("Heavens, I recognize the place, I know it!"), even though, she confides to us, "Those particular geese and cows / are naturally before my time." From these appealing, even chatty reflections, she moves into an identification of Uncle George's "view" (as shown in his painting) and her own, memory-imperfect sense, when a young child, of the "life" he had rendered into art: "our looks, / two looks: / art 'copying from life' and life itself, / life and the memory of it so compressed / they've turned into each other." "Which is which?" she asks, then moves into a concluding tribute as moving in my judgment as anything she ever wrote:

> Life and the memory of it cramped,
> dim, on a piece of Bristol board,
> dim, but how live, how touching in detail
> —the little that we get for free,
> the little of our earthly trust. Not much.
> About the size of our abidance
> along with theirs: the munching cows,
> the iris, crisp and shivering, the water
> still standing from spring freshets,
> the yet-to-be-dismantled elms, the geese.

What a model of not saying too much but just enough—of "radiance," twisted enough to be wry, yet gracefully so. Once more it is "timing" that is central: the crucial repetitions of "dim," of "Life and the memory of it," of "the little . . . the little." The really astonishing effect occurs after the reflection about how our "abidance," a slightly remote and dignified word for the earthly dwelling we share "along with theirs"—the natural and animal inhabitants denoted in the painting. "Theirs" is what fills up the last three and a half lines, individual items separated only by the neutral, nondiscriminatory comma and concluding in the most unspectacular of ways with (merely) "the geese."

Merrill also wrote a poem in homage to Bishop ("Overdue Pilgrimage to Nova Scotia") of five connected sonnets, the third of which begins, "In living as in poetry, your art / Refused to tip the scale of being human / By adding unearned weight." These lines fit perfectly the human scale ruefully celebrated in "Poem." In her own life she was not likely to add "unearned weight" to the scale; writing to Pearl Kazin in 1953, she remarks in a throwaway sentence, "It is a little hard to get used to being happy after forty-two years . . . of being almost consistently unhappy." The final poem in *Geography III*, "Five Flights Up," assesses the human scale in its daily resumption, by contrasting it with the sounds of little animals heard upon waking:

> Still dark.
> The unknown bird sits on his usual branch.

The little dog next door barks in his sleep
inquiringly, just once.
Perhaps, in his sleep, too, the bird inquires
once or twice, quavering.
Questions—if that is what they are—
answered directly, simply,
by day itself.
Enormous morning, ponderous, meticulous;
gray light streaking each bare branch,
each single twig, along one side,
making another tree, of glassy veins . . .
The bird still sits there. Now he seems to yawn.

The little black dog runs in his yard.
His owner's voice arises, stern,
"You ought to be ashamed!"
What has he done?
He bounces cheerfully up and down;
he rushes in circles in the fallen leaves.

Obviously he has no sense of shame.
He and the bird know everything is answered,
all taken care of,
no need to ask again.
—Yesterday brought to today so lightly!
(A yesterday I find almost impossible to lift.)

In his review of *North & South,* Jarrell wrote that Bishop's poems instead of crying "This is a world in which no one can get along" show that "it is barely but perfectly possible—has been, that is, for her." At the end of "Five Flights Up," in that juxtaposition of the exclamatory wonder at what the bird and the dog know ("everything is answered, / All taken care of"), and the final confiding, murmur within the parentheses, the getting along of a new day seems possible—but just barely. Here the "human scale" is all but overtaken by the weight of the burden.

She wrote Jarrell a wonderful letter in 1965, the year he published his last book, *The Lost World,* and the year of his death. Whatever her reservations about Frost and his poetry ("a malicious old bore," she called him in one of her letters), she must have heartened Jarrell by calling him "the real one and only successor to Frost," not the folksy-wisdom side of Frost, but "all the good, the beautiful writing, the sympathy, the touching and real detail, etc." She says she could almost write a piece about this if she were a more skillful critic: "You're both [Jarrell and Frost] very sorrowful, and yet not the anguish-school that Cal [Lowell] seems innocently to have inspired—the self-pitiers. . . . It is more human, less specialized, and yet deep." However truly it fits the best of Jarrell, she was also, in these sentences, writing her own epitaph.

NOTES

1. Reviews of Bishop may be found in *Elizabeth Bishop and Her Art*, ed. Lloyd Schwartz and Sybil P. Estes (Ann Arbor: University of Michigan Press, 1983). David Kalstone's book is *Becoming a Poet* (New York: Farrar, Straus, and Giroux, 1989). Brett Millier's biography is *Elizabeth Bishop: Life and the Memory of It* (Berkeley: University of California Press, 1995). Thomas Travisano's book is *Elizabeth Bishop: Her Artistic Development* (Charlottesville: University of Virginia Press, 1988).

2. Bonnie Costello, "The Impersonal and the Interrogative in the Poetry of Elizabeth Bishop," in *Elizabeth Bishop and Her Art*, 119–32.

3. The best account of Bishop's poetic rhythm is Penelope Laurans, "Elizabeth Bishop, 'Old Correspondences': Prosodic Transformations in Elizabeth Bishop," *Elizabeth Bishop and Her Art*, 75–95.

4. In *Conversations with Elizabeth Bishop*, ed. George Monteiro (Jackson: University Press of Mississippi, 1996), 41.

The Poetry of Randall Jarrell

*I*n 1990 I published a biographical and critical study of Randall Jarrell. It was my feeling then that although Jarrell was agreed to be perhaps the best critic of poetry of the post–Second World War decades, there was no such agreement about his work as a poet. In reviewing his *Collected Poems* (1969), Helen Vendler had come up with a since often-quoted formulation—that Jarrell put his genius into his criticism, his talent, merely, into his poetry. And although his friend Robert Lowell judged that Elizabeth Bishop and Jarrell were the best poets of the postwar era (Lowell modestly passed over himself), Jarrell's reputation had not kept pace with theirs. My book was an attempt to remedy things, but why did I think it would do that? Since then—a few years ago—Brad Leithauser's excellent and generous selection of Jarrell's criticism, titled *No Other Book*, elicited appreciative reviews but did nothing that made his poetry freshly available. In a recent anthology of twentieth-century American poetry edited by Dana Gioia, David Mason, and Meg Schoerke, part of the introductory note to Jarrell reads this way: "His poetry was sometimes faulted for sentimentality—and it is often drenched in nostalgia, sadness, or regret—but at its best it achieves surprising and memorable moments of deep sympathy." The "but" effects some recovery, by way of observing that even though the poetry is drenched in sentimental attitudes it still, at moments, achieves "deep sympathy." Yet such a conflicted judgment is notably absent when the editors consider Lowell and Bishop, such masters of form as Richard Wilbur and James Merrill, or practitioners like John Ashbery and Adrienne Rich, whose output is prolific even though the free verse they write would be considered by Robert Frost as playing tennis with the net down.

Jarrell's *Complete Poems* runs to 500 pages, the last 150 pages of them uncollected or unpublished work his publisher decided to include. That's

First published in *Literary Imagination* 8, no. 2 (2006): 175–93 (as "Randall Jarrell's Poetry")

a lot of poems to have been written by a man who died at fifty-one, and there is no excuse for not being severe, though judicious, in our estimate of their value. Perhaps Jarrell would have wanted us to be severe, since he once wrote to Bishop that his favorite poet, Rilke, was "monstrously self-indulgent a lot of the time." But, he continued, the good poems made up for that and "really one expects most of a good poet's work to be quite bad—if that isn't so it's the 30th of February." In his own critical practice he followed this principle by telling us that we should be tempted to throw away one third—the bad third—of Frost's *Complete Poems;* that Wallace Stevens's late volume, *The Auroras of Autumn,* was arid and repetitive, was G. E. Moore at the spinet; that Whitman, of course, was impossible most of the time; and that William Carlos Williams was a "*very* limited poet" on his way to becoming overvalued. Remember that Jarrell wrote admiring essays on each of these four poets, indeed was instrumental, in the case of Frost and Whitman, in suggesting new terms for their proper appreciation.

The most severe but also judicious review of Jarrell's own poetry was provided by James Dickey, himself a poet and critic, on the occasion of Jarrell's publishing, in 1955, a large selection from his first four volumes of verse. The review is notable in that Dickey created two fictive speakers, gave them the bland but unprejudicial names A and B, then set them loose at each other in the belief that, as he put it, it was good for writers "to have the most violent possible arguments brought into play against them." Or, we might add, *for* them, since speaker A calls the *Selected Poems* a "triumph," "the work of an honest, witty, intelligent, and deeply gifted man, a man who knows more about poetry, and knows it in better, more human ways, than any other of our time." To which B responds that he finds the book "dull beyond all dullness of stupefaction or petrification," and that Jarrell's poems seem to him "the most untalentedly sentimental, self-indulgent, and insensitive writings that I can remember." The ensuing exchange between the two voices revolves on questions of whether and to what extent Jarrell has "the poet's deep instinctive feel for language" (B says he hasn't); whether his poems put us in touch with a "real" world (A thinks they do); whether there are people in these poems or merely face-less abstractions; whether, in B's summary terms, "he has . . . the power, or

the genius, or the talent, or the inclination, or whatever, to make experi-
ence rise to its own most intense, concentrated and meaningful level, a
level impossible without the poet's having caught it in *those* words."

For most of the argument B seems to be winning, at least margin-
ally. Yet at the very end of the exchange, A is given a long concluding
paragraph, the last word, in which he sums up what he sees as Jarrell's
"relevance," his staying power as a poet "who will have something to say
to people for a very long time to come." A insists that the poems give us
"the feel of a time, our time, as no other poetry of our century does."
They show us "the uncomprehending stare of the individual caught in
the State's machinery"; they show us the child's "slow, horrified, magni-
ficently un-understanding and growing loss of innocence"—indeed they
are "one long look through this expression, into a child's face." Despite
all objections to his poems, Jarrell "gives you, as all great or good writers
do, a foothold in a realm where literature itself is inessential, where your
own world is more yours than you could ever have thought, or even felt,
but is one you have always known." With this positive, indeed passionate
summing up of the case—in a style that reminds of no one's so much as
Jarrell's own in his criticism—Dickey ends his "review."

Dickey wrote that review before the appearance of two volumes of verse
Jarrell published in the last ten years of his life: the first of these, *The Woman
at the Washington Zoo*, won the National Book Award for 1960, while the
second—*The Lost World*, published the year he died—seems to many readers,
including this one, his best, most original book of poems. Still, Dickey's
criticism of the poetry overall remains the most inventively probing of any
Jarrell received during his life or after his death. And the fact that in his
numerous reviews of other contemporaries Dickey made no use of the dia-
logue of opposing voices suggests that it was a response dictated by prob-
lems and challenges that any reader should encounter reading Jarrell's work.
In fact, I have come to believe that a reader of his poems who does not, and
repeatedly, feel divided or uncertain about how good or bad, successful or
not so, moving or banal they are, fails in truly taking their measure.

Since more than one critic has accused Jarrell's poetry of sentimentality,
we should note what a murky area that term of opprobrium connotes.
I say opprobrium, since those of my generation, and perhaps some later

ones, who were brought up under the aegis of the New Criticism, learned to regard sentimentality as a besetting sin both in poetry and in life, against which the only protection was, we came to believe, irony. Jarrell began to write poetry in the 1930s when the notion of sentimentality was very much under fire. In *Practical Criticism* (1929), I. A. Richards devoted a chapter to anatomizing it and decided that a response was sentimental when "it is too great for the occasion," when "it is inappropriate to the situation that calls it forth." Of course, as Richards knew, it is no easy task to define clearly the "occasion" or "situation" a particular poem presents or enacts. A decade later Brooks and Warren, in their enormously influential first edition of *Understanding Poetry*, found sentimentality to lie in an "obsession with one's own emotions—an exclusive interest which blinds the person involved to everything except the sweet intensity of the emotion in question." (A poem of Shelley's was selected to exhibit this pernicious quality.)

Remember that Dickey's speaker B judged Jarrell's writing to be "the most untalentedly sentimental, self-indulgent and insensitive that I can remember." When the poet Donald Hall reviewed *Woman at the Washington Zoo*, he charged it with "radical sentimentality" and reserved particular contempt for the final line of the earlier, heavily anthologized "Death of the Ball-Turret Gunner": "When I died they washed me out of the turret with a hose." Hall referred to that line as "the portentous ending of a tiny poem," and alluding to a popular TV show of the period said that "like the oracular remarks of Sergeant Friday on *Dragnet* . . . it chokes with the softness of toughness." Hall says the detail of the hose is pure sentimentality. The man is dead, and he is no deader for being in fragments that have stuck to the metal and plexiglas—thus the last line is, in Richards's terms, "an inappropriate response to the situation." And yet, we might wonder, what *is* an appropriate response to the situation of being shot to death in the air, especially if you, the dead ball-turret gunner, are invited to comment on the event, as this one was? Couldn't one think of the poem's final utterance as, at least, an *interesting* or unobvious thing to have said—not what any listener would expect to hear?

Donald Hall was especially displeased by Jarrell's endings, and he cites "In Those Days," from the *Washington Zoo* volume, as an example of a poem that starts well but ends badly:

In those days—they were long ago—
The snow was cold, the night was black.
I licked from my cracked lips
A snowflake, as I looked back

Through branches, the last uneasy snow.
Your shadow, there in the light, was still.
In a little the light went out.
I went on, stumbling—till at last the hill

Hid the house. And, yawning,
In bed in my room, alone,
I would look out: over the quilted
Rooftops, the clear stars shone.

How poor and miserable we were,
How seldom together!
And yet after so long one thinks:
In those days everything was better.

Hall zeroes in on the last stanza, saying, "It isn't the writing that is bad here" but the way we are left with a "trivial announcement of feeling": "The rush of self-pity in the last line . . . blinds him to the questions it raises."

I remember Lionel Trilling once setting a Columbia class back on its heels by asking them what was wrong with self-pity anyway? Wasn't it an important emotion that should be represented in literature without apology? Without pursuing that query, we can say more about that final stanza than does Hall, who disclaims minimally that "It isn't the writing that is bad here." On the contrary, the writing seems to me quite good, and good writing makes good poetry: for here the flat, wistful, if you will self-pitying voice of "In those days everything was better," is ushered in by a more musing, confiding one in "And yet after so long one thinks: / In those days everything was better." One may think so, but surely the poem leaves room for the possibility that, really, the past wasn't "better" than the present, just different, and attractive simply because it is now the past, to which we can journey only in imagination. Like D. H. Lawrence's "Piano," which it resembles in other respects as well, "In Those Days" is the richer for making a response that is "too great for the occasion" and doing something artful with it.

The richest of Jarrell's poems, which both courts the risks of sentimentality and makes capital out of those risks, is one he wrote when he turned forty. I've more than once tried to say why "Aging" seems to me a remarkable, always returnable-to poem, and I want to try again here, with a brief look at an earlier poem of his, to suggest the kind of achievement in "Aging":

> I wake, but before I know it it is done,
> The day, I sleep. And of days like these the years,
> A life is made. I nod, consenting to my life.
> . . . But who can live in these quick-passing hours?
> I need to find again, to make a life,
> A child's Sunday afternoon, the Pleasure Drive
> Where everything went by but time; the Study Hour
> Spent at a desk, with folded hands, in waiting.
> In those I could make. Did I not make in them
> Myself? The Grown One whose time shortens,
> Breath quickens, heart beats faster, till at last
> It catches, skips. . . . Yet those hours that seemed, were endless
> Were still not long enough to have remade
> My childish heart: the heart that must have, always,
> To make anything of anything, not time,
> Not time but—
>   but, alas! eternity.

How do you write a fresh poem about aging when, as Jarrell did, you knew the beginning of Yeats's "The Tower":

> What shall I do with this absurdity—
> O heart, O troubled heart—this caricature
> Decrepit age that has been tied to me
> As to a dog's tail?

Or have absorbed T. S. Eliot's "Gerontion":

> I have lost my passion: why should I need to keep it
> Since what is kept must be adulterated?

> I have lost my sight, smell, hearing, taste and touch:
> How should I use them for your closer contact?

Or noted the lines from Wallace Stevens's "Le Monocle de Mon Oncle" about a forty-year-old man and his wife:

> Our bloom is gone. We are the fruit thereof.
> Two golden gourds distended on our vines,
> Into the autumn weather, splashed with frost,
> Distorted by hale fatness, turned grotesque.
> We hang like warty squashes, streaked and rayed [. . .]

Fourteen years previous to writing "Aging," when he was twenty-six, Jarrell wrote "A Note on Poetry," which argued that Modernist poetry was the logical extension of Romantic poetry, carrying to the fullest extreme its tendencies. Typical "modernistic" poetry, he wrote, contained the following qualities: "very interesting language; a great emphasis on connotation, "texture"; extreme intensity, forced emotion—violence; a good deal of obscurity; emphasis on sensation, perceptual nuances; experimental or novel qualities of some sort . . . all tendencies are forced to their limits . . . the thoroughly subjective." When he wrote that essay, Jarrell's own poetry sounded like this in lines excerpted from a longer poem:

>   . . . Tomorrow puffs
> From its iron centers into the moonlight, men move masked
> Through streets abrupt with excavations, the explosive triumphs
> Of a new architecture: the twelve-floor dumps
> Of smashed stone starred with limbs, the monumental
> Tombs of a whole age.
>
>   ("The Winter's Tale")

And so on in ever more extravagant figuration, by way of depicting "our" plight.

Returning to "Aging" after such extravagances in Jarrell's predecessors and in his own modernistic verse, we may dismiss the usefulness of "sentimental" as a term for devaluing a poem by admitting the futility of trying to decide whether the utterances of Yeats's tortured elder, or Eliot's little old man, or the florid rhetorician in Stevens's poem, or

Jarrell's own apocalyptic speaker in "The Winter's Tale" with his list of excavations—smashed stone starred with limbs, monuments and tombs of a whole age—are in excess of whatever respective "occasion" called them forth. And when we note the qualities that fifteen years previously Jarrell had claimed were to be found in typically modernistic poems, we can see how un-modernistic a poem is "Aging": no words that require a dictionary, only a couple of ordinary ones of more than two syllables; a "form" that is indeed unexceptional—two eight-line unrhymed stanzas; a speaker who is anything but strongly individuated (he might be any of us at a certain moment in life); not terribly "interesting language," not much noticeable "texture," no obscurity. Just a reiteration of common words and their families: make and made; life; time; five buts and one yet.

And yet, as his admired Frost liked to say, Jarrell might well claim on the basis of "Aging": "I am not undesigning." For there is art in the voice of this poem that aspires to speak for all of us inasmuch as we have all experienced those (endless) Pleasure Drives and Study Hours set off in capital letters, to be contemplated with a remembrance—in the sense we could never appreciate back then—of how endless they were. (Enforced Sunday drives with parents were a torture I at least endured.) "Aging" is a Wordsworthian poem in which The Child turns out to be Father of the Man in a way not suggested by Wordsworth's epigraph to the Immortality Ode. Or maybe behind it is Goethe, who warned us to beware of youthful wishes because we were apt to get them later on. Viewing things from the long perspective of adulthood makes us think that, in those days of childhood, everything was better, or at least shapeable just by being imaginable. "In those I could make," says the man, suddenly empowered as an artist, a maker, only to slip into the perfectly irrefutable question/answer—"Did I not make in them / Myself?" And this self is but a pathetic and flimsy personification of weakness and vulnerability, "the Grown One whose time shortens, / Breath quickens," and who concludes, choking on his own attempted eloquence by invoking his still childish heart—"the heart that must have, always, / To make anything of anything, not time, / Not time but—but alas! eternity."

"Aging" is the sort of poem that distinguishes Jarrell from his contemporaries, poets of the self like Lowell or Berryman or Roethke or Sexton or Plath. Its language is "ordinary" language, the posture of its dramatic speaker is not eccentric or overwhelming or lurid or farcical; its tone stays fairly steady; its prosody or "technique" isn't something that asks to be noticed or much commented on. Could it be merely the subject matter—getting older, thinking about death—that takes in the reader? To say so would be to ignore what in the poem should not be ignored—its humor. For all its pathos, "Aging" is also darkly humorous, a grim joke emphasized by those ironic capital letters, and by an ingenious speaker whose train of thought does itself and himself in.

I noted earlier that Jarrell's *Collected Poems* runs to five hundred pages, and when I wrote my literary life of him I also edited a selection of his poems—a rather severe selection consisting of what in my judgment were the "best": most interesting, memorable, vivid—fifty of them. A perceptive reviewer of the selection noted not only how much I'd left out but also my own predilection for a certain kind of literary life, in his words "the ordinary, bourgeois, academic life . . . a life rooted in reading, civil in its pleasures and dedicated to understanding rather than to change." With this bias, I had excluded much work by a "lonely and extravagant author," and had presented a poet more sensible and less daring than the poet Jarrell really was. This may well be true, and in concentrating on just a few poems here I run the risk even more of limiting and reducing this poet of large ambitions, often ambitions that don't seem to me to get realized in the verse. So one poem that went by the boards in my selection was "The Night Before the Night Before Christmas," one of Jarrell's longest poems, in which (in the words of an unfriendly reviewer) "a 14-year-old girl—mother dead, pet squirrel dead, brother sick, snow falling—sits in her cold room over *Das Kapital* weeping for poor people." When Jarrell enclosed the poem to William Carlos Williams he told Williams that "I find that by having irregular line lengths, a good deal of irregularity of scansion, and lots of rhyming, not just perfect regular rhymes, musical forms, repetitions, 'paragraphing,' speech-like effects . . . you can make a long poem seem a lot shorter and livelier." Maybe so, but this is one of a number of poems that, to my taste, goes on too long in a prosody just not strong enough to take hold of the reader.

Jarrell published "The Night Before . . ." in 1949, the year after he had gone to Europe for the first time, spent some weeks teaching at the Salzburg Seminar in Austria, and fallen in love with a woman for whom he would almost but not quite leave his wife (he soon left his wife anyway and married Mary Von Schrader, still alive and keeper of the flame). The discovery, as it were, of Europe involved many things of vivid interest: folk and fairytales; Romanticism, especially of the German variety; a passion for the music of Richard Strauss; and generally an interest in writing tone poems. The poems that resulted were dense, highly allusive (some of them needed the identificatory notes he provided in his 1955 *Selected Poems*), full of dream and legend, murmurs of, in the title of one of them, "The Märchen." I have found and continue to find them extremely hard going, "other," expressive doubtless of a lonely man looking determinedly elsewhere for imaginative sustenance, but still in the main unpalatable to my un-Middle-Europish sensibility. Defending himself against Allen Tate's reservations about Jarrell's lack of prosody in some of his early poems, he told Tate he'd "rather seem limp and prosaic than false or rhetorical. I want to be rather like speech." Insofar as he had managed to shuck off the high (and false) rhetorical mode he inherited from Auden and that permeates early poems like "The Winter's Tale," well and good. But limp prosaicism has its own defects, probably just as debilitating, and many of the poems from his middle period—from *Losses* (1948) through *The Seven-League Crutches* (1951)—suffer from them.

More positively, coming between the early high-Auden apocalyptic mode and the postwar European/fabulistic one, are the poems Jarrell wrote in his three years of service as a flight instructor in the air force. Many of them are relatively lengthy narratives that don't lend themselves well to excerpting in an essay such as this one. They are also, I suspect, not all that much read except by literary scholars, one of whom, Lorrie Goldensohn, in her recent book about war poetry, *Dismantling Glory*, has written about them pointedly and at length. At any rate, when Jarrell began in the spring of 1943, some months after he had enlisted, to write poetry every night (as he said in a letter), he confronted a subject matter that felt too large, serious, and grave for it ever to be well served by neatly turned formal effects and regular insistent patterns of rhyme and stanza—patterns he was not all that good at achieving anyway. Jarrell's war poems have been more respected than read and returned to, because they lack the poignant expressiveness of the personal voice he would find in his later domestic narratives. But generally they have been admired as the most impressive and enduring poems by an American about World War II.

James Dickey's speaker B, however, dissents, finding no individuals in the poems, just faceless types in uniform that Jarrell could "pity . . . in a kind of monstrous, abstract, complacent and inhuman Compassion." It is not enough to say in response that, since Jarrell is writing about a war fought by great machines we are all the slaves of, including that greatest of all machines, The State—that therefore the absence of particular people in the poems is appropriate. (He himself noted at one point how foolish it would be to introduce an "I" into such a scene.) In his memorial tribute to Jarrell, the critic R. W. Flint, himself a ship's company gunner on a carrier, thus closer to the experiences Jarrell wrote about than was the poet himself (who never left the States), seems almost surprised that the war poems told him, Flint, what he did not know he knew, and he reminds himself that the civilians Whitman and Melville were our Civil War poets.

Flint writes accurately of what he terms the poems' "general monotony of effect . . . their static grandeur of sentience: A ground tone of swaying iambics varied by spondees and syncopation, paired and tripled adjectives in wistful or angry clumps, a recurring litany of abstractions: the State, the States, Death, Dream, fire, the years, the cities—the soldier-prisoner-patient, his wife, mail, and cat." This is indeed the landscape of Jarrell's poems, as illustrated by the following swatches of lines I've torn out of individual ones:

> from "Losses," speaking of pilots:

> > We read our mail and counted up our missions—
> > In bombers named for girls, we burned
> > The cities we had learned about in school—
> > Till our lives wore out; our bodies lay among
> > The people we had killed and never seen.
> > When we lasted long enough they gave us medals;
> > When we died they said, "Our casualties were low."

> from "Transient Barracks," speaking of an airman returned from combat:

Summer. Sunset. Someone is playing
The ocarina in the latrine:
You Are My Sunshine. A man shaving
Sees—past the day-room, past the night K.P.'s
Bent over a G.I. can of beets
In the yard of the mess—the red and green
Lights of a runway full of 24's.
The first night flight goes over with a roar
And disappears, a star, among mountains.

from "Second Air Force," speaking of the planes:

(At twilight they wink over men like stars
And hour by hour, through the night, some see
The great lights floating in—from Mars, from Mars.)
How emptily the watchers see them gone.

And from my favorite of them all, "Absent with Official Leave," about a
soldier sleeping at night in the barracks:

He moans like a bear in his enchanted sleep,
And the grave mysterious beings of his years—

The causes who mourn above his agony like trees—
Are moved for their child, and bend across his limbs
The one face opening for his life, the eyes
That look without shame even into his.

And the man awakes, and sees around his life
The night that is never silent, broken with the sighs
And patient breathing of the dark companions
With whom he labors, sleeps, and dies.

A single poem may serve to illustrate the "ground tone of swaying
iambics varied by spondees and syncopation" R. W. Flint speaks of, along
with the repetitions of words and phrases that give coherence and for-
ward motion to the narrative. Also important are the—only occasional—
rhymes heard powerfully at the end of "Absent with Official Leave" that
carry with them, because of their rarity, more than usual force beyond

any purely semantic aspect of the words. "A Front" is about a fogged-in base at which one plane lands, while the rest head south for a more accessible landing field—except for one plane whose radio has gone out and that crashes:

> Fog over the base: the beams ranging
> From the five towers pull home from the night
> The crews cold in fur, the bombers banging
> Like lost trucks down the levels of the ice.
> A glow drifts in like mist (how many tons of it?),
> Bounces to a roll, turns suddenly to steel
> And tires and turrets, huge in the trembling light.
> The next is high, and pulls up with a wail,
> Comes round again—no use. And no use for the rest
> In drifting circles out along the range;
> Holding no longer, changed to a kinder course;
> The flights drone southward through the steady rain.
> The base is closed . . . But one voice keeps on calling,
> The lowering pattern of the engine grows;
> The roar gropes downward in its shaky orbit
> For the lives the season quenches. Here below
> They beg, order, are not heard; and hear the darker
> Voice rising: *Can't you hear me? Over, Over*—
> All the air quivers, and the east sky glows.

There is no "comment" here about war, no pity for the men involved in its execution; for Jarrell, unlike Wilfred Owen, the poetry is *not* in the pity, at least not in "A Front." And if there are no "people" here, as Dickey's speaker complains, there is a master mind or voice that sees it all and sets it all down, that makes the voice call out and animates the darker voice that is not heard. And who speaks that final line: "All the air quivers, and the east sky glows." Like the latrine, the ocarina, the G.I. can of beets of "Transient Barracks"—and in the words of that poem, now applied to "A Front"—"These are. Are what? Are." If it is a defeat to be forced into saying about a poem like this one, why it's *real*, we are more than once tempted to say it about Jarrell's war poems. To a reader like myself who at age eleven, twelve, thirteen, read every morning in the small-town paper news of heroisms and deaths so many miles away, who was himself learning in schools about the cities that were being bombed, who saw innumerable movies on Saturday afternoon in which our boys prevailed or died gallantly—it may be impossible to read these poems with the disinterested eye of the true critic. Matthew Arnold's cherished "real estimate," in which poems are valued for themselves and apart from the circumstances of history and of personal biography, is an ideal difficult to attain in a situation where the claims of both the historical and the personal are so strong.

If the war poems represent one peak of Jarrell's achievement as a poet, the other one is surely reached in those poems he wrote near the end of his life about what he called the lost world. These poems can be seen as an answer, if not exactly a triumphant one, to the recurring complaint in the relatively few poems he produced in the 1950s—the complaint of a self grown old we hear in "Aging." For complicated reasons, Jarrell in life was overcome by his own aging, falling into prolonged depression as he neared fifty, a depression that was elevated, through mood-enhancing drugs, into manic behavior. Eventually there was a suicide attempt, hospitalization, a partial recovery, then the deadly encounter with a car into whose path he stepped, or which inadvertently sideswiped him. Reviewing my book, Helen Vendler, in a corrective counter to my perhaps too sanguine assumption that this late depression came out of the blue, called him, with a capital letter, an "Inconsolable," chronically depressed as a child. "The Inconsolable," she said, "attracts many friends because he seems to want so intensely to be consoled . . . responds to friendships gratefully and vividly—and if he is clever, winning, intuitive, interested, and talkative like Jarrell, he and his friends forget his inconsolableness for a while. Then the void returns, yawning below." This seems to me as good a try as any to speak about a mystery: how so much wit, intelligence, and life went along with a dark companion.

His wife Mary, from whom he was soon to be temporarily estranged, recalls her husband's rush of creativity in the spring of 1963, sparked by his mother's sending him a Christmas box of the letters he had written home to her from Los Angeles when, in a magic year, 1926–27, he visited his grandparents there. Before the worst of Jarrell's nervous collapses came on, Mary Jarrell writes, "he was granted a few magic weeks of Lisztian virtuosity. . . . [P]oems flew at him, short ones, quatrains . . . ideas for poems until just words beat at his head like many wings." The results from this time include, most notably, "Next Day"; "The Lost Children"; the three-part poem that would be the title of his final volume, "The Lost World"; its sequel, "Thinking of the Lost World"; and "The Player Piano." The volume appeared in February 1965 and received appreciative reviews; but one of the first to appear, by Joseph Bennett in the *New York Times*, was a savage and scornful dismissal that surely contributed to Jarrell's self-inflicted cutting of his wrist a few days after reading it. It was, once more, the old charge of sentimentality, as Bennett spoke of "familiar, clanging vulgarity, corny cliches, cutenesses," and "the intolerable self-indulgence of his tear-jerking, bourgeois sentimentality. Folksy, pathetic, affected—there is no depth to which he will not sink if shown the hole."

You would never guess from Bennett's trashing of the book that it contained lines like the following from "Children's Arms," from the first part of "The Lost World," and not untypical of other passages that could be quoted from that poem. In these lines, the boy Randall, as we may certainly call him, waits to be picked up and taken to a public library in Los Angeles by a friend of his grandparents, a Mrs. Mercer who sports an electric car and is accompanied by a large dog named Lucky. One of the books the boy is returning, his favorite, is H. G. Wells's *The Food of the Gods*, about which he says,

> Liking that world where
> The children eat, and grow giant and good,
> I swear as I've often sworn: "*I'll* never forget
> What it's like, when *I've* grown up." A prelude
> By Chopin, hammered note by note, like alphabet
> Blocks, comes from next door. It's played with real feeling,
> The feeling of being indoors practicing. "And yet
> It's not as if—" a gray electric, stealing

To the curb on silent wheels, has come; and I
See on the back seat (sight more appealing
Than any human sight!) my own friend Lucky,
Half wolf, half police-dog. And he can play the piano—
Play that he does, that is—and jump so high
For a ball that he turns a somersault. "Hello,"
I say to the lady, and hug Lucky . . . In my
Talk with the world, in which it tells me what I know
And I tell it, "I know—" how strange that I
Know nothing, and yet it tells me what I know!—

Part of the wit here is surely enabled by the terza rima, with some variation, that gives linkage and forward movement (also backward) to the composition. But what's mainly appealing is the interplay and interdependence of the precocious twelve-year-old, happy with the things in his world, and the poet looking over this child's shoulder and getting in that fine quip about playing with real feeling (the feeling of being indoors practicing), or the complicated play between child and world around the rich phrase, "I know."

In an earlier passage from "Children's Arms" (the line "O arms that Arm, for a child's wars, the child" summons up the *Aeneid* to stand behind this mini-epic), the boy is waked up by his grandmother for breakfast: "We eat in the lighted kitchen. And what is play / For me, for them is habit." Jarrell made such play most fully his own in "The Lost Children," which has a lovely instance of an adult talking with a world that tells her what she knows. A mother looking at pictures of her two daughters as children—one of them is dead, the other alive and looking at these pictures with her—makes a connection with these differently lost children:

I look too
And I realize the girl in the matching blue
Mother-daughter dress, the fair one carrying
The tin lunch box with the half-pint thermos bottle
Or training her pet duck to go down the slide
Is lost just as the dark one, who is dead, is lost.
But the world in which the two wear their flared coats
And the hats that match, exists so uncannily

That, after I've seen its pictures for an hour,
I believe in it: the bandage coming loose
One has in the picture of the other's birthday,
The castles they are building, at the beach for asthma.
I look at them and all the old sure knowledge
Floods over me, when I put the album down
I keep saying inside: "I *did* know those children.
I braided those braids. I was driving the car
The day that she stepped in the can of grease
We were taking to the butcher for our ration points.
I *know* those children. I know all about them.
Where are they?"

All knowledge in minute particulars, as William Blake knew. The poem
ends when, dreaming of her little girls, the mother thinks of it as a game of
hide-and-seek, with each daughter just out of reach. It is a tiring game:

> I am tired
> As a mother who's played all day, some rainy day.
> I don't want to play it any more, I don't want to.
> But the child keeps on playing, so I play.

Such "play" reaches perhaps its most unapologetic embodiment in the
poem that concludes *The Lost World*. In "Thinking of the Lost World," the
speaker—Randall Jarrell in no disguise at all—has a Proustian, or parody
of a Proustian experience:

> This spoonful of chocolate tapioca
> Tastes like—like peanut butter, like the vanilla
> Extract Mama told me not to drink.
> Swallowing the spoonful, I have already traveled
> Through time to my childhood. It puzzles me
> That age is like it.

And yet, age is not like it, things are missing that once were:

> Back in Los Angeles
> We missed Los Angeles. The sunshine

Of the Land of Sunshine is a grey mist now, the atmosphere
Of some factory planet: when you stand and look
You see a block or two, and your eyes water.
The orange groves are all cut down.

Not just *les lauriers sont coupés,* so it is the poem's Proustian job of recovery
to bring it all back, but to do so in a style that, even as it threatens to fall
into bathos, sheer heart- and hand-wringing, just manages to stay on the
side of life and wit—of poetry. I realize this is assertion merely, and that
Joseph Bennett and others hear as folksy, pathetic, and affected what I
hear as the true voice of feeling, indeed as a supreme moment in Jarrell's
poetry. I am speaking of the recovery enacted by the closing thirty or so
lines in which the boy sees his grandmother (Mama) decapitate a chicken
in the back yard, preparatory to cooking it, and conflates it with a science
fiction tale he is reading about the end of the world. Where do these lost
things exist, asks the man, and answers:

> All of them are gone
> Except for me; and for me nothing is gone—
> The chicken's body is still going round
> And round in widening circles, a satellite
> From which, as the sun sets, the scientist bends
> A look of evil on the unsuspecting earth.
> Mom and Pop and Dandeen are still there
> In the Gay Twenties.
>
> The Gay Twenties! You say
> The Gay Nineties . . . But it's all right, they *were* gay,
> O so gay! A certain number of years after,
> Any time is Gay, to the new ones who ask:
> "Was that the first World War or the second?"
> Moving between the first world and the second,
> I hear a boy call, now that my beard's gray:
> "Santa Claus! Hi, Santa Claus!" It *is* miraculous
> To have the children call you Santa Claus.
> I wave back. When my hand drops to the wheel,
> It is brown and spotted, and its nails are ridged

Like Mama's. Where's my own hand? My smooth
White bitten-fingernailed one? I seem to see
A shape in tennis shoes and khaki riding-pants
Standing there empty-handed; I reach out to it
Empty handed, my hand comes back empty,
And yet my emptiness is traded for its emptiness,
I have found that Lost World in the Lost and Found
Columns whose gray illegible advertisements
My soul has memorized world after world:
LOST—NOTHING, STRAYED FROM NOWHERE.
   NO REWARD
I hold in my own hands, in happiness,
Nothing: the nothing for which there's no reward.

In his introduction to Edwin Arlington Robinson's posthumously pub-
lished long poem *King Jasper*, Robert Frost speaks of Robinson's "sadness"
(calling him "a prince of heartachers") which is at the same time, in his
poems, "so happy an achievement." Frost ends his essay by directing the
powers that be, "Give us immedicable woes—woes that nothing can be done
for—woes flat and final. And then to play. The play's the thing. Play's the
thing. All virtue in 'as if.'" In his writings about Frost, Jarrell never alludes
to these remarks, yet the recurring invokings of "play" in his own last
poems—in their range of tone and gesture, their line-by-line behavior
in which a word, a remark spins off, puts a move on, tropes a previous
one—are both a confirmation of Frost's motto (courtesy of *Hamlet*) and
an expression of Jarrell's happy achievement made out of sadness.

"It's played with real feeling, / The feeling of being indoors practic-
ing." So the poet helps the child think about that Chopin prelude being
hammered out next door. Maybe no one but Jarrell would have thought
to say it in a poem, this playful stroke of quiet wit that also invites us
into a world of real feeling, a feeling we never before knew we had. In
these last poems of Jarrell there is a merging of the satiric and comic with
the lyric, as if to vindicate Robert Lowell, who once called him a com-
bination of Pope and Matthew Arnold. Or to answer his contemporary
Delmore Schwartz, who, reviewing an early volume of Jarrell's, wished
that the wit of his prose essays could become part of his verse. (What

a "modernist Pope" we would then have, wrote Schwartz.) Or to prove another contemporary's, Karl Shapiro's, seemingly extravagant claim that Jarrell was the only poet of his generation "who made an art out of American speech as it is, who advanced beyond Frost in using not only contemporary idiom . . . but the actual rhythm of our speech." One asks immediately, what of Lowell, of Bishop? But it could be argued that in its combination of geniality and darker portent, Jarrell's actual rhythms of speech were unique.

In his life the darker side eventually had its innings. We remember Coleridge in his "Dejection" ode:

> My genial spirits fail;
> And what can these avail
> To lift the smothering weight from off my breast?

In August of 1965, as Jarrell prepared to resume teaching for the last time, he wrote to Robert Penn Warren to answer a concerned letter Warren had written him about his health. He told Warren that he had always wanted to change, "but not to change into what you become when you're mentally ill." And he concluded by saying that he hadn't written any poems recently, "but I've been thinking so much about the passage of time, and what it's like to live a certain number of years in the world, that I think it's sure to turn into some poems in the long run." There was to be no long run, but the triumph of Jarrell's poetry, though not his life, was that it had already turned into those poems. One of the very last of them, published after his death, "The Player Piano" is supposed to be spoken by an elderly woman, a grandmother. But as usual with Jarrell's dramatic monologues, the grandmother sounds like Randall Jarrell as she addresses and expresses real feelings that, we do not doubt, must have been his own:

> I ate pancakes one night in a Pancake House
> Run by a lady my age. She was gay.
> When I told her that I came from Pasadena
> She laughed and said, "I lived in Pasadena
> When Fatty Arbuckle drove the El Molino bus."
>
> I felt that I had met someone from home.
> No, not Pasadena, Fatty Arbuckle.

Who's that? Oh, something that we had in common
Like—like—the false armistice. Piano rolls.
She told me her house was the first Pancake House

East of the Mississippi, and I showed her
A picture of my grandson. Going home—
Home to the hotel—I began to hum,
"Smile a while, I bid you sad adieu,
When the clouds roll back I'll come to you."

Let's brush our hair before we go to bed,
I say to the old friend who lives in my mirror.
I remember how I'd brush my mother's hair
Before she bobbed it. How long has it been
Since I hit my funnybone? had a scab on my knee?

Here are Mother and Father in a photograph,
Father's holding me . . . They both look so *young.*
I'm so much older than they are. Look at them,
Two babies with their baby. I don't blame you,
You weren't old enough to know any better;

If I could I'd go back, sit down by you both,
And sign our true armistice: you weren't to blame.
I shut my eyes and there's our living room.
The piano's playing something by Chopin,
And Mother and Father and their little girl

Listen. Look, the keys go down by themselves!
I go over, hold my hands out, play I play—
If only, somehow, I had learned to live!
The three of us sit watching, as my waltz
Plays itself out a half-inch from my fingers.

Robert Lowell: *Collected Poems*, edited by Frank Bidart and David Gewanter

"*I* am tired. Everyone's tired of my turmoil." The final line of Robert Lowell's "Eye and Tooth," one of the many poems about depression in *For the Union Dead* (1964), feels ominously prescient of a decline in the poet's reputation after his death in 1977. Something like it happened to both Frost and Eliot after their deaths in the mid-1960s. In Lowell's case, biographical accounts of his clinical dementia and concomitant unhappiness inflicted on others ("not avoiding injury to others, / not avoiding injury to myself," as words from "Dolphin" put it) alienated some readers. In particular he was criticized for using, as material for poems, letters from his second wife, Elizabeth Hardwick, from whom he had separated. Although books and articles continued to appear about Lowell's life and poetry (biographies by Ian Hamilton and Paul Mariani; a collection of essays and memoirs about him edited by Jeffrey Meyers; an incisive short book, *Damaged Grandeur*, by Richard Tillinghast), claims for Lowell's centrality were less often made. It was as if, being early on crowned as America's premier poet and a "political" one to boot, there was no place to go but down.

Frank Bidart, who writes the introduction to the *Collected Poems* he and David Gewanter have edited, was a student of Lowell's at Harvard in the 1960s and went on to become not only his friend but both "amanuensis and sounding board" for the poet's work. Mr. Bidart's efforts as a sounding board on Lowell's behalf were called into play particularly in the late 1960s and early '70s, when Lowell wrote and rewrote the hundreds of unrhymed sonnets that appeared first in *Notebook 1967–68*, then in a revised *Notebook* (1970), then three years later—rearranged, and with many new sonnets—in *History*, *For Lizzie and Harriet*, and *The Dolphin*. In

First published in the *New York Times Book Review*, June 29, 2003, 11–12 one of the three sonnets from *History* titled "Randall Jarrell," Lowell has his friend and fellow-poet say to him, "You didn't write, you *re*-wrote." Bidart quotes this at the beginning of his introduction by way of admitting his own active participation in the process of Lowell's rewritings. That introduction (quite properly) doesn't make a case for Lowell's preeminence as a twentieth-century American poet, but stresses instead the editors' attempt to look at every published instance of a Lowell poem and to include, in their notes, versions and lines that appeared elsewhere than in the published volumes. It is good to have included, among many other things in the notes and appendices, magazine versions of such central poems to the Lowell canon as "Beyond the Alps" and "Waking Early Sunday Morning." But I would hazard that, no more than is the case with Yeats or Auden—other great revisers of their own verse—does Lowell's interest for us depend upon his revisionary zealousness or obsession.

Collected Poems includes ten books of Lowell's, from *Lord Weary's Castle* (1946) to *Day by Day* (1977); *Imitations,* Lowell's renderings of other poets, is included, but not his first book, *Land of Unlikeness,* which occupies the first of various appendices. These contain versions of poems by Akhmatova and Mandelstam; magazine versions of some Lowell poems plus various uncollected ones and others in manuscript; a short, delightful essay, "After Enjoying Six or Seven Essays on Me," which Lowell wrote near the end of his life; and a useful essay, "On Confessional Poetry," in which Bidart describes the sequence of the last four poems in the final section of *Life Studies.* There then follow 165 pages of notes, ranging from the very useful to the scarcely necessary. These notes avoid interpretations of individual poems and do not attempt to account for all textual changes. A model example is the note to Lowell's early "Colloquy in Black Rock" ("Here the jack-hammer jabs into the ocean"), which locates the Connecticut neighborhood near Bridgeport where Lowell lived after his imprisonment for draft resistance. Black Rock was populated in part by workers at the Sikorsky helicopter factory, many of Hungarian descent, who attended St. Stephen's Catholic Church—thus the allusion to Hungary's first king and patron saint as well as to another Stephen, the first Christian martyr ("In Black mud / Hungarian workmen gave their blood / For the martyre Stephen who was stoned to death"). Lowell's account of the poem's genesis is given, as well as a letter published in the *Black Rock News* about the geographical proximity of his house to the church. A query by T. S. Eliot, Lowell's editor at Faber, about the word "detritus" is mentioned, along with other bits of annotation that serious readers of Lowell will be informed by. At the other extreme, one wonders what conceivable reader of this volume will need to have Lent and Pax Romana glossed, to be informed that Tacitus and Juvenal are Roman writers, Thoreau and Emerson American ones, that *Tess of the D'Urbervilles* is by Thomas Hardy, and that Trollope is a "novelist." Still, assembling these notes is an achievement not to be minimized.

Bidart singles out Helen Vendler for her insistence that this edition of Lowell have notes, and Vendler has over the past thirty-five years provided, in a number of valuable essays that are the equivalent of a short book, the strongest case for Lowell's preeminence as the American poet of his time. The preeminence is clearly not a matter of superior technique—in this realm he is excelled, at least equaled, by his contemporaries Wilbur, Bishop, Merrill, and Hecht. But as Eliot put it, complicatedly, in *The Sacred Wood*, "we cannot say at what point 'technique' begins or where it ends." Consideration of Lowell's technique as a poet must include the sense of how wide he cast his net; of how many men, women, and events he engaged with; and of how much history or "life" he aspired to take in and send out in the poems. He once called Hart Crane the great poet of his [Crane's] generation in that "[h]e got out more than anybody else[;] . . . he somehow got New York City; he was at the center of things in the way that no other poet was." In his poems and prose tributes, many of them to other writers, Lowell "got" more out of the midcentury American scene—literary, cultural, political—than anyone else. Vendler's name for his peculiar quality was "difficult grandeur." No one will deny the grandeur, from *Lord Weary* through the hundreds of sonnets; but assessments of the difficulty that went along with it vary, as seen in the divergent verdicts by serious poets and critics of his contribution to poetry overall.

That important poets show a power of development over their careers has been the assumption on which we measure the major-ness of a Yeats, an Eliot. But the notion has also been countered by as major a poet as Philip Larkin, who once alluded to Oscar Wilde's quip about how only mediocrities develop. There is no question that Lowell "developed" in the sense of a gradual stylistic unfolding over a career of books: from the rhymed, brutally enjambed pentameters of *Lord Weary*, to the modified free verse of *Life Studies*, to the public address of octosyllabic couplets in *Near the Ocean*, to the clotted unrhymed abruptness of the sonnets, to the final free verse explorations of *Day by Day*. But Lowell's development in the sense of an achieved maturity, a higher instance of the display of human powers in poetry, is a more contested subject, especially with reference to the poems written after *For the Union Dead*. I have in mind not only what Larkin most likely thought about Lowell's sonnets, but also what such good poets and critics of poetry as Donald Hall and Donald Davie, Denis Donoghue and Clive James, said about them and about *Day by Day* in print. But then, as Jarrell once put it, "if you never look *just* wrong to your contemporaries, you'll never look just right to posterity."

For this reader, a trip through the collected poems, read in the order they appeared, enforces Lowell's sense of tonic—and Eliotic—restlessness with any perfected style ("For last year's words belong to last year's language /And next year's words await another voice"—"Little Gidding"). So the unyielding rhetorical overkill of *Lord Weary* and its successor narratives in *The Mills of the Kavanaughs* ("The Quaker Graveyard in Nantucket," "Between the Porch and the Altar," "After the Surprising Conversions," "Her Dead Brother") provokes, with "Beyond the Alps" as a hinge or pivot, the rueful, humorous, ironic voice of the "Life Studies" section of *Life Studies*, from which lines like the following are as fresh and irresistible as when I first encountered them forty-five years ago: "Anchors Aweigh, Daddy boomed in his bathtub"; "Dearest I cannot loiter here /in lather like a polar bear"; "Tamed by *Miltown* we lie on mother's bed"; "There are no Mayflower /screwballs in the Catholic church." Humor is a feeble word for the deeply satisfying twists made by such lines—and they are all over *Life Studies*. Five years later, again "frizzled, stale and small," we hear the depressed regretful tenor of most of the poems in *For the Union Dead*; then at book's end the title poem, which moves beyond private turmoil into civic, momentous statement. About a large number of poems in these two volumes it can be said what Jarrell said about "one or two" of them in *Lord Weary*—that they "will be read as long as men remember English."

No such consensus exists about the late Lowell. After I. A. Richards read and reread *Notebook 1967–68*, he wrote a letter to the poet that was probably not sent, and one can see why Richards might have held it back as he explains to Lowell why he can't "understand justly" these poems: "The tone, the address, the reiteration, the *lacunae* in convexity, the privacy of the allusions, the use of references which only the Ph.D. duties of the 1990s will explain, the recourse to contemporary crudities, the personal note, the 'it's enough if I say it' air, the assumption that 'you must sympathize with *my* moans, *my* boredom, *my* belches' . . . puzzle me." This from the great construer himself! Recurrent readings of those sonnets and further ones in *The Dolphin* never quite do put Richards's complaints to rest. Even Lowell's loyal friend from Kenyon College days, John Thompson, noted that the form's brevity "relieves the poet of the burden of exposition and encourages him to get lyric about anything that catches his fancy." My own favorite sonnets are the ones about older writers— Frost, Eliot, Pound, Williams, Ford, and others—where the "connexity" Richards had trouble with feels stronger and where Lowell's mischievous humor is most evident. ("Robert Frost at midnight, the audience gone / to vapor, the great act laid on the shelf in mothballs.") Still, one could name thirty or forty of the sonnets with passages gripping enough to lodge them in our minds and ears.

Bishop once told Lowell she envied him the authority granted him as a poet just by being a Lowell rather than, say, her Uncle Artie. A mixed blessing of course, but if the equivalent of Uncle Artie had written *Day by Day*, published shortly before Lowell died, it would have been—as the book was judged to be by some reviewers—slack and listless. Only when we read *Day by Day* as a *Life Studies* written twenty years later by a poet who knows his career as a writer and his life as a man is about to end does its beauty and pathos emerge. Some would call this special pleading; but read in this splendid edition and after the noise and flash of the sonnets, Lowell's final book has the ring of inevitability about it as a last reinvention, painful and sometimes breathtakingly delicate, of the man who said to Bidart months before he died, "I don't know the value of what I've written, but I know that I changed the game."

Robert Lowell: *Collected Prose,*
edited by Robert Giroux

Writing about Yvor Winters in 1961, Robert Lowell saluted his genius, as a literary critic, for finding the right quotation. By contrast, Lowell said, he himself was not a "practiced critic" and had "no gift, for the authoritative and lucid comment that somehow makes a quotation sail." Yet in the very act of disclaiming the gift for criticism he finds a last word to make his own sentence sail. The strategy—or happy impulse—is characteristic of Lowell as a writer of prose. Now his friend and editor, Robert Giroux, has gathered together the various instances of his practice as a critic, an elegist of dead friends, a memoirist and autobiographer. Included are such incidentally fascinating documents as the letter he wrote to President Roosevelt, refusing induction into the army ("I very much regret that I must refuse the opportunity you offer me," it begins, with proper or mock-proper Bostonian courtesy). The book contains as well two revealing and attractive interviews, plus thirty packed pages (edited by Giroux) of what was to have been a book about New England writers, from Cotton Mather to T. S. Eliot.

Lowell was concerned not to be mistaken for an academic critic who wrote standard analytical essays; he liked rather, as he remarks in one of the interviews, to produce "sloppier and more intuitive" criticism. This was his way of reminding us that he was first a poet, only secondly a critic. Like his friend Jarrell, whose name is evoked time and again in these pages and about whom he wrote his most moving tribute, Lowell almost never wrote a sentence that is "straight," that doesn't have the twist of wit—some slight alteration of language into memorableness. He says of Frost, "There was music in his voice, in the way he made

First published in the *Boston Globe,* March 22, 1989 (as "The Prose Voice of Poet Robert Lowell")

his quotations ring, in the spin on his language, in the strange, intuitive waywardness of his toleration." The same could be said of Lowell (those who heard him speak will agree), especially with regard to that spin on the language. He calls his ancestor James Russell Lowell "a poet pedestalled for oblivion," and the quotation not only rings, but rings with a witty and forlorn truth. Two sentences juxtaposed say something equally fresh and apt about Longfellow: "A good storyteller, our cultured metrical technician. Tennyson without gin."

The collection is divided into three parts, the first of them—and perhaps the richest—consisting of Lowell on individual poets. It ranges from his early reviews from the 1940s of Stevens's *Transport to Summer,* Eliot's *Quartets,* and Williams's *Paterson* (Books 1 and 2), to the later well-known appreciative essays on dead friends such as Frost, John Crowe Ransom, Jarrell, and John Berryman. He makes just observations and distinctions about individual poems, but as with the sentences quoted above on James Russell Lowell and Longfellow, he is most memorable when speaking about the poet's person and character. Inevitably it is a witty speaking, the twist and jab almost unobtrusive, as when Jarrell's "romantic" nature is contrasted with Ransom's, the former "educated in the preoccupations of the '30s, Marx, Auden, Empson, Kafka, plane design, anthropology since Fraser, and news of the day. He knew everything except Ransom's close, provincial world of Greek, Latin, Aristotle, and Oxford." A significant "except," and surely there is a double-edge in speaking of the classics and of Aristotle as a "provincial world" compared to plane design. In his 1965 eulogy of Eliot, he registers how Eliot's "air of a slightly square *poète maudit* missionary suited no one else." Putting together words that don't usually belong with one another (*"poète maudit"* with "missionary") gives the sentence that "intuitive" feel Lowell strove for, rather than academic analytical caution. Of Ford Madox Ford, who kicks off the collection (chronology is not observed by the editor), Lowell writes: "His humility was edged with a mumbling insolence. His fanatical life-and-death dedication to the arts was messy, British, and amused." Again the words clash invigoratingly ("humility" with "insolence," "dedication" with "messy and amused") to give us the contradictory Ford whom Lowell had earlier addressed in a poem as "Master, mammoth mumbler."

The essays were designed to sound sloppy as well as intuitive, but at times there is something rather mechanical in the piling up of tripartite clusters of adjectives or nouns, as in the "messy, British, and amused" assigned to Ford above. Lowell describes Ford's poetry as "tame, absent-minded and cautious"; "his memory, pace, and tastes were conservative." Jarrell's "soul" is characterized as "noble, difficult, and beautiful." Often in Lowell's poems, the group of three surprisingly combined words make for authentic killer lines, as in "Hairy, muscular, suburban," or "Flabby, bald, lobotomized" from "Memories of West Street and Lepke." But eventually the tripling became bureaucratized into a habit or tic, which, instead of sounding "sloppy" in an appealing sense, sounds as if Lowell has switched onto automatic three-step pilot.

At his best, as in the wonderful 1962 essay on Williams, he combines intuitive brilliance as a reader with the informal ("sloppy" if he prefers) sound of a voice that cares about real speech. He recalls being directed by James Laughlin to Williams's "The Catholic Bells," which begins

> 'Tho I'm no Catholic
> I listen hard when the bells
> in the yellow-brick tower
> of their new church
> ring down the leaves
> ring in the frost upon them[.]

And later "ring in / the new baby of Mr. and Mrs. / Krantz which cannot / for the fat of its cheeks / open well its eyes . . ." In a paragraph bristling with humorous trenchancy, Lowell describes his bemused response to it:

> What I liked about "The Catholic Bells" were the irrelevant as-
> sociations I hung on the word *frost* and *Catholic,* and still more its
> misleading similarity to the "Ring out wild bells" section of "In
> Memoriam." Other things upset and fascinated me and made me
> feel I was in a world I would never quite understand. . . . There had
> to be something outside the poem I could hang on to because what
> was inside dizzied me: the shocking scramble of the august and the
> crass in making the Catholic church "new' and "yellow-brick," the

cherubic ugliness of the baby, belonging rather horribly to "Mr. and Mrs. / Krantz," and seen by the experienced mature pediatrician as unable to see "for the fat of its cheeks"—this last a cunning shift into anapests.

After something as lovingly complicated and candid as this shrewd glimpse into the psychology of reading a poem, Lowell has softened us up to the point where his concluding sentence to a paragraph has enormous, indeed moving impact, when, speaking of Williams, he says, "His flowers rustle by the superhighways and pick up all our voices."

In a charming moment from a *Life Studies* poem, "Home after Three Months Away" (those months spent in a mental hospital), Lowell addresses his young daughter, having her bath while he is shaving: "Dearest, I cannot loiter here / in lather like a polar bear." His strain of comic ingenuity has not been recognized enough; it informs these essays in their wryly funny accounts of bringing Jarrell and Berryman together, with unhumorous consequences; or of visiting the Tates, when a brash young man, and pitching a tent in their front yard. And it informs the pages titled "New England and Further," flashing into life as he writes about Thoreau's claim to have seen the whole world just by rambling about Concord: "Who but St. Anthony or a catatonic really wants to 'see the world in a grain of sand'? We long for a little weakness, darkness, and fiction, for the crowded, the smut, the closeness, and malice of things." Henry James is presented as a compound of Proust's idealized narrator and the conspiring Baron Charlus, "a whale in society"; while Lowell ends a brief portrait of Santayana by praising not only his "Montaigne-like moderation," but his "civilized, philosophic love of scandal." Emerson is invoked as "Robert Frost's sweeter, thinner, more celestial forerunner," and Frost himself is called "an actor . . . who might have made Yeats seem a model of artless simplicity." About that New England poet's late poem "Directive," Lowell says it is "an aging Frost's 'Tintern Abbey'—written as he journeyed to the destroyed homestead of his early marriage, his lost wife and children." Here, as with so many moments in Lowell's poems, we are face to face with the sort of inventive audacity—tamer names for it are imagination, or intelligence—that made him a worthy successor to the New England writers he catches so memorably.

The Letters of Robert Lowell,
edited by Saskia Hamilton

"*H*ave you ever tried to stop writing? It's harder than alcohol, which I also forswear as the very early sun crashes at about four through faults in the blinds." So Robert Lowell wrote to his old friend and Kenyon College classmate Peter Taylor, the year before Lowell died. He was talking about poems, but he ceaselessly wrote letters as well, and Saskia Hamilton, herself a poet, has undertaken the heroic task of editing a generous selection of them. These 724 examples of Lowell's epistolary art begin in 1936, when he was a freshman at Harvard, with a letter to Ezra Pound in which Lowell proposes to come to Italy if Pound will accept him as a student. They conclude with a fragment written to his third wife, Lady Caroline Blackwood, as he prepares to fly to New York, there to rejoin his second wife, Elizabeth Hardwick. He would die of a heart attack in a taxi on the way to her apartment.

The editor has not only with great diligence provided 131 pages of notes to the letters, but also written a shrewd introduction directed at bringing out the nature of Lowell as a correspondent. "[He] often overcame his inertia and engaged his will by attending to the musical problems in sentence making. He typed as fast as he could, but his ear reached for work," she notes by way of suggesting similarities in the energetic and original reach of Lowell's "work" both in poetry and prose composition. Often that work commanded a fusion of opposites to create the power of a sentence, as when in an early letter to his former teacher at St. Mark's School, the poet Richard Eberhart, he tells Eberhart to read *Snooty Baronet* (a little-read novel by Wyndham Lewis), which, though at times "hardly articulate," deserves reading for "the conversations, the firm satire, and the rough hewn craftsmanship of the prose." Rough-hewn craftsmanship

First published in the *Boston Globe*, June 19, 2005

works as a kind of oxymoron perhaps prompted by Hamlet's conviction that "There's a divinity that shapes our ends / Rough hew them how we will."

Lowell's craftsmanship is evident in these letters, but anyone who persists through 800 pages of them will experience a feeling he himself expressed at the end of a fierce poem in *For the Union Dead:* "I am tired. Everyone's tired of my turmoil." His first major breakdown, a manic episode with its subsequent depression, happened in 1949, one of a series that only abated—and then temporarily—when the drug Lithium was prescribed in 1967. Yet as his devoted friend and editor Frank Bidart put it, when Lowell was well, he was "more 'well' than most people I know." Most of these letters were written in such periods of wellness, and the character that emerges from them, as Hamilton says rightly, "is full of affection and candor, funny, gregarious, hungry for fathers, hungry for conversation about writing." The "fathers," beginning with Pound, include Frost ("the first real writer I had ever met"), Eliot, George Santayana—to whom some of his best letters are written—and William Carlos Williams. The "conversation about writing" he hungered for took place mainly with his friends and contemporaries—with Randall Jarrell, Peter Taylor, Theodore Roethke, but above all with Elizabeth Bishop. His relationship with the latter went deeper than with anyone else, except for the other Elizabeth—Hardwick. (An edition of the full correspondence between Lowell and Bishop is in the works.) Notable omissions from the present volume—destroyed or gone missing—are the letters to his first wife, Jean Stafford, and to Blackwood (the volume ends with fragments of letters to her that were first published by Ian Hamilton in his 1982 biography).

Yet few readers will finish the volume wanting more, since God's, or Lowell's, plenty in various workings has been plentifully displayed. Especially salient and unsparing are his self-characterizations. Writing to Robert Fitzgerald after the first breakdown, he says of the experience, not yet fully digested, that it contained "terrific lifts, insights, pourings in of new energy, but no work on my part, only more and more self-indulgence, lack of objectivity; and so, into literal madness i.e. I had to be locked up." Years previously he had written Merrill Moore, the psychologist-poet he consulted, "My career, I hope, will be exceptional rather than queer." But

increasingly he recognized his own exceptional queerness, writing to San-
tayana that "the peculiarity I seem to have been born with is a character
made up of stiffness and disorder, or lethargy and passion." Eventually
he would declare to John Berryman, apropos of their generation, "What
queer lives we've had even for poets!" When one of that generation,
Roethke, suffered a breakdown, Lowell wrote him that what was lost
would be returned and that "[w]e even bring back certain treasure from
our visits to the bottom." Perhaps the main treasure he brought back was
a sharpened sense of how far down the bottom was, and how precarious
life at the top thus became.

But when he was "well," he was really well, and this ebullient sense of
life at the top comes through magnificently in the rich humor of so many
of these letters. One of his favorite gambits is to make the second half of
a sentence cast a funny look on the claim made in its first half. He writes
to John Crowe Ransom, when Lowell and Stafford were living in Black
Rock, Connecticut, while he served his C.O. sentence mopping floors,
"We are living in a really splendid apartment with great windows, but it
rests on a dump and looks out on a mud-flat." A 1950 letter to Bishop
about visiting Santayana in Rome declares, "The meetings were delightful
for me and perfect; except that he is deaf and couldn't hear a word—
shouted or whispered—that I said." From his innumerable, marvelous
brief portraits of other writers, here he is (again to Bishop) on Robert
Graves's poems: "There is not a banality, I think anywhere, though a
somewhat sparring, boxerlike and too steely man . . . each poem knocks
me in a corner with a wet towel over my head." We hear of Adrienne Rich
"having a third baby . . . reading Simone de Beauvoir and bursting with
benzedrine and emancipation," or of Edmund Wilson, who "drinks like
an ox, like Ted Roethke, and yet it does no harm. Only at about 11.30 he
becomes rather speechless." My own favorite moment comes in a letter
to Taylor about their mutual friend, Jarrell, and his inordinate affection
for his cat, Kitten: "Doesn't it chill your blood to think that Kitten is
still alive, both Stalin and Queen Mary looked so flourishing, then to be
survived by Kitten."

Such genial spirits animate much of this rewarding book. But as
Coleridge put it in "Dejection," "My genial spirits fail," and Lowell's

failed him increasingly in the last years of his life, as he shuttled between Britain and Harvard, between what he once called the "unending nervous strife" of his marriage to Hardwick, and the mounting pains and confusions of his marriage to Blackwood ("I don't know what to say, our problems have become so many-headed and insuperable"). Writing to Taylor after a breakdown in 1970 when he was living with Blackwood, he reached for a summing-up beyond the local occasion: "There was great joy in it all, great harm to everyone." Death, as it does, put an end to Lowell's insuperable problems, to harm and joy. Life remains vibrant in these letters.

Philip Larkin: R.I.P.

*T*he death of Philip Larkin at age sixty-three deprived us not only of the finest poet writing in English, but of a particularly resourceful imaginer of the idea of death. He was also a resister of death as a fact; his great friend Kingsley Amis (*Lucky Jim* was dedicated to Larkin) wrote a novel titled *The Anti-Death League*, and Larkin was a charter member of that organization. "Beneath it all, desire of oblivion runs," ran a line from his first mature book of poems, *The Less Deceived* (1955). From the beginning Larkin was exceptionally sensitive to, and moved by, the oblivion into which things fall, while the "all" continues on its way. His poems were acts of resistance directed at that oblivion, from which (in "Maiden Name") he beautifully rescued a married woman's former name ("Now it's a phrase applicable to no one") by affirming eventually, "It means what we feel now about you then: / How beautiful you were, and near, and young." Or, in the final poem from *The Less Deceived* ("At Grass"), he contemplated racehorses fifteen years past their prime: "Do memories plague their ears like flies? / They shake their heads"—but shake them, not in response to the question, only against the flies. Thus it is left for the poet to memorialize them: "Almanacked, their names live; they / Have slipped their names, and stand at ease . . . And not a fieldglass sees them home."

I first became aware of Larkin sometime in the middle 1950s, when I had worn out both my recording of Dylan Thomas reading his poems and most of my enthusiasm for Dylan Thomas. Thomas was certainly full of stirring challenges and directives to death with a capital D ("And Death Shall Have No Dominion," "Do Not Go Gentle Into That Good Night"), but the music was too loud, the voice too thrilling for my own

---

First published in *The New Republic*, January 6 and 13, 1986 (as "The Least Deceived")

good. Without raising his voice, Larkin spoke about death (in his poem "The Old Fools") with a small d, in a tone of regretful evenhandedness, making his subject all the more inescapable and unarguable with, even as he argued about it:

> At death, you break up: the bits that were you
> Start speeding away from each other for ever
> With no one to see. It's only oblivion, true:
> We had it before, but then it was going to end,
> And was all the time merging with a unique endeavour
> To bring to bloom the million-petalled flower
> Of being here.

No one has said anything truer and wiser about the difference between birth and death: between the "unique endeavour" that someone—a mother, a father, a doctor—is there to see, and the much later lonely breaking up of that "million-petalled flower" we scarcely knew we were part of in being here.

Like Hardy, the poet of all poets he admired most, Larkin wrote rhymed verse, and when the occasional poem didn't rhyme it only proved the rule. Like Frost, he had no use for free verse and would as soon have written poems that delighted in not making "sense" (John Ashbery's delight) as he would have visited a foreign country, say the United States ("And of course I'm so deaf now that I shouldn't dare. Someone would say, What about Ashbery, and I'd say, I'd prefer strawberry, that kind of thing"). For Larkin, rhyme and stanza and making sense were the cement that held together both the poem and the poet's relation to his reader, as in the following lines from "Aubade," published a few years after his last book of poems, *High Windows*, appeared in 1974. This is a different, grimmer song than the aubades sung at dawn, usually to a lover; here the man wakes at 4 a.m., in the grip of "unresting death, a whole day nearer now," the dread of which "Flashes afresh to hold and horrify." He goes on to explore this "special way of feeling afraid / No trick dispels":

> Religion used to try,
> That vast moth-eaten musical brocade
> Created to pretend we never die,
> And specious stuff that says *No rational being*

> *Can fear a thing it will not feel,* not seeing
> That this is what we fear—no sight, no sound,
> No touch or taste or smell, nothing to think with,
> Nothing to love or link with,
> The anaesthetic from which none come round.

The specious stuff of religion and philosophy is dismissed, but there is nothing specious about the rhyming, especially the double one of "think with" and "link with," which touchingly links itself with the reader who both sees and hears a life-affirming connection made in the midst of death.

Larkin loved American jazz of the 1920s and 1930s (before Charlie Parker): Armstrong and Fats Waller, Big Sid Catlett and especially Pee Wee Russell, who figured for him and Amis and their Oxford pals as "mutatis mutandis, our Swinburne and our Byron." He concluded his introduction to *All That Jazz*, a collection of his reviews, by imagining the audience to whom this music could speak: "Men whose first coronary is coming like Christmas; who drift, loaded helplessly with commitments and obligations and necessary observances, into the darkening avenues of age and incapacity, deserted by everything that once made life sweet." One almost yearns to be such a man, just to live up to that prose, or to the figure in one of the last poems he published, "Continuing to Live," in which life as it continues is seen as "nearly always losing, or going without":

> This loss of interest, hair, and enterprise
> Ah, if the game were poker, yes,
> You might discard them, draw a full house!
> But it's chess.

And, the poem continues, "Once you have walked the length of your mind / What you command is clear as a lading-list." Larkin felt he had walked the length of his own mind, that he had no more—or hardly any more—poems to write, and that the only profit of continuing to live was that, in the poem's words, we may in time "half-identify the blind impress / All our behavings bear." But it concludes ruefully:

> . . . to confess,
> On that green evening when our death begins,

> Just what it was, is hardly satisfying,
>   Since it applies only to one man once,
>   And that one dying.

Cold comfort farm. One likes, nevertheless, to think Larkin may once or twice have had an inkling of how much pleasure and satisfaction he gave to readers, most of them not aging men headed for coronaries, but younger readers of both sexes who, in the words of his best-known poem, "Church Going," recognize in themselves "[a] hunger . . . to be more serious." He declined to succeed Betjeman as poet laureate; like Hardy, Larkin was something better.

Philip Larkin: *Collected Poems,*
edited by Anthony Thwaite

When Philip Larkin died, his poetry-writing self had been at least terminally ill. His last book of verse, *High Windows* (1974) was followed by very few published poems, and when that book was added to previous ones—*The Whitsun Weddings* (1964) and *The Less Deceived* (1955)—the total number of poems on which, it appeared, his reputation would be based came to fewer than 100. (An early volume, *The North Ship*, figures as juvenilia.) Now, having waited patiently for the *Collected Poems* to appear, we are gratified by this substantial volume of 242 poems. After marveling at the scrupulousness with which Larkin held off from including many of them between his earlier hardcovers, what are we to make of the new expanded oeuvre?

In his introduction to the volume, its editor Anthony Thwaite gives a clear rationale for his procedure. The major section (titled "Poems 1946–83") consists of "mature" Larkin, beginning with "Going" ("There is an evening coming in / Across the field, one never seen before, / That lights no lamps,") and ending with "Party Politics" ("I never remember holding a full drink. / My first look shows the level half-way down"). The two poems appropriately frame Larkin as, to put it mildly, the poet of transience. Then follows a smaller but fairly thick section consisting of "Early Poems, 1938–45" (*The North Ship* was published in that latter year.) Since, thankfully, Larkin was careful about appending completion dates to the poems as they appeared in his manuscript notebooks, each poem is followed by its year of composition and place (if any) of previous publication.

We have then a *Collected Poems* in which the order of arrangement Larkin chose for his individual volumes is no longer present; and since—especially

---

First published in the *Boston Globe*, April 14, 1989 (as "The Astringent Vision of Philip Larkin")

in *High Windows*—that order was an artful one, something has been lost. On the other hand, we gain from the chronological ordering a better sense both of Larkin's productive and fallow periods as a writer and of the interesting congruities between one poem and another. For example: January 1954 was a greatly productive month as he wrote or brought to completion "I Remember, I Remember," "For Sidney Bechet," "Born Yesterday," and "Poetry of Departures." But between January 1957, when he finished the beautiful "Love Songs in Age," and October 1958, which brought "The Whitsun Weddings," there is not a single poem. We may learn something from Larkin's biographer, Andrew Motion, about such silences and productivities.

A simplified overview of Larkin's earlier career, drawn from the group of 1938–45 poems at the back of the book, shows first some Tennysonian-Swinburnian efforts published in his school magazine, *The Coventrian*, in 1939, with lines like "Now night perfumes lie upon the air, / As rests the blossom on the loaded bough"; or "Pale Winter draws away his white hands, loathed, / And creeps, a leper, to the cave of time." In 1940, there is an extended burst of Audenesque writing, with poems that begin "And the walker sees the sunlit battlefield," or "Tired of a landscape known too well when young," or "Out in the lane I pause"—see Auden's "Out on the lawn I lie"—and with imitations of Auden's off-rhymings and wearily knowing manner (Larkin was all of eighteen years old at the time). These forceful-enough poems are nevertheless empty of what will later be identified as typical Larkin content. After Auden, Yeats makes his appearance with some horses and horsemen, swans and stony places, spoken through a tough-bittersweet voice: "To write one song, I said, / As sad as the sad wind / That walks around my bed." It would be no exaggeration to say that nothing in these poems prepares us in any way for the work soon to come.

At the end of 1947, Larkin put together and submitted to publishers a manuscript titled *In the Grip of Light*, the result of which was a series of rejections. Looking at the poems included in it (Thwaite provides a list of them), one has to sympathize with the publishers, since the poems are in the main humorless, sometimes pretentious, and generally rather dry—though without the astringent dryness Larkin was soon to achieve.

Then—it feels miraculous—four months into 1948, he wrote the follow-ing poem:

> An April Sunday brings the snow
> Making the blossom on the plum trees green,
> Not white. An hour or two, and it will go.
> Strange that I spend that hour moving between
> Cupboard and cupboard, shifting; the store
> Of jam you made of fruit from these same trees:
> Five loads—a hundred pounds or more—
> More than enough for all next summer's teas,
> Which now you will not sit and eat.
> Behind the glass, under the cellophane
> Remains your final summer—sweet
> And meaningless, and not to come again.

Larkin has been quoted as saying once that he wrote his first good poem at age twenty-six, and it may have been this one about his father's death, so perfectly managed in its voice and rhythm, and with that final epitaph ("sweet / And meaningless, and not to come again") striking the authen-tic Larkin note. Seven poems later and less than two years after "An April Sunday . . ." the reader encounters "At Grass," Larkin's first masterpiece and the final poem in what would be "The Less Deceived." "At Grass" is about horses, not Yeatsian apocalyptic ones but old racehorses now subsided into something else. Of them, the poet asks,

> Do memories plague their ears like flies?
> They shake their heads. Dusk brims the shadows,
> Summer by summer all stole away,
> The starting-gates, the crowds and cries—
> All but the unmolesting meadows.

The unobtrusive wit of having those horses obliviously shake their heads, the splendid rightness of having meadows be "unmolesting"— such qualities began to show up, more often than not, in every poem Larkin went on to write.

Perhaps the most interesting single new one in this collection is an un-finished piece titled "The Dance," begun in 1963 and abandoned almost a year later. Written in the spacious stanza Larkin had recently employed in "The Whitsun Weddings" and "Dockery and Son"—and that the finest of his poems to come, like "The Old Fools" and "Aubade," would also use—"The Dance" is about a man's attending such an occasion only because a desired woman will be there. Although this event, as the protagonist says to himself, dilutes "Drink, sex and jazz—all sweet things, brother," these things are moving along well enough on the dance floor as, under "the slug / And snarl of music," and with "a few permitted movements," his partner suggests "A whole consenting language." Suddenly, things fall apart: "Your fingers tighten, tug, // Then slacken altogether, I am caught / By some shoptalking shit who leads me off / To supper and his bearded wife," as the moment passes and the evening falters. "The Dance" has the richness of a good novel (we may recall the great dance chapters in Amis's *Lucky Jim*), with the additional bonus of watching a poet execute his engaging sounds of sense over an exacting stanzaic grid. By this time, of course, Larkin's presence had fully declared itself and continued to do so until the end of 1973 when the lode was evidently mined out.

"I didn't abandon poetry; it abandoned me," as he put it, and his final twelve years show a total of seventeen poems, of which—in addition to "Aubade"—four or five are real and chilling additions to his best work. They show us, if we hadn't suspected it before, that Larkin was a love poet, of love somehow gone wrong and of sex both hungrily desired and impossible of fulfillment. He was also a bachelor, in a way that gives that quaint old term a vivid and troubling life. The chill of absence, felt as things moved further and further out of reach, is literally present in a late poem, titled "The Winter Palace," which begins "Most people know more as they get older; / I give all that the cold shoulder." The poem's speaker—Larkin in no disguise at all—having lost what he learnt at university, having refused to take in what has happened since, and having forgotten the names and faces and places he is supposed to be remembering, consoles himself at the poem's end with this bleak recompense:

> It will be worth it, if in the end I manage
> To blank out whatever it is that is doing them damage.

> Then there will be nothing I know.
> My mind will fold into itself, like fields, like snow.

The recompense makes late Yeats or Stevens sound positively rosy by comparison. But like their work—if in no other respect—Larkin's is a whole that hangs together and reveals a life, even as, in the title of another grim late poem, it was "The Life with a Hole in It."

Philip Larkin: A Writer's Life,
by Andrew Motion

*P*hilip Larkin's death in 1985 was greeted by readers of po-
etry with more or less universal sorrowing, a sense that
something precious had been taken away whose like wouldn't be seen again.
Even though no significant poem of his had appeared since the great
"Aubade" eight years previously, the possibility of one more slim volume
didn't seem beyond imagining. In between "Aubade" and his death there
was *Required Writing* (1983), a collection of his miscellaneous prose that
provided many attractive formulations about how Larkin's creativity was
fueled by absences rather than presences: "Deprivation is for me what
daffodils were for Wordsworth" was one of his memorable ways of put-
ting it. It was easy, perhaps too easy, to take to our hearts the grumpy, hu-
morously complaining, self-depreciating figure who existed in the prose:
the Hermit of Hull; the man who mock-innocently asked an interviewer,
on mention of Borges, "Who's Jorge Luis Borges?"; the nontraveler who
said he'd like to visit China if he could come back the same day. These
comic simplifications added up to a portrait of the artist as wonderful
old curmudgeon.

Then came—in 1992, in Britain—a fat selection of Larkin's correspon-
dence, confirming rumors that the old curmudgeon was, earlier on, also a
young one whose slashing, sometimes virulent remarks at the expense of
other races, other places, the other sex, almost any brand of "otherness,"
were egregiously and unabashedly on display. Farrar, Straus and Giroux
has intelligently decided to delay publication of the letters until after this
biography appeared. But advance notice of Andrew Motion's *Philip Larkin:
A Writer's Life* in this country has already directed attention to Larkin's

First published in the *New York Times Book Review*, August 1, 1993 (as "The
Bleakest Poet")

bad attitudes, with the effect of alerting people who had no interest in reading his poems anyway to the scandal of the poet as unacceptable human being.

In one of Larkin's most painful poems, "Love Again," written late and published posthumously, he speaks, gravely, of an "element / That spreads through other lives like a tree / And sways them on in a sort of sense," then adds, "And say why it never worked for me." If this could be read as a challenge to the biographer somehow to "explain" the distorted lack of sense Larkin often felt about his life, particularly in its sexual aspect, Andrew Motion—who knew Larkin at the University of Hull in his last nine years and wrote one splendid poem about him ("This Is Your Subject Speaking")—is aware of the pitfalls of latching on to some biographical key that would unlock the mystery.

To be sure, there is the parental key: Larkin's father, Sydney, an effective city official in Coventry with a contemptuous attitude toward women and an admiration for Hitler and 1930s Germany; or his mother, Eva, whose "monotonous whining monologue" (Larkin wrote, in an unpublished autobiographical fragment from the 1950s) "I mustn't under any circumstances risk encountering again." But Motion argues saliently that Sydney Larkin's influence on his son (he encouraged Philip's literary and musical life, kept D. H. Lawrence novels in the house and even took out a subscription to the American jazz magazine *Down Beat,* while buying his son a set of drums) was by no means negative; and that complaining about his mother's personality was also Larkin's way of keeping her near him in imagination. "My mother, not content with being motionless, deaf and speechless, is now going blind," he wrote Amis in 1977, the year she died. Even so, Eva Larkin's presence is behind the energy of many of his finest poems, including "Aubade," published shortly after her death.

Larkin's time at Oxford coincided with World War II (he was exempted from service because of bad eyes); he established himself, in Motion's words, as an "opinionated and even flamboyant personality," complete with cerise trousers (supposedly on advice given by Lawrence in *Lady Chatterley's Lover*). In company with his friend and fellow writer Amis ("a talent greater than my own," Larkin confessed to feeling when they first met), Larkin played the bad undergraduate, mocking and deriding tutors, lecturers, and official education generally. His real education was extracurricular, "off the syllabus," and the Bodleian Library's day books show that most of the books he read had nothing to do with tutorials.

But his most off-the-syllabus educative experience was listening to American jazz, as he and Amis contrived to turn English Romantic poets into a recorded session by Bill Wordsworth and his Hot Six, featuring Lord Byron (trumpet), Sam (Tea) Coleridge (piano), and others. Larkin later reviewed jazz for the *Daily Telegraph*, wrote an appreciation of Cole Porter, and echoed, in some of his best lines, the diction and rhythms of popular lyric. Against his prediction he took a first-class degree at Oxford and then, by somewhat less than firm decision making, landed a job as a librarian in a provincial town in Shropshire. It would be followed by stints in Leicester, in Belfast, and finally at the Brynmor Jones Library in Hull, where he settled in 1955 to live out his life.

Motion skillfully alternates his narrative of Larkin's careers: as novelist, which came to an end after *A Girl in Winter* was published in 1947 but (surprise) included two unpublished lesbian spoof-romances; as poet; as a highly successful librarian, admired by his staff; and as a lover. Except for a brief single-sex attachment at Oxford, the objects of his affection were women and the circumstances never less than complicated, not to say agonized. He could perform his agonies with fine and funny bravado in letters, especially to Amis: "Everything about the ree-lay-shun-ship between men and women makes me *angry*. . . . It might have been planned by the army, or the Ministry of Food." To another friend, James Sutton, he wrote more soberly in 1946: "I find, myself, that this letting in of a second person spells death to perception and the desire to express, as well as the ability." Relations between the sexes, in other words, were likely to be disastrous if marriage was in the offing. In a famous letter, Henry James once wrote that he could never marry because it would imply he thought too well of life. Larkin says something like this when in "Reasons for Attendance" he looks through a window at couples dancing and finds that unlike them, he has been singled out by "that lifted, rough-tongued bell /(Art, if you like) whose individual sound/Insists I too am individual."

But sex and at least occasional companionship called Larkin also. At one point, fairly late in his life, he is balancing "ree-lay-shun-ships" with his long-term love Monica Jones, who said, on first meeting him, "He looks like a snorer," and who destroyed his diaries when he died; with Maeve Brennan, a member of his staff at Hull and also a lover, though their affair remained unconsummated for many years; and with Betty Mackereth, his secretary at the library. Both Monica and Maeve write at length, and trenchantly, about the man they shared—or a part of him. With no ingratitude for Motion's labors, I should say that in future we need hear no further about Larkin and the women.

Motion says cleverly that, especially in the years at Hull, Larkin contrived to sound "like a sexually disappointed Eeyore," and the historian A. L. Rowse once grumbled, "What the hell was the matter with him? . . . I mean, he hadn't much to complain about. He was tall." Larkin's genius in the poems for freezing his life, as Motion puts it, in "postures of continuing unhappiness" that were also beautiful and valuable to contemplate gradually hardened—in his life outside the poems—into all he'd got, like the speaker of "Dockery and Son." Palliatives were only that: his interest in pornography, ministered to by the poet Robert Conquest, who turned up choice items to send him, is one with his celebration of the bathing-suited girl on the billboard in "Sunny Prestatyn," defaced by real-life cynics ("She was too good for this life"). The tortoise-shell spyglass he kept on the windowsill of his Hull library office was there, Betty Mackereth told Motion, "so that he could examine pretty students as they passed by"—and not too close up, thank you. He once quoted A. E. Housman approvingly to the effect that anybody who thinks he has loved more than one person has probably never loved at all. What did such a view, too good for any life, have to do with his own imperfect, multiple erotic attachments?

His last years, especially the last months, in which his esophagus was removed and a further inoperable cancer discovered (the knowledge kept from him), are very sad to read about: continuing deafness; a deepening dependence on alcohol ("I get up at 6 A.M. [to write a poem]. It's the only time I'm not drunk," he wrote Amis); general physical decay (he characterized his "sagging face" in a 1984 photograph as "an egg sculpted in lard, with goggles on—depressing, depressing, depressing"); and the drying up of everything, except for a few close friends, "which had once

entertained or diverted him. . . . Jazz. Poems. The countryside. Work."
While he was in hospital recovering from the operation, someone, in a
near replaying of Apthorpe's fate in Evelyn Waugh's novel *Men at Arms*,
brought him a bottle of whisky that, once drunk, caused him to vomit
and flood his lungs. He recovered, but it was not to be for long. "I am
going to the inevitable," he said as he was dying, squeezing the hand
of his nurse.

Why, some might ask, would one want to read all this when the match-
less poems are there, still fresh and glittering as creation itself? Because,
if we decide that these poems constitute a great creative achievement, we
want to know everything, even too much, about the man who wrote them.
How great a creative achievement are they? His biographer ranks Larkin
with Hardy, Yeats, Eliot, and Auden as the premier poets of this cen-
tury. Let us add to them an American component of Frost and Stevens,
perhaps Robert Lowell, and say that more than any of them, excepting
Hardy, Larkin is the poet of death who, since death is the mother of
beauty, brings us most vividly to life. "At Grass," "Church Going," "Love
Songs in Age," "The Whitsun Weddings," "An Arundel Tomb," "To the
Sea," "The Old Fools," "The Explosion," "Aubade"—these and twenty
or thirty more will be read, as Randall Jarrell once said about some of
Lowell's poems, as long as we remember English.

Richard Wilbur:
Collected Poems, 1943–2004

*I*n his introductory note to this handsome and in every sense
weighty volume, Richard Wilbur, surveying the fruits of
sixty-one years of poems, announces with some pride, "Nothing has been
thrown out, and any changes of wording are too few and too slight to
mention." Nothing need be thrown out, we might add, because from the
outset of his career Wilbur has never published a poem that was merely
tossed off, hoping somehow to catch the eye of a sympathetic reader.
Once he had submitted words to the authority of print, few further changes
of wording were needed, since the poem had attained what Robert Frost
called its "figure""—"a clarification of life," "a momentary stay against
confusion." Frost also said, in his brief manifesto "The Figure a Poem
Makes," that the figure was the same as for love. So it makes wholly
appropriate sense that this edition begins and ends with poems clearly
occasioned by the presence of Charlotte Ward Wilbur, to whom the col-
lection is dedicated. (They were married in 1942, and Wilbur went off to
war the following year.)

Since *Collected Poems* follows the current common practice of printing
the work in reverse order of its appearance, it ends with the title poem to
Wilbur's first volume, *The Beautiful Changes,* and begins with "The Reader,"
published in the *New Yorker* not long ago. Without simplifying the ca-
reer and achievement unduly, these two poems juxtaposed say something
about the nature and value of that achievement. "The Beautiful Changes"
consists of three six-line stanzas in loose iambics with an anapestic lilt.
The first stanza observes such changes in nature: a meadow of Queen
Anne's lace suddenly becoming, to the viewer's eye, a lake; a forest chang-
ing and deepening its color because of a mantis's presence on a single

First published in *Commonweal*, April 22, 2005 (as "A Master") green leaf. The third stanza observes similar effects as produced by an unnamed you:

> Your hands hold roses always in a way that says
> They are not only yours; the beautiful changes
> In such kind ways,
> Wishing ever to sunder
> Things and things' selves for a second finding, to lose
> For a moment all that it touches back to wonder.

This is a love poem about losing one's self, and the things of nature and human nature, into a new finding—a sundering that results in wonder, as the woman's hands make the roses new, enlarged in their beauty and power. Paraphrase doesn't work well to convey the suggestion and implication of such a poem, which shows, in matchless fashion, Wilbur's early and unswerving commitment to the corresponding figures of love and poetry.

"The Reader" more directly and fully imagines a woman who is rereading the "great stories that charmed her younger mind." The poet looks on and, seeing the pages turn, imagines the characters who appear once more to her, such as, perhaps, James's Isabel Archer and Thackeray's Becky Sharp, "The serious girl, once more, who would live nobly, / The sly one who aspires to marry so." He compares the woman as reader to a god who knows both the "first and final selves" of these heroes and heroines she engages with, then ends at the heart of the matter:

> But the true wonder of it is that she,
> For all that she may know of consequences,
> Still turns enchanted to the next bright page
> Like some Natasha in the ballroom door—
> Caught in the flow of things wherever bound,
> The blind delight of being, ready still
> To enter life on life and see them through.

Wilbur saves his blank verse for special occasions, often for longer poems, like "The Mind-Reader" or "Lying," which propound and elucidate large human experiences. In "The Reader," the challenge, splendidly met in my judgment, is to enter the mind of a beloved without violating it by simplifying or sentimentalizing. Rather the approach to "true wonder" (that final word from "The Beautiful Changes" reappears) is effected in lines that make up an original sentiment, something truly found only when the poem has found its end. "It is a trick poem and no poem at all if the best of it was thought of first and saved for the last," said Frost. Wilbur's art lies in bringing us into the presence of the genuine article: "Like a good fiddle, like the rose's scent, / Like a rose window or the firmament," as another late poem, "For C.," ends.

Since the publication of his last collected volume in 1987, Wilbur has produced relatively few new poems, thirty or so, many of them short, a few of them slight as well—one thinks again of Frost and his penchant for brevity in the work of his late volumes. The contrast with such fluent ease, as was revealed in the hundred and more poems that appeared over a nine-year period of his first three books—from *The Beautiful Changes* through *Things of This World*—is patent but not to be regretted. Aside from the steady translation of poems and plays Wilbur has pursued from early on (this volume contains the prologue to his 1995 translation of Moliere's *Amphitryon*) he has also latterly written a good deal of light verse, illustrated by himself. Wilbur takes these poems seriously enough to conclude his *Collected* with 100 pages of them, and he once remarked in an interview that he wished some critic would connect those "playful books with the rest of me." Anyone who reads, say, *The Disappearing Alphabet*, perhaps the most delightful of these books, will be rewarded by one feat of witty association after another, as the poet imagines consequences of each letter disappearing: "Hail, letter F! If it were not for you, / Our raincoats would be merely 'WATERPROO,' / And that is such a stupid word, I doubt / That it would help to keep the water out." Or there is U: "Without the letter U, you couldn't say, / 'I think I'd like to visit URUGUAY,' / And so you'd stay forever in NORTH PLATTE, / NEW PALTZ, or SCRANTON, or some place like that." These efforts are priceless, but in one sense no more, or no more merely, "playful" than the serious books. It's all serious play, as Hamlet, for whom the play's the thing, was perhaps the first to inform us.

After the deaths of James Merrill and most recently of Anthony Hecht, American poetry is left with its one elder formalist master, Richard

Wilbur (no one writing in England bears comparison with any of these three). Yet although his genius as a maker of rhyme and stanza or the sheer inventiveness of his way with words has been conceded, some have found less than appealing his determination to say yes to life, indeed yes to life in America. In an interview he once mildly defended himself from the charge of thinking too well of things: "I have an inclination to be positive, but I hope that in most of my work I'm not a cheerleader for the universe but a describer of how it feels to be in it." In this respect the American contemporary he most brings to mind is John Updike, whose unwavering determination that we were put in the world to pay attention and to give praise has also not elicited unanimous assent. Like Updike, Wilbur thinks of himself as a Protestant Christian, although the moral nerve of his poems is wide and unsectarian.

Readers of this rich volume are invited to test out that nerve by reviewing some of Wilbur's early poems, then turning to the front of the book and reading ones as densely satisfying as "The Reader," "Man Running," "The Sleepwalker," "For C.," and—perhaps the finest of the late ones—"This Pleasing, Anxious Being." For my purposes the conclusion to "Mayflies" provides the right gloss on Richard Wilbur's contribution as a poet: there a man in a forest, after watching a glittering mist of flies and comparing them in their dance to a crowd of stars, suddenly feels himself alone, "more mortal in my separateness than they." The poem's closing lines, however, effect an enormous and gratifying reprieve:

> Unless, I thought, I had been called to be
>   Not fly or star
> But one whose task is joyfully to see
> How fair the fiats of the caller are.

Donald Hall: *White Apples and the Taste of Stone: Selected Poems, 1946–2006*

*H*ere are sixty years' worth of Donald Hall's poetry. In 2004, Richard Wilbur brought out a collection of his poems from the same decades, and Hall now joins him as the two living American poets who have provided us, over an extended period, with oeuvres of amplitude and distinction. Both bring to their poems, in addition to memorable lyric cadence, a critical intelligence that also reveals itself in their prose: Hall's books of memoirs (the most interesting being *Life Work*, 1993) and biographical studies are especially notable. But the resemblance ends there, since Hall's verse, increasingly in recent years, has become relentlessly autobiographical, personal in its focus on the man and those loved ones he has lost—particularly his wife, Jane Kenyon, herself a poet, who died in 1995 at age forty-seven.

Frost once called poetry "a measured amount of all we can say," and suggested that among the things not to be said—subjects to be kept back rather—might well be "friends, wife, children, and self." Hall made the decision, after his wife's death, to keep back nothing and to expose the self in all its buffetings, its sufferings. In "Distressed Haiku" he imagines someone asking about his enterprise, "Will Hall ever write / lines that do anything / but whine and complain?" The question, in its willingness to imagine something other than a pious response to expressions of grief, makes it evident that humor, black as it is, can check the uninhibited flow of sad reflection. Hall's humor can sometimes shock, as when in "Letter after a Year," written as so many of the poems are to the dead Jane Kenyon, he visits her grave in April, the spot having been inaccessible in winter weather. He is accompanied, he tells her, by his dog: "Every day

---

First published in the *Washington Times*, May 28, 2006

Gus and I / take a walk in the graveyard. / I'm the one who doesn't / piss on your stone." He then imagines her asking him, "Where the hell are you?" to which the answer is, "In hell." At times Hall takes a less than uplifting look at the whole business of putting words on the page, especially when the subject is close to unendurable. In the longish and very fine "Letter at Christmas," he steps outside to check the weather and pass on the news to the absent woman; then it is "Time for the desk again. / I tell Gus, 'Poetryman / is suiting up!'"

As a poetry man Hall suited up early, publishing his first book when he was a junior fellow at Harvard and even before that taking an Oxford degree and an active role in introducing the English to what was happening in American verse. He wrote lively essays about his experiences and interviews with significant predecessors—Eliot, Pound, Frost—and turned out at regular intervals slim volumes in changing styles, from tersely ironic to more psychologically open, "deep image" (as it was called) ventures. But it was when he wrote about his own life, especially the summers spent with his grandparents on the New Hampshire farm where he still lives, that his poetry became more expansive and humanly explorative. In a three-part long poem, *The One Day*, he managed to combine Whitman-like range of perception with moments of satiric and passionate anger at what was happening to the American landscape: "Survey, cut a road, subdivide, bulldoze / the unpainted barn . . . build Slope 'n' Shore, name the new / road Blueberry Muffin Lane . . . ."

In *The Museum of Clear Ideas* (1993), Hall showed himself a brilliant formalist, writing a superb poem about baseball ("Baseball") in an ingenious syllabic verse where each "inning" is composed of nine stanzas of nine lines each, and in which the witty and serious are wholly intertwined. At about this time, he fell dangerously ill, had part of a cancerous liver removed, and survived—only to have Kenyon stricken with the leukemia that, after a failed bone marrow transplant, would kill her. The last hundred pages of *White Apples and the Taste of Stone* are about her illness, her death, and the husband-poet's retrospective formulations, musings, and outcries, in "letters" written to her four days, four months, a year afterward: "Your presence in this house / is almost as enormous / and painful as your absence" ("Letter with No Address"). Hall's ear for the line is so strong and delicate that individual poems take on distinctive rhythms, even though their prevailing mode is free verse. (Some of these are handsomely realized in the CD of Hall reading his poems that accompanies this volume.)

Perhaps the most striking of these late poems is "Without," the title poem to a volume published in 1998. It consists of eight unrhymed stanzas of seven lines each, the whole without capital letters or punctuation: "we lived in a small island stone nation / without color under gray clouds and wind / distant the unlimited ocean acute / lymphoblastic leukemia without seagulls / or palm trees without vegetation." It is a tour de force that overall feels more humanly affecting than loudly theatrical. More often the poems are cast as quotidian news items—the weather, gossip about friends, visits to children and grandchildren—sent beyond the grave from the man who remains this side of it. A sequence of them, in rhyme and stanzas, almost explicitly recalls Thomas Hardy's *Poems of 1912–13*, written to his dead wife Emma. "Her Garden" begins

> I let her garden go.
> *let it go, let it go*
> How can I watch the hummingbird
> Hover to sip
> With its beak's tip
> The purple bee balm—whirring as we heard
> It years ago?

But it isn't only the few poems in formal measures that justify comparison with Hardy, since no verse that I'm aware of, written since *Poems of 1912–13* matches Hall's in its exploration of what it is like to live without the loved woman. One of the demands Wallace Stevens put on poetry in his "Notes toward a Supreme Fiction" was that "[i]t must give pleasure." Grim as is the subject of these late poems from a poet's old age, their sustained and sad achievement gives pleasure to the reader while making most contemporary poems look minor, even trivial, by comparison.

THREE

Three Critics of Poets and Poetry

Eliot's Mischievous Prose

*I*n a handwritten note to his copy of Ezra Pound's *Selected Poems* edited by T. S. Eliot, I. A. Richards took up a side of Eliot that greatly dissatisfied him:

> Must "come out" about Eliot's prose. His unfortunate inability to comprehend what he is implying; what he must be taken as intending to assume; the vast liabilities he so often (thoughtlessly? no not without thought but without the right kind of thought) incurs.
>
> The pontification, the impossible claims, the ridiculously too conscious humilities, the gauche misrepresentations of other people's fairly obvious remarks—these things I am persuaded are not in Mr Eliot's mind so much as in his prose style: an instrument he can never keep on the right terms with for long.

At the end of his catalogue of how Eliot's prose failed to produce disciplined thought, Richards, who much admired Eliot's poems, called his prose "an amusing trail of logically incompetent manipulations of bogus information." We may assume from this assault that Richards thought of himself as, on the contrary, a writer of logically competent, disciplined, fair-minded prose whose disinterested procedures were not unlike those of the scientist. If we look at what is probably Richards's most lasting book, *Practical Criticism* (1929), we find such procedures exhibited in its later chapters, which bear titles such as "The Four Kinds of Meaning" or "Irrelevant Associations and Stock Responses" and amount to 150 pages of reflective generalizations from the "experiment" Richards had conducted with his Cambridge students. As is well known, that experiment consisted in eliciting commentary from the students on thirteen poems, untitled and undated, names of the poets withheld. Writing up the

First published in the *Hopkins Review* 1, no. 3 (Summer 2008): 383–402 results, Richards quotes from what he called the students' "protocols," making it clear which he admires and which he does not. This commentary makes up the first half of *Practical Criticism* and is what we remember and reread from the book; its memorability has much to do with Richards's willingness to cultivate a humorously ironic tone in his remarks about the students' contributions. Such a tone is almost completely absent from the sober, "scientific" manner of the book's second half.

Without attempting to refute his enumerations of why Eliot's prose is faulty, we can at least entertain the idea that Richards's own prose is most rewarding when he allows himself some of the unscientific play he found so annoying in Eliot. Since I am convinced that Eliot's greatness as a critic is inseparable from the style in which his prose operates, I want to take up some examples of that style from reviews, essays, and other commentary that have never been collected between hard covers. Even sympathetic readers of the poet may know relatively little about the seven hundred or so items that remain uncollected or unpublished, and my endeavor is spurred by a recent announcement that Eliot's publisher, Faber, in collaboration with the Johns Hopkins University Press in this country, are projecting a seven-volume edition of his complete prose, supervised by Ronald Schuchard, a first-rate scholar and critic.

Most of the following collections of prose have been available since before and after Eliot's death: *The Sacred Wood* (1920) and *Selected Essays* (1932) were and are still the major ones through which he made his enormous impact. *The Use of Poetry and the Use of Criticism* (1933), his Norton lectures at Harvard, was followed by another series of lectures given at the University of Virginia and published as *After Strange Gods* (1934). Eliot never reprinted the latter, probably because of its infamous remark about "free-thinking Jews" being dangerous to a traditional society. *On Poetry and Poets* (1957) gathered up some fine essays on individual writers—Samuel Johnson and Byron, Milton and Yeats—plus a number of salient reflections on poetry, in particular "Poetry and Drama" and "The Three Voices of Poetry." A posthumous collection, *To Criticize the Critic*, appeared in 1965. Eliot's social and political thought are to be found in *The Idea of a Christian Society* and *Notes towards the Definition of Culture*, books that have remained in print while exerting little influence. In 1994 Ronald Schuchard introduced and edited with generous commentary Eliot's 1925 Clark Lectures at Cambridge and his Turnbull lectures at Johns Hopkins. This volume, *The Varieties of Metaphysical Poetry*, set a standard for editorial scrupulousness that the promised *Complete Prose* will strive to emulate.

I shall describe briefly some high spots in the uncollected prose, aware of having doubtless missed out on other interesting material, pieces which, in Faber's announcement, "remain scattered in numerous libraries and institutional collections around the world." Of the uncollected material I'm aware of, most appealing are the pieces that appeared in two English periodicals, *The Egoist* (1917–18) and *The Athenaeum* (1919). Only a very small portion of these found its way into Eliot's published collections. In 1919 he began reviewing anonymously for the *Times Literary Supplement*, there producing his most famous essays—those on Ben Jonson, Dryden, Marvell, Blake, Swinburne—which appeared in *The Sacred Wood* and *Selected Essays*. Entirely uncollected are the London Letters he wrote for the American magazine *The Dial* (1922) and, in a similar vein of cultural commentary, his many items signed and unsigned about the state of things in London and elsewhere as they appeared in his magazine *The Criterion* beginning in 1922.

In his excellent chapter on Eliot's criticism in *The Invisible Poet*, Hugh Kenner laid great stress on the anonymity provided by reviewing for the *TLS* as central to Eliot's daring brilliance as a critic. Kenner believes that after about 1925, when Eliot had become a recognized big name, his criticism became less vital. While it is true that Eliot would never surpass the essays mentioned above—those written anonymously for the *TLS*—Kenner's explanation may be too simple. It doesn't give sufficient credit to the signed, earlier pieces in *The Egoist* and *The Athenaeum*, and it doesn't explain why the anonymous pieces he continued to write for the *TLS* are less weighty than the great ones of 1920–21. It is a fact that after *The Waste Land* appeared in 1922 and he became a literary power, Eliot was solicited by a wide variety of periodicals both English and American, such as, among others, *The Dial, Books and Bookmen, Nation and Athenaeum, Vanity Fair, Time and Tide, The Listener*, above all *The Criterion*—thus the *TLS* became just another place where he appeared. But it is certainly the case that as, in Kenner's phrase, the invisible poet and critic turned into a highly visible and extremely influential one, Eliot became more wary and circumspect in his pronouncements. There is, notwithstanding, valuable uncollected work appearing in the later 1920s and early 1930s. Foremost are twelve brief talks he delivered over the BBC and published in *The Listener* in 1929–30. Partly the fruits of his Clark Lectures, they take up various aspects of English writing in the late sixteenth and early seventeenth centuries. In 1931 he gave three further BBC talks, again published in *The Listener* and collected in a small volume published by an obscure American press (Terence and Elsa Holliday). This volume, *John Dryden: The Poet, The Dramatist, The Critic* has been unavailable for decades except in good libraries.

At least since Randall Jarrell's tribute to Eliot in his 1962 lecture at the National Gallery in Washington, "Fifty Years of American Poetry," we knew that Eliot as poet was a very different figure from the devotee of various causes he championed: Classicism, Orthodoxy, Marvellian Wit (tough reasonableness beneath slight lyric grace). Instead of a poet who had effected a total severance between the man who suffered and the artistic creation, Jarrell, in the form of an enormous, disbelieving question, proposed a quite different Eliot:

> Won't the future say to us in helpless astonishment: "But did you actually believe that all these things about objective correlatives, classicism, the tradition, applied to *his* poetry? Surely you must have seen that he was one of the most subjective and daemonic poets who ever lived, the victim and helpless beneficiary of his own inexorable compulsions, obsessions?"

Although it would be mistaken to claim that such a wide divergence between truth and myth is to be found in Eliot the critic as well, there is more wildness, more anarchy, more sheer mischief in his prose writings than has been charted by those who see him as the steely-eyed scourge of Romanticism, the spokesman for all that is sane and orderly in the English tradition. As Graham Hough pointed out some time ago in his searching essay "The Poet as Critic," Eliot admitted in "The Three Voices of Poetry" that his poetry had always been, in Hough's words, "radically dependent on unconscious and uncontrollable processes." To some extent this was also true of his criticism, which in its early manifestations depended much upon serendipitous opportunities to review books for *The Egoist, The Athenaeum,* and *TLS.* The results, when some were gathered together in hard covers, made the whole operation look more systematic and planned than in fact it was. Hough also admired what he called, particularly with respect to the early reviews, a pervading quality of "intellectual charm." "Intellectual" may not be quite the adequate word for a manner that is by turns sly and feline, then suddenly revelatory in the occasional sentence that seems to have popped out from nowhere. A head-shaking at human—especially English—literary folly alternates with the equivalent of practical jokes, of which in his later employment at Faber he was a great practitioner. In *The Invisible Poet* Kenner drew our attention to the letters Eliot wrote to *The Egoist,* full of preposterous sentiment that supposedly issued from British worthies with names and addresses like Charles Augustus Conybeare, The Carlton Club, Liverpool. The poetic sensibility that was indulging itself in the obscene "King Bolo" poems he shared with Pound and Wyndham Lewis, or the later humorist of *Old Possum's Book of Practical Cats* who composed a poem beginning "How unpleasant to meet Mr. Eliot," must have enjoyed writing prose in which he could say extravagant things and get paid for saying them. I don't mean to imply that Eliot as critic was frivolous or given to the trivial; rather that, as his rival Robert Frost liked to claim about himself, "I am never more serious than when joking."

"Joking" sounds much too loud and merry for the kind of humor in Eliot's reviews from these years. In one of them he has at hand an anthology of sixteen contemporary poets, and he places it in a context of three older generations of what he calls "verse-producing units":

> The first, the aged, represented by the great name of Hardy, but including several figures in process of oblivesence; the middle-aged, including Mr Yeats and a small number of honored names; the ageing, including the Georgian poets and the curious shapes of Mr Eliot and Mr Pound: all these ages have already lined their nests or dug their graves. We could, at will, pronounce a fitting obituary over any one of these writers except the first mentioned.

In *Lives of the Modern Poets* I wrote about this paragraph,

> One is struck by the civilized humor tending toward mordancy,
> expressing itself sharply in particulars of diction and idiom; as in
> choosing an automaton-like phrase, "Verse-producing units," to
> neutralize the creative pretensions of all these poets: or "oblives-
> ence," imparting a suavely gentle air of decline to the "aged"; or
> "ageing" as a mock-weary epithet for himself and Pound (both in
> their early thirties) and with a nod to the Georgian poets whom
> Eliot mocks elsewhere and of whom everyone (such is the air) is
> by now tired. Finally there is the one-two punch of yoking these
> "units" together, all of them having "lined their nests or dug their
> graves," and the concluding boast about how the reviewer could
> write an obituary for any of them, except of course—in a grace-
> ful bow—Hardy, the first mentioned. The surface of this prose
> is so engaging and resourceful, the reader feels so flattered to be
> addressed in such a knowingly urbane way, that he is unlikely to
> have much interest in disputing Eliot's distinctions, even when they
> are more disputable than the ones brought forth here.

Eliot's criticism in the years 1917–19 is mainly a dissolvent of various
terms and assumptions that other writers have too credulously invested
in. His skeptical and astringent humor is directed at any sort of literary
writing—creative or critical—that has emanated from minds more il-
lusioned and less knowing than his own. In one of his earliest *Egoist* pieces
in October 1917, the second of three "Reflections on Contemporary
Poetry," he introduced a distinction he would elaborate two years later
in "Tradition and the Individual Talent." He is comparing the poems of
his London contemporary, Harold Monro, with those of a French poet,
Jean de Bosschère. Monro's poems, Eliot writes, seek to present human
emotions by decorating them in thoughts and images; De Bosschère, by
contrast, "is an intellectual by his obstinate refusal to adulterate his poetic
emotions with human emotions." De Bosschère aims not to tell us how
we feel about a situation, "but how it is." His "austerity is terrifying"; his
direct aim at "emotions of art," rather than human emotions, sometimes
issues in "an intense frigidity which I find altogether admirable." We

recall that when Eliot wrote this and similar pronouncements in praise of austerity, frigidity, poetic rather than human emotions, he was undergoing marital chaos, miserable health, and exhausting work that made him feel, as he put it in a letter, that he was living in a novel by Dostoyevsky rather than one by Jane Austen. The aims of art as against the claims of life he would formulate in memorable sentences from the "Tradition" essay:

> Poetry is not a turning loose of emotion, but an escape from emotion; it is not the expression of personality, but an escape from personality. But, of course, only those who have personality and emotions know what it means to want to escape from those things.

When the American poet John Gould Fletcher read the opening chapter of *The Sacred Wood* ("The Perfect Critic"), he found it insufficiently generous to the claims of emotion. Eliot wrote Fletcher back that he would not deny the importance of emotion, but that he often found it "present to me when other people find only 'frigidity.'"

The sentence is typically Eliot in that it is both serious and humorous—a trace of mischief is surely visible. At about the same time Frost declared in a letter that humor was the "most engaging cowardice," a "form of guardedness" that kept "some of my enemy in play far out of gunshot." The "play" in Eliot sentences is not without its aggressive component, as when in a review of an anthology of recent poetry he ends a paragraph by stating, innocently, "Rupert Brooke is not absent." He then composed a letter to *The Egoist* by a presumably surprised woman who had taken offense at this abrupt dismissal of Brooke:

> Brooke's early poems exhibit a youthful exuberance of passions, and an occasional coarseness of utterance, which offended finer tastes; but those were but dross which, as his last sonnets show, was purged away (if I may be permitted the word) in the fire of the recent Ordeal which is proving the well-spring of a Renaissance of English poetry.

It was signed Helen B. Trundlett, Batton, Kent, and its mock daring parenthetical apology ("if I may be permitted the word") marks it as an Eliotic spoof.

Sometimes a sentence of his has to be read twice in order to catch the dismissive thing being said, as when, in the beginning of a review of a certain Guy Rawlence, author of *Covent Garden, and Others*, Eliot observes, "One is annoyed with him for not having rewritten the small book," as if it were merely annoying of poor Rawlence to overlook such a crucial matter. From Alec Waugh's poems Eliot quotes some undistinguished lines and announces that "Mr. Waugh is said to be very young, and to have written a novel. That is a bad beginning, but something might be made of him." The list of such *mots* could be extended, and if the habit of facetiousness seems no more than something to be deplored as the arrogance of a young reviewer feeling his oats, it can also indicate something deeper, what Wyndham Lewis in *Tarr* called "the curse of humor," something its owner couldn't get rid of if he tried.

Eliot's ironic humor is dry enough to exclude readers who if asked would insist that of course they had a good sense of humor. A related exclusiveness shows up in odd ways at unexpected moments in the early criticism, perhaps the most surprising of which occurs in a review of a book by George Saintsbury on the nineteenth-century French novel. Titled "Beyle and Balzac," it is dedicated partly to making the highest claims for Stendhal and Flaubert as opposed to Balzac. We may speak, Eliot writes, about how Balzac unites imagination with observation, carrying us—though not profoundly—through the pages of *Cousin Bette*. On the other hand, and with reference to *Le Rouge et le Noir*:

> It is impossible to say that certain scenes between Julien and Mathilde de la Mole are a union of imagination, etc; they go too deep for that. Stendhal's scenes, some of them, and some of his phrases, read like cutting one's own throat; they are a terrible humiliation to read, in the understanding of human feelings and human illusions of feeling that they force upon the reader.

This is extraordinary for the way it suggests a disturbing depth of feeling in the critic, which we (at least this reader) can't begin to lay claim to. What *are* those scenes in Stendhal that demand to be read in the extreme way Eliot reads them? And how do they produce the "terrible humiliation" he says they produce? If, as he claims, "Beyle and Flaubert strip the world;

and they were men of far more than the common intensity of feeling, of passion," then can readers like the rest of us rise only to a common intensity—something a good deal less than stripping the world as Eliot says Stendhal does?

In a less extreme way, reviewing the letters of J. B. Yeats as edited by Pound, Eliot concludes by quoting some sentences that could, he suggests, be said of the man who wrote them:

> The solitary has charm whereas the companionable compels his followers. When the companionable says I am your friend and will help you, or to a girl that he loves her, his voice does not penetrate so deeply and so touchingly as when the solitary speaks.

So much for the penetration of the merely companionable person like you or me (or Balzac?). Something of a similar exclusivity is revealed in one of his most surprising turns of pronouncement in a review of a volume of Kipling's. After various fertile and unobvious comparisons of the writer with Swinburne, with Tennyson, with Joseph Conrad, Eliot concludes with this consideration of Kipling's audience:

> It is wrong, of course, for Mr. Kipling to address a large audience; but it is a better thing than to address a small one. The only better thing is to address the one hypothetical Intelligent Man who does not exist and who is the audience of the Artist.

Eliot never said this again; it was something that overtook him at the end of a review. If for a second at the opening of it we pride ourselves on being on the side of "minority" art, we immediately stand corrected when told that addressing a large audience, wrong as it is, is better than addressing a small one. Who would be bold enough to translate this pronouncement into more easily available terms? How enlivening but difficult it is to summon up this Intelligent Man who does not exist? Graham Hough's phrase "intellectual charm" as a way of taking Eliot's temperature in these early pieces is as good as any, as long as we don't try to say exactly what that means.

After the First World War, in 1921, the year in which appeared his seminal essays on Marvell, Dryden, and the Metaphysical Poets, Eliot introduced himself to an American audience in *The Dial*, where *The Waste Land* would appear the following year. He did this through a series of London Letters in which he reported on the state of things, cultural and otherwise, in England. The manner in which he conducted himself in these relaxed expatiations was in some ways a continuation of the dead-pan humor of the *Egoist* and *Athenaeum* pieces, but, less tethered to a particular book or writer, the prose's effect was more purely an independent creation. Here is part of the first paragraph of the letter of July 1921:

> The vacant term of wit set in early this year with a fine hot rainless spring; the crop of murders and divorces has been poor compared with that of last autumn. . . . Einstein the Great has visited England, and delivered lectures to uncomprehending audiences, and been photographed for the newspapers smiling at Lord Haldane. We wonder how much that smile implies; but Einstein has not confided its meaning to the press. He has met Mr. Bernard Shaw, but made no public comment on that subject. Einstein has taken his place in the newspapers with the comet, the sun-spots, the poisonous jellyfish and octopus at Margate, and other natural phenomena. Mr. Robert Lynd has announced that only two living men have given their names to a school of poetry: King George V and Mr. J.C. Squire. A new form of influenza has been discovered which leaves extreme dryness and a bitter taste in the mouth.

The innocent juxtapositions, or rather the sequence of sentences that are and are not sequential—from Einstein to Bernard Shaw to the poisonous jellyfish and the discovery of a new form of influenza—must have caused some readers new to the writer to wonder exactly what was going on in these communicated "facts" about London, 1921. Never did Eliot put himself forth as more unillusioned, weary (or mock-weary) of the spectacle of human follies and wishes, than in these bulletins. "The man who is tired of London is tired of life," Samuel Johnson's dictum, is all too resolute for the tone Eliot captured in a paragraph such as the above.

You would not guess, from the enervated, thoroughly-small-and-dry atmosphere of the London Letters, that their author was being an extremely productive figure on a number of fronts. In January 1922 he returned from his three-month visit to the clinic in Lausanne, had accepted Pound's excisions and revisions of the *Waste Land* manuscript, and was preparing to launch *The Criterion*, where *The Waste Land* would be published in England. In April 1922 he began a London Letter by saying that, after his time away, he found London unchanged, "the same things one liked, the same things one detested, and the same things to which one was indifferent." He decided to contemplate the particular "torpor" that struck him on becoming again a citizen of London, and ascribed it to English provinciality, the complacent belief that English literature was already so good that adventure and experiment were too risky. Such "torpid indifference" distinguished London negatively from other cities, which as they decayed "extend a rich odour of putrefaction; London merely shrivels, like a little bookkeeper grown old."

Dispiritedly, or such is the pose, he considers an anthology of contemporary American poets edited by Louis Untermeyer. In this he fails to find "one or two of the writers who interest me most" (they are unnamed) and finds in those present the same "commonplace and conventionality" as is present in current English poets. One by one he ticks them off—Sandburg, Vachel Lindsay, Edgar Lee Masters, Amy Lowell, eventually arriving at Frost, at which point the letter doubles back on itself by alluding to the condition with which it began:

> Mr. Frost seems the nearest equivalent to an English poet, specializing in New England torpor; his verse, it is regretfully said, is uninteresting, and what is uninteresting is unreadable, and what is unreadable is not read. There, that is done.

Although he makes a serious mistake about Frost, the really irritating thing here is the tone: the passive voice excusing itself as it performs an unpleasant task; the pained sigh of relief at the end. It represents, I should say, some extreme of cultivated, yawning insolence, and would provide food for despisers of Eliot did they but know of the item tucked away in a never-republished London Letter. The only claim that might be made for it is that as insolence it is absolutely distinctive: no one but Eliot would have been capable of it.

The urbane spectator of human foibles, a persona developed in the London Letters, made many appearances in the Commentaries, signed and unsigned, Eliot wrote for *The Criterion* during his editorship at that magazine. Usually his observations were directed at things going on in England, particularly in London, and special note was taken of the fate of various churches condemned to disuse and dereliction. The most vividly amusing of these is a commentary of January 1928, the year after Eliot had entered the Anglican church. In it he addresses himself to the "problem" of Westminster Abbey, "particularly the fear that available space for interring great men will soon be exhausted (if, that is, we go on producing great men at the present alarming rate)." He is skeptical of plans for extending the space, and also points out that the Abbey was designed originally as a church, not a Pantheon. He then cocks a wary eye at the fact that, increasingly, the great men memorialized were not only not Church of England but had dissociated themselves from any communion, and he asks, "why should great men be buried in a church of which they are not members?" The concluding paragraph proposes a brilliant solution to the whole difficulty:

> Fortunately, there is a way out, which has just occurred to us, and which is both more practical and more sensational than anything the newspapers have thought of yet. The French have a poor little Pantheon at the end of the Rue Soufflot in Paris. Let us have one six times the size, and prove that we have six times as many great men. Some piece of waste ground could be provided, near London (Wembley would be a good spot, if it is not engrossed by greyhound courses; and the greyhounds would be an attraction). Our Pantheon should be built of course of reinforced concrete, with statuary by Frampton. But let this monument for the World's Finest Pantheon be set on foot at once, so that the edifice may be ready for Mr. Bernard Shaw, and Mr. H.G. Wells, and the Dean of St. Paul's.

I have no doubt Eliot was troubled by the fact that Westminster Abbey was both a church and a tourist attraction (patronized by visiting Americans), but his "solution" turns the whole matter into farce by building a creative fantasy that becomes increasingly bizarre as it develops. After the "piece of waste ground," currently put to no good use, has been activated in Wembley, the possible difficulty caused by the dog races quickly becomes an asset to tourists—"the greyhounds would be an attraction." Tilting at what passes for great men in the modern world—Shaw, Wells, and Dean Inge are always favorite targets for Eliot's condescension—he puts a crown on the whole edifice of reinforced concrete. Satire is deliberately unfair, said Eliot's friend Wyndham Lewis; Eliot is quite deliberate and ingenious about his unfairness, and we may think of Jonathan Swift.

In selecting for inspection sentences and paragraph from "early" Eliot prose, I may be laying disproportionate emphasis on his performances as an ironist, a satirist, while paying insufficient attention to his ideas and principles, his "positive" contributions as a literary and cultural critic. Yet since matters of "content" in Eliot have received more attention than the manner of style, I attempt to redress the balance. The fact that Eliot never reprinted the bulk of his early writing (he did include "Reflections on *vers libre*," one of his most humorous ventures, in *To Criticize the Critic*, but that was the exception) probably meant that he thought them slighter efforts than the pieces collected in *The Sacred Wood* and *Selected Essays*. It may also have been that after his conversion in 1927, he looked somewhat more severely on youthful mischief. At any rate the writings he produced at the end of the 1920s and early '30s are contemporaneous with "Ash-Wednesday," with its parenthetical question "(Why should the aged eagle stretch its wings?)." The prose equivalent of this resigned posture seeks to inform and direct a reader, rather than shake him up, and is accordingly mainly devoid of fireworks and mock heroics.

But there is an easier, less speculative answer to this question about Eliot's changed manner, and it has to do with the medium he employed. Both the eleven talks he gave in 1929–30 on Renaissance and early seventeenth century writers, and the three talks on Dryden in 1931, were delivered over the BBC and published in its organ, *The Listener*. The aim of each talk was to address something like the general listener, no specialist in Renaissance writers or in Dryden, but ready to be informed. The sort of teasing that Eliot liked to do in the early pieces and the London Letters was to be avoided in favor of something altogether more straightforward.

He succeeded admirably in adapting his style to the possibilities of a still relatively untried medium of communication. These expository talks, very much pitched at an introductory though not simplified level, were undeniably enhanced by Eliot's drawing upon his experience of giving extension lectures in London and elsewhere fifteen or so years previously. Unlike these earlier lectures, Eliot knows nothing of the individuals in his radio audience, so must address something like, to modify an earlier formulation, the Intelligent Man who does not exist but is the audience for the lecturer. For example, in "The Genesis of Philosophic Prose: Bacon and Hooker," Eliot begins by apologizing for the forbidding sound of his title, then surveys in an opening paragraph some of the chief prose writers who flourished at the end of Elizabeth's reign and the beginning of the seventeenth century. Some of these he has discussed in earlier lectures: the lively prose of the Tudor translators; the popular journalism of Greene, Dekker, and Nashe; the prose of the great dramatist Ben Jonson ("the most intelligent man of his time") and of Shakespeare, whose unique prose is unsurpassable ("There is no finer prose than Shakespeare's"). He then introduces the contributions of Richard Hooker and Francis Bacon by suggesting what, if these two writers were ignored, would be left:

> I think that you would find in all of it either a certain boyishness, as in the people we looked at last week, or a certain pedantry and quaint stiffness, as in Donne and Andrewes, or a kind of luxuriance of style, as in Donne and Andrewes and later in Jeremy Taylor, and especially Browne and Burton, all of which are qualities to be enjoyed, but which seem to us antique. Of all the writers we examine, Bacon and Hooker seem to me among the most modern. That they are the fathers of modern philosophy and theology respectively is not the point with which I have to deal: my point here is that they are the fathers of the modern abstract style. We do not all study philosophy, but we must all make use of a kind of writing which these two men made possible; make use of it, I mean, either when we write or read. Any kind of argument, legal, political, or general; any kind of scientific exposition or explanation, from the theory of relativity to how to clean a typewriter or oil a motor car, owes something to Bacon and Hooker.

"I think . . . ," "seem to me," "my point here is," "I mean,"—this is the cautious, uneventful style of the patient expositor making a thoughtful presentation of material in the time allotted him. Even if the listener or reader has heard or read the previous lectures, quite a lot is demanded of him: the assumption that he will nod his head, in reference to the preachers Donne and Lancelot Andrewes, at their "quaint stiffness"; or that Sir Thomas Browne and Robert Burton and Jeremy Taylor had "luxuriance" of style that was also (compared to the prose of Hooker or Bacon) "antique." The "modern"aspect of the two central subjects of this talk is brought out by invoking their utility as makers of an argument—from explaining the theory of relativity to instructing one how to clean a typewriter or oil a motor car. It is the opposite of tendentiousness: nothing is declared from on high, as in so many of Eliot's early pronouncements. The effect rather is quietly persuasive—one wants to agree with such low-keyed, modest judgments.

Even as Eliot invites us to look, in these old poets and prose writers of the early seventeenth century, for evidences of "life," the life of his own prose is patent. Except for one or two specialists, no one reads the late Elizabethan pamphleteer, novelist, and poet Thomas Nashe, but Eliot makes a case for why this writer might just possibly be rewarding by quoting a paragraph from Nashe's *Piers Penniless His Supplication to the Devil:* "With the enemies of poetry I care not if I have a bout, and those are they that term our best writers but babbling ballad makers, holding them fantastical fools, that have wit, but cannot tell how to use it." He then focuses:

> But when one becomes a little used to the long breathing sentences, the torrential phrases, and the perpetual surprises of conceit, one finds something more than archaic quaintness: one finds life in this style, a life from which our language can still be renewed.

And he proceeds to make a case for the qualities we look to find in such "old prose."

His 1921 essay on Dryden, occasioned by Mark Van Doren's book, contained a memorable formulation: "To enjoy Dryden means to pass beyond the limitations of the nineteenth century into a new freedom."

Ten years later he returned to the subject more fully in the radio talks on Dryden as poet, as dramatist, and as critic. It is a model of just, perspicuous observation, dedicated to no more and no less than what its final sentence sums up: "But it is worth while to know what Dryden did for the English language in verse and in prose, because we shall understand better what that language is, and of what it is still capable." The essays are mainly written in a manner similar to the talks on Renaissance writers noted above. But there is one extraordinary moment in which Eliot's critical genius shines forth. He is comparing Dryden's *All for Love* with Shakespeare's *Antony and Cleopatra* and is occupied by what it means to use the words "poetic" and "dramatic" in speaking about these plays. To elucidate the tricky matter, he focuses on the moment at the end of the play when, Cleopatra having poisoned herself and died, her maid Charmian (Charmion in Dryden) herself utters last words. In Shakespeare she says,

> It is well done, and fitting for a princess
> Descended of so many royal kings.
> Ah, soldier!

Dryden has it thus:

> Yes, 'tis well done, and like a Queen, the last
> Of her great race. I follow her.

Eliot says that if you take the passages by themselves you cannot say that Dryden's lines are any less dramatic, or poetic, than Shakespeare's, and that a great actress could make much of either of them. Then he asks us to consider "Shakespeare's remarkable addition to the original text of North, the two plain words *ah, soldier*":

> You cannot say that there is anything peculiarly *poetic* about these two words, and if you isolate the dramatic from the poetic, you cannot say that there is anything peculiarly dramatic either, because there is nothing in them for the actress to convey in action; she can at best enunciate them clearly. I could not myself put into words the difference I feel between the passage if these two words *ah, soldier* were omitted and with them. But I know there is a difference, and that only Shakespeare could have made it.

Christopher Ricks, who first drew my attention to the passage, writes that if he had to adduce a single paragraph to prove Eliot was a great critic, this would be the one. To his excellent account of the passage in *T. S. Eliot and Prejudice*, I would add that what generates the special power and surprise of Eliot's writing here occurs at the end of the paragraph: first his confession that he can't put into words (what? Eliot at a loss for words?) the difference made by the addition "Ah, soldier!"; second that he insists there is such a difference and only Shakespeare could have made it. A lesser critic could not have gotten away with this, much less done it triumphantly by making the very inability to put something into words—surely the critic's task—an indication of how powerful is the dramatic and poetic effect, the kind of effect only Shakespeare could have brought off.

These are some examples of uncollected Eliot that will be welcomed back into print as of permanent value. One should add to them the brief but trenchant essay of 1930 titled "Johnson's *London* and *The Vanity of Human Wishes*," later titled "Poetry in the Eighteenth Century." (He would expand some of its insights in his much longer essay "Johnson as Poet and Critic" published in *On Poetry and Poets*.) It is most notable for some remarks about how the virtues of later eighteenth- century poetry such as Goldsmith's and Samuel Johnson's are in part the virtues of good prose. He lays down the following caveat:

> Those who condemn or ignore en bloc the poetry of the eighteenth century on the ground that it is "prosaic" are stumbling over an uncertainty of meaning of the word "prosaic" to arrive at exactly the wrong conclusion. One does not need to examine a great deal of the inferior verse of the eighteenth century to realize that the trouble with it is that it is not prosaic enough. We are inclined to use "prosaic" as meaning not only "like prose" but as "lacking poetic beauty." . . . Only, we ought to distinguish between poetry which is like *good* prose, and poetry which is like *bad* prose.

"To have the virtues of good prose," he concludes, "is the first and minimum requirement of good poetry." This is surely a response to Matthew Arnold's downgrading of the eighteenth century as an age of prose and reason that, for all its virtues, lacked the higher virtues to be found in the Elizabethans, Milton, and the Romantics. Both Eliot and Pound had been insisting that poetry should be, in Pound's phrase, at least as well-written as prose; to my knowledge Eliot was the first to make a case in these terms for some eighteenth-century poetry.

In the later 1930s and '40s, when his attention became more and more focused on religion and its current relation to culture and society, his memorable literary efforts became fewer and farther between, the main ones to be found in *On Poetry and Poets*. In 1937 he gave a lecture in Edinburgh titled "The Development of Shakespeare's Verse," never published but from which significant parts were used in "Poetry and Drama." Near the end of his life he produced a pamphlet for the British Council on George Herbert, who by that time had become just about his favorite English poet. Despite that fact, the pamphlet is undistinguished as criticism. More rewarding, partly because more pointedly sardonic, are his reflections in 1962 on the new English Bible. After producing various examples of its "monotonous inferiority of phrasing" ("sweated all day in the blazing sun" having replaced "borne the burden and heat of the day"), he ends with the following paragraph:

> It is good that those who aspire to write good English prose or verse should be prepared by the study of Greek and Latin. It would also be good if those who have authority to translate a dead language could show understanding and appreciation of their own.

Finally, in a compendium of Eliot's formulations, many of which take their bite from a somewhat acidulous humor, we can note how, in his way with questionnaires, he maintained an admirably skeptical temper. One of his most provocative definitions of poetry, that it was "not a career, but a mug's game," has been preserved in *The Use of Poetry and the Use of Criticism*. Not as well known are three responses to well-meaning and pointless questions from a variety of publications. In 1922, responding to the *Chapbook*'s query about the particular function of poetry, as distinguished from other kinds of literature, his answer was that it "[t]akes up less space," an appropriately space-saving response. When in 1938 *transition* wondered whether he had ever felt the need of a new language to express the experiences of his "night mind" (*Finnegans Wake* was on the horizon), he said definitely not, adding that he was not "particularly interested in my 'night mind,'" but qualified this by disclaiming any suggestion about "other people's interest in their night-minds." "It is only that I find my own quite uninteresting," he concluded, with a most notable use of "only." Finally, in 1949, after *The Cocktail Party* had been performed at the Edinburgh Festival, he was provided with a list of fourteen questions, the final one of which invited him to give "a definition of Comedy which seems to you precise for our time and place." His answer may give the right note on which to end:

> Instead of answering the question, I should like to suggest to you a useful exercise. Imagine that you have just seen the first performance of *Hamlet*, and try to set down fourteen questions for Shakespeare to answer, parallel to these fourteen. Then consider whether it is not all for the best that Shakespeare never answered these questions, or if he did, that the answers have not been preserved.

Hugh Kenner's Achievement

*T*he late Hugh Kenner's (d. November 2003) contributions to literary studies were immeasurable, but I hope here to make a few measurements, particularly of his rethinking of how to think about poetry in English. Those who know his work know it mainly through his pioneering studies of what he liked to call International Modernism, as it was created by Pound, Joyce, Eliot, Wyndham Lewis, and Samuel Beckett. Viewed in this light, his masterwork is *The Pound Era* (1971), the massive compendium of analysis and anecdote devoted to establishing the centrality of The Men of 1914 (Lewis's name for them) and, as focal point of energy in the literary vortex they formed, the galvanizing presence of Ezra Pound. Yet some readers, including this one, have found it difficult to make the enormous investment Kenner has made in every part of Pound's work. For these less intrepid readers it is impossible to see the *Cantos* as always brilliant, to be admired throughout; or to see Pound's criticism—literary and social—as inevitably shrewd, relevant, useful; or his excursions in the literatures of other times and other lands—Provençal lyric, Confucian analects, Greek tragedy newly translated—as excursions only pedants and timid preservers of the status quo could be less than enthusiastic about.

Attempts to grapple with the whole of Kenner's oeuvre bring out one's readerly limitations. Mine reveal themselves most notably in the failure to take up, or take on, his guide to Buckminister Fuller (*Bucky*, 1973) or his *Geodesic Math and How to Use It* (1976). Sections of *The Pound Era*, notably the ones on China, or on Major C. H. Douglas's economic theories, or on the British biologist D'Arcy Wentworth Thompson's *On Growth and Form*—whose "economies and transformations" Kenner uses to describe, by analogy, Pound's transactions with Latin in *Homage to Sextus Propertius*—

First published in the *Hudson Review* 57, no. 3 (Autumn 2004): 383–400 these mainly go past my head. Kenner can be downright intimidating, too much for anyone except perhaps his loyal disciple, Guy Davenport, to assimilate. After all, we learn that as an undergraduate at the University of Toronto he was torn between concentrating in English or in Mathematics, deciding upon the former because (one of his sons has said) he would never be more than a competent mathematician. This particular reader, incompetent as a scientist, is further intimidated by what feels in Kenner's writings like a rich familiarity with physics, with electronics (he assembled his own computer), with "science" generally and particularly. The remarkable thing is that he shows a similar inwardness not just with literature, but with music, fine art, architecture. That he wrote forty-odd columns for the magazine *Art and Antiques* is no more surprising than is his expert fascination with the art of stoic screen comedians like Buster Keaton and W. C. Fields, or his approach to the movie *King Kong* with the help of *Paradise Lost*.

Enough throat-clearing. I can at least recall and describe the impact Kenner made nearly fifty years ago on the sensibility of a graduate student of English at Harvard, circa 1958. In that year Kenner published his first collection of essays—many of them having appeared in *Hudson Review*—titled provocatively *Gnomon: Essays in Contemporary Literature* and dedicated to his friend and colleague at the University of California, Santa Barbara, Marvin Mudrick.[1] *Gnomon* contained a number of pieces about recently published works of Pound's, but what first engaged me was its opening essay on Yeats, in which Kenner put forth the notion that some of Yeats's individual books of poetry should be read as sequentially organized, rather than arranged chronologically or just willy-nilly. To demonstrate, he described the organic continuity exhibited by the first five poems in *The Wild Swans at Coole*, and to introduce that procedure began his essay not in the traditional academic way ("I shall be concerned here to show etc."), but with a dialogue between speakers A and B. In this dialogue, A begins to expound his theory that there is much method to Yeats's placing a poem *here* rather than *there*; after a short while B interrupts him with "Stop, you grow prolix. Write it out, write it out as an explanation that I may read at my leisure. And please refrain from putting in many footnotes that tire the eyes." The ensuing essay does contain three footnotes, not at all hard on the eyes, but unexpectedly witty and arresting, just as was the dialogue that began things. No one at Harvard, certainly no English professor, had told me I should read Kenner; he had been mine to discover, and I was pleased and excited by the discovery.

Gnomon featured useful measurings of Conrad's virtues and limitations as a novelist; of Ford Madox Ford's just reissued *Parade's End;* and of Wyndham Lewis's climactic work, *The Human Age.* It also included a less than reverent look at Freud as he appeared in Ernest Jones's biography ("Tales from the Vienna Woods" was the review's excellent title) and a hilarious survey of nine recent textbook-anthologies of poetry. There were also essays on two contemporary critics, and as a reader brought up to revere William Empson and R. P. Blackmur as consummate analysts of poetry (they had been exalted in Stanley Edgar Hyman's survey of modern critics, *The Armed Vision*), I was surprised, indeed disturbed, by Kenner's less than admiring treatment of them. The Blackmur essay, a review of *Language as Gesture,* began with a flourish:

> Despite his habitual doodling with other men's idioms ("The menace and caress of waves that breaks on water; for does not a menace caress? does not a caress menace?"—p. 204) in the hope that something critically significant will occur, Mr. Blackmur has achieved institutional status among the company, not inconsiderable in number, for whom "words alone are certain good."

There follows, after praise of some of Blackmur's early essays on modern poets, a severe but just critique of his fatal fondness for irritating verbal self-displays. Kenner notes that Blackmur "achieves divinations . . . by inspecting the entrails of his own formulations," points out his penchant for "alliterative jingles" and "compulsive repetition of quotations that catch his fancy," and deplores his "intolerably kittenish" essay titled "Lord Tennyson's Scissors," with its "pseudo-wisdom" toying so idly with quotations as to produce "a sort of thwarted poetry": "His hair-trigger pen, tickled by some homonym or cadence, is free to twitch out dozens of words at a spurt." In a word, Kenner is at odds with the "poetry" of a criticism that achieves its effects through words interacting in a closed system, and is to that degree irresponsible and irrelevant to words on the page out there. This was sufficient at least to make me question Blackmur's unshakeable place on the pedestal I had arranged for him.

As for Empson ("Alice in Empsonland"), Kenner begins his review of *The Structure of Complex Words* with another killer sentence that salutes Empson's earlier *Seven Types of Ambiguity*, even as it distances Kenner from its procedures: "In 1930 William Empson published a book of criticism which had the unique distinction of reducing the passivity before poetry of hundreds of readers without imposing—or proposing—a single critical judgment of any salience." Could this be true? As for *The Structure of Complex Words*, a book whose individual chapters I had found myself starting but not finishing, Kenner asserted that for all the impressive lexicographical feats performed in them the chapters were dull, "because the method is wrong for discussing poetry. Long poems deploy a far more complex weight than Mr. Empson appears to suppose. They can't really be reduced to the intricacies of their key words—it is a little like discussing an automobile solely in terms of the weight borne by its ball-bearings." It was surely possible for an admirer of Blackmur or Empson to take issue with Kenner's judgments, but there's no doubt that judgments they were indeed, guaranteed to shake up previous valuations of each critic's work.[2] The jacket blurbs to *Gnomon* included one by Marianne Moore that went like this: "Hugh Kenner, upon technicalities of the trade, is commanding; and when intent upon what he respects, the facets gleam. Entertaining and fearless, he can be too fearless, but we need him." Too fearless in his undeniable penchant for being entertaining? Whatever Moore mischievously meant, she brought out something essential in the aggressive— though good-humoredly so—posture of Kenner's criticism.

In the months that followed my discovery of *Gnomon,* I looked up the three books Kenner had published in a remarkable five-year period from earlier in the decade. These studies, all of which deserve the overused word "pioneering," were devoted to three of the Men of 1914: *The Poetry of Ezra Pound* (1951), *Wyndham Lewis* (1954), and *Dublin's Joyce* (1956). (I failed to locate a copy of his earliest publication, from 1948, *Paradox in Chesterton*, with an introductory essay by Herbert Marshall McLuhan.) The book on Joyce was a rewritten version of Kenner's doctoral dissertation at Yale in 1950, supervised by Cleanth Brooks; the book on Pound, really the first book-length study of that poet's work, was prompted by a visit to Pound at St. Elizabeths he and McLuhan made in 1948. That summer, Kenner tells us later, working at a picnic table overlooking a Canadian lake, he typed out (on a Smith-Corona) in six weeks what became a 342-page book on the poet, including a substantial section on the *Cantos* right down to the recently published Pisan ones. The shorter book on Lewis—156 fully packed pages—was, as with Pound, the first serious book about that controversial writer.

It is no less than astonishing to note that Kenner wrote these books when he was in his twenties (b. 1923). They show throughout an irrepressible self-confidence in their descriptive and critical pronouncements; one thinks, by contrast, of Blackmur's and Empson's interest in teasing out and exploiting the ambiguities they discover in poems, as well as ambiguities discovered (in Kenner's words about Blackmur) by consulting the entrails of their own formulations. Kenner, on the other hand, from the beginning was convinced that, like the created universe, art possessed an intelligible structure that was there to be revealed by the intelligent reader-critic. His business was exegesis—explanation and interpretation of the structures made by significant artists like Pound, Joyce, and Lewis. It is perhaps legitimate to note here that, although he never addressed it explicitly in his writings, Kenner became a Roman Catholic sometime in his formative years, and his procedures in scouting out the intelligible forms in works he admires are as energetic and untroubled by doubts or second thoughts as appears to be the case with Thomas Aquinas on metaphysics.

A related aspect of Kenner's criticism, evident early on, is its commitment to Eliot's principle, enunciated in "Tradition and the Individual Talent," that "[h]onest criticism and sensitive appreciation is directed not upon the poet but upon the poetry." Tutelage under McLuhan, then under W. K. Wimsatt and Brooks at Yale, could only have confirmed this emphasis; but in Kenner's case it involved a lifelong disinclination (to use a mild word for it) to practice biographical criticism. The introductory note to his Lewis book begins with a warning:

> I had better make it clear that this book is not a biography but an account of a career, and that the Wyndham Lewis that figures in it, not always resplendently, is a personality informing a series of

books and paintings, not the London resident of the same name who created that personality and may be inadequately described as its business manager and amanuensis.

This conviction that a too sanguine acceptance of biographical appraisal would inevitably result in "explanations" of a writer's work that simplified and distorted it comes out most fully in his less than admiring review of Richard Ellmann's biography of Joyce, universally lauded when it appeared in 1959. Needless to say, Kenner never wrote a biography, even as, in later works like *A Sinking Island* or *The Mechanic Muse*, he is adept at placing his writerly subjects in various cultural, philosophical, and historical contexts.

Although, in the opening sentence to *Wyndham Lewis*, Kenner claims that the Lewis of its pages figures "not always resplendently," his standard practice was to assume an imaginative coherence in Lewis's, Pound's, Joyce's, and, later, Eliot's work as a whole, so that even if some of a writer's books are less highly charged than others, they still demonstrate the emerging pattern of a literary career. In a sense then, the chosen writer can do no serious wrong, and although Kenner judges a minor piece of fiction by Lewis, *Snooty Baronet* (1932), to be "a peppy and pointless novel," it also reveals—in the coldness with which Lewis renders a sex grapple between his hero and a woman—"a technical feat," a prose under "better control" than it was in *The Apes of God*, the novel just preceding *Snooty*. Kenner's "holistic" bent in approaching his writers, each of them treated as heroic in his intransigence and audacity, may be contrasted with that of the man he and Mudrick brought to Santa Barbara to join the English department for a year, Donald Davie. Perhaps the leading scholar of Pound after Kenner, Davie, in his *Ezra Pound: Poet as Sculptor* (1964), a still valuable book about the poet, showed a much more mixed response to Pound's writing than did Kenner. For example, Davie found large portions of the *Cantos* indigestible, raised questions about how *Hugh Selwyn Mauberley* did and did not go together, talked about Pound's ruinous anti-Semitism, and in general—while benefitting enormously from Kenner's book—strove to take a more balanced, more qualified judgment of Pound.

Kenner completed his cycle of books about the Men of 1914 when he published *The Invisible Poet* (1959), his substantial account of T. S. Eliot's literary career. This superb book, still the best overall treatment of Eliot's poetry and prose, has lost none of its freshness four decades and more later. At the time it was notable for its commentaries not only on "Prufrock," on "Gerontion," on *The Waste Land* and *Four Quartets,* but on related matters that hadn't yet been explored: like the significance of Eliot's Harvard dissertation on the philosopher F. H. Bradley, a dissertation that would not be published until 1964; or the importance of anonymity (the invisible poet) in the essays Eliot published as a young critic in the *Times Literary Supplement.* Kenner also brought out, as had no one previously, the incorrigibly humorous character of Eliot's temperament, as displayed, for example, in the fatuous letters he fabricated (in *The Egoist*), written under the following names: J.A.D. Spence, Thridlingston Grammar School; Helen B. Trundlett, Batton, Kent; Charles James Grimble, The Vicarage, Leays.; Charles Augustus Conybeare, The Carlton Club, Liverpool; and Muriel A. Schwarz, 60 Alexandra Gardens, Hampstead, N.W. Not only the names and addresses but the tones of voice—from high-minded approval to outrage—are fine comic achievements. Here, for example, is the contribution from Charles Augustus Conybeare:

> The philosophical articles interest me enormously; though they make me reflect that much water has flowed under many bridges since the days of my dear old Oxford tutor, Thomas Hill Green. And I am accustomed to more documentation; I like to know where writers get their ideas from. . . .

The book provides a lively and continuous narrative of Eliot's literary life, combined with exegesis ("Comparison and analysis," the tools of the critic, said T.S.E.) and supplemented by glances at relevant events in the world outside Eliot's head. In the views of this particular reader, *The Invisible Poet* stands at the peak of Kenner's critical work, even as it is less ambitious and wide-ranging than *The Pound Era.*

In the same year that *The Invisible Poet* appeared, Kenner brought out his unfortunately short-lived *The Art of Poetry,* a textbook for students and their teachers in introductory poetry courses. I myself used it once in such a course, but as is the case with 99 percent of such textbooks, it soon fell out of print for good. This is unfortunate, since *The Art of Poetry* is notable for its good sense and for the taste with which poems are assembled to form an anthology of illustrative specimens. It contains pithy formulations throughout that stick in the mind, like this one about taste: "Taste is comparison performed with the certainty of habit." Other formulations deal with the notion of "pace"—"the rate at which the poem reveals itself"—or with the reading of poetry generally: "The first requisite is not analytic skill but a trained sensibility." Kenner had no illusions about how easy it was to train sensibilities. In his mainly dismissive survey (in *Gnomon*) of poetry textbooks, he concluded by wondering about the whole enterprise of studying poetry: "To study Poetry requires an unusually tenacious mind, fortified by a wide acquaintance with poems. It is doubtful whether very many people should be encouraged to undertake such a study." The "elitist" ring of this is likely to be troublesome to those teachers of literature who *know* that reading poetry is a good thing and try to sell that line to often unconvinced students.

The clear model for Kenner's textbook was its highly successful predecessor, to be reprinted many times, Brooks and Warren's *Understanding Poetry*. But Kenner manages to avoid their somewhat humorless and often relentless tone of instruction. For example, Brooks and Warren devote three pages to showing the student why a slight poem of Shelley's ("The Indian Serenade") is hopelessly sentimental, and they point out the dangers of such a state of mind: "We also use the term *sentimentalist* occasionally to indicate a person whose emotions are on hairtrigger. And we also use it to indicate a person who likes to indulge in emotion for its own sake." So beware. Kenner's intervening commentary is typically less rigid than theirs. In an introductory note to the teacher he says wryly, "Much of the commentary has been kept sufficiently gnomic not to impede the teacher who wants to modify or dissent from it." Such a note is borne out by what follows. Every so often, however, he raises a warning finger, as when suggesting that poetry should be "nutritive": "Some kinds of poetry are like chocolates, in individual instances pleasant and harmless, but as a staple diet destructive to the sense, the digestion, and the appetite." This witty admonition is followed by some lines from Tennyson's "The Lotos-Eaters" and an example of late Swinburne, "A Ballad of Burdens" ("And love self-slain in some sweet shameful way, / And sorrowful old age that comes by night / As a thief comes that has no heart by day"). There follows a one-sentence paragraph: "Probably everyone should read enough of Swinburne to get tired of him." (We remember Eliot's declaration that reading the poet gives one the effect of repeated doses of gin and water.) Kenner's remark holds off the poet a bit but doesn't really disparage him. Yes, we say, I too should read enough Swinburne to get tired of him.

What is perhaps most engaging and convincing about *The Art of Poetry* is the way Kenner refuses to encumber "the student" with all sorts of names and terms that will presumably help in reading poetry. He does introduce a few useful ones, like the names for poetry's different feet, but pretty quickly draws back from systematizing by declaring, "With a sufficiently elaborate system of marks and names it is possible to affix labels to most of the things that happen in lines of verse, and construct uninteresting models of them, but the usefulness of this procedure is not evident." Instead he delivers this terse advice: "*Listen* to the way the verse moves." The emphasis on listening is very much a Poundian one, and the master's voice may be detected behind the following tip from Kenner:

> Insensibility reveals itself more surely in rhythmic forcing (or else in the absence of any rhythmic assurance at all) than in any other way. You can tell a live poem from a dead one just as you can tell a heart beating from a watch ticking.

His message is, trust your ear to detect the difference between live and dead work. An unstated corollary is that most of the verse from any period is immediately disposable—is dead—on grounds of its rhythmic insensibility.

Trusting the ear goes along, in Kenner's recipe for alert response to poems, with trusting that the words in a poem mean what they say. In a section titled "The Image," he points out that much of the time we get through swatches of printed matter by *not* bothering about the meanings of words—as in the politician's "There exists a solid argument favoring such a course." But when, for example, Shakespeare has Romeo say "Night's candles are burnt out," we should think of candles. Rather than enforcing distinctions between metaphor, simile, and other specialized terms for poetic figures, he adopts the all-purpose "image" to designate "the thing the words actually name." We are not to think of expression as "a colorful way of saying something rather commonplace," which may then be translated into some equivalent; rather, "The poet writes down what he means. Poetry is the only mode of written communication in which it is normal for all the words to mean what they say."

More than once in his commentary in the anthology Kenner suggests a historical view of what happened to English poetry, his suggestion surely influenced by, though distinct from, Eliot's emphasis on the "dissociation of sensibility" that occurred in the mid-seventeenth century. Kenner's warning that some kinds of poetry were, like chocolates, destructive as a staple diet comes out of a historical conjecture that a relishing of rhythm and sound for their own sake had roots in "the fact that in its period of greatest life so much English verse was written to be declaimed from a stage." This fact he found not to be "wholly fortunate," and indeed, three years previously, he had addressed the fact more fully in a lecture delivered in England to the Royal Society of Literature. It was published in *Essays by Divers Hands* (1958) but never reprinted by Kenner in any of his collections, so it has been somewhat overlooked. Its title, "Words in the Dark," alludes to what he called a poetry of "majestic imprecision and incantation" that originated in the Elizabethan era, more precisely in the great speeches from Marlowe's and Shakespeare's plays. By way of demonstration he quotes the famous speech from *Doctor Faustus* about Helen of Troy:

> Was this the face that launch'd a thousand ships,
> And burnt the topless towers of Ilium?—
>
> . . . .
> O, thou art fairer than the evening air
> Clad in the beauty of a thousand stars;
> Brighter art thou than flaming Jupiter
> When he appear'd to hapless Semele;
> More lovely than the monarch of the sky
> In wanton Arethusa's azur'd arms;
> And none but thou shalt be my paramour!

and says about it:

These words don't make us see the vision, they are a verbal substitute for the vision. What they achieve by incantation the vision, could we be shown it, would, it is understood, achieve directly. What the audience *saw* was the costumed and painted boy; the words however don't encourage it to examine what can be seen, but to dream away from the visible. . . . A "face" is mentioned but it is not shown; we see ships and towers. And while the words evoke hapless Semele and wanton Arethusa, Helen is not compared to either of them, but to a brightness and a loveliness: the loveliness of the monarch of the sky and the brightness of flaming Jupiter.

What this "parable" shows, in Kenner's view, is that these dramatists were engaged in creating "an illusion more powerful than the testimony of the senses," through words that "sound well in the dark."

By contrast, some different verse of Marlowe's shows that dreaming away from the visible is not the only way for poets to proceed:

Now in her tender arms I sweetly bide,
'If ever, now well lies she by my side,
The air is cold, and sleep is sweetest now,
And birds send forth shrill notes from every bough:
Whither runn'st thou, that men and women love not?
Hold in thy rosy horses that they move not.

These lines from Marlowe's rendering of one of Ovid's elegies, lines written 180 years after the death of Chaucer, remind us that in the poetry of Marlowe's predecessors, the "visible" was something to be presented rather than dreamed away from. Such Chaucerian potentialities involved "a close fit between the word and its object and a certain plainness and clarity of sense and definition in the refusal to let every phrase run almost unbidden into metaphor." This last formulation is not from "Words in the Dark" but from Charles Tomlinson's 1989 essay "The Presence of Translation: A View of English Poetry."[3] There Tomlinson describes how he was struck when Kenner pointed out, in the 1956 lecture, that the poetry of Marianne Moore and William Carlos Williams, neither of whom had made much impact on English readers, might seem difficult to ears coming to poetry with Shakespearean expectations. Since,

Tomlinson said, his own poems were being written with the examples of Moore and Williams very much in mind, Kenner's evoking of them was excitingly germane.

. "Words in the Dark" would presumably have been part of—probably a key part of—a historical survey of English poetry to be titled *The Night World*. The book never got written, probably because Kenner had so many competing projects in his head that did get written, also perhaps because his interesting idea about the influence of Elizabethan dramatic verse on suceeding poets resisted being worked up into a large-scale argument. (How, for example, Kenner would have handled the poetry of Wordsworth in these terms is a chapter from that unwritten book we would have loved to have seen.)[4] The essays about earlier English poetry he did publish—the introduction to his anthology of seventeenth-century poetry, *The Schools of Donne and Jonson;* a fascinating account of rhyming in Pope ("Pope's Reasonable Rhymes"); an essay on syntax in poetry ("Post-Symbolist Structures") with examples drawn from Ben Jonson, Tennyson, Yeats, and Eliot—provide glimpses of remarkable insights into certain instances of English verse. But it may well have been that he found the three centuries of poetry between Jonson and Yeats to be more various and ungeneralizable about than "Words in the Dark" had suggested.

It's likely though that Kenner's rather exclusive attention to certain twentieth-century English and American poets rather than to others—often better-regarded ones—has everything to do with his distrust of language running "unbidden into metaphor" and his admiration for the plain style, the clarity of sense and definition to be found in Chaucer and Ben Jonson, in Pound, Moore, Williams, and some of their more recent descendants. In *A Homemade World* (1975), his survey of last century's American writers—the first in a trilogy of books that includes surveys of Irish and English ones—a major chapter of some length is devoted to American poets who are, to say the least, less than household names. Louis Zukofsky, George Oppen, Charles Reznikoff, Carl Rakosi are the post-Poundian poets who matter to Kenner more than what might be called the descendants of Frost, Stevens, or Hart Crane. Among those descendants are the post–World War II generation of vivid individual talents—Lowell, Bishop, Jarrell, Berryman; and the formalist masters,

Richard Wilbur, Anthony Hecht, James Merrill. Kenner's preference for poetry he calls "modernist" (the subtitle of *A Homemade World* is "The American Modernist Writers") rather than what might be called modern / traditional, with its willingness still to risk eloquence in presenting a human dramatic situation, is something of which he is not unaware. On occasion he makes his bias explicit, as when he admits, in the introduction to *A Homemade World*, "There are distinguished bodies of achievement—Robert Lowell's, Robert Frost's—through which the vectors it traces do not run." His study of these "vectors" does not claim to be "a survey nor an honor roll," but his extremely high valuation of modernism earlier in the century means that there will be a falling-off from high achievement into something a good deal lower down. Or so it appears to me the case if (as Kenner does) you ignore Lowell, Wilbur, Bishop, and Merrill in favor of the Zukofsky-Oppen group. *A Homemade World* ends with chapters on these Objectivists and on Faulkner as "the last novelist" whose work shows "the last mutation . . . of the procedures that dominated the novel for many decades." Kenner's references to post-Faulknerian novelists such as John Barth or Thomas Pynchon or William Gaddis are a brief and less than enthusiastic recognition of these deconstructors of the traditional novel. But what, we might ask, of Bellow or Updike or Philip Roth, who write as if that tradition were very much alive? We remember that Kenner's interest in novels focused itself on Flaubert, on Joyce, on Beckett (as studied in *The Stoic Comedians*, 1964, and elsewhere) rather than on Dickens, George Eliot, Henry James, Thomas Hardy: on verbal structures that are comic and satiric, rather than "exploratory-creative" (F. R. Leavis's term) in their tracing of moral issues and human destinies (Leavis's "great tradition").

Even more precipitous is the decline (or sinking) Kenner finds in the Modern English Writers, the subject of *A Sinking Island* (1988). In some ways his most entertaining book, especially in its presentation of different English reading publics at the beginning of the last century, it is also tendentiously and programmatically mischievous, scrupulously "unfair," as Wyndham Lewis said all satire had to be. In Kenner's account, English literature after World War II not only declined, it ceased to exist. Of course there are admirable exceptions, such as Charles Tomlinson and Basil Bunting, the poets with whom the book concludes, but they only prove the rule. This process of disintegration had been going on since the 1930s, when Auden was the rage ("undergraduate callowness merges with unschooled self-esteem"), and the trumpery modernism of *The Waves* confused with the real thing ("Bloomsbury self-congratulation, unreal from end to end, voice after voice finely straining for fineness of perception"). Although Kenner admits in a preface that his treatment of twentieth-century English writers will be "highly selective" (he mentions Ivy Compton-Burnett as an example of one of many "good writers who simply did their job"), the urge to sink the island so infects him as to make his dismissal of or nonattention to modern (rather than modernist) writers blatant, and more revealing of his limitations as a reader than he might have wished. Nonmodernist, un-Poundian poets from earlier in the century fare poorly: Hardy is just barely mentioned; there is no Lawrence (as poet), no Robert Graves, no Louis MacNeice. Philip Larkin is treated as a "portent" of Philistia—Larkin claimed, provocatively, that he didn't know who Jorge Luis Borges was, and Kenner pretends to believe him—and his work is dismissed with the faintest of praise ("Not that his best poems are negligible"). Such grudging admission consorts with other swipes at writers who have in fact pleased many readers not merely susceptible to the whims of fashion. Evelyn Waugh survives, in Kenner's book, on the basis of a single novel, *A Handful of Dust* ("a popular novel for the mid-thirties. Not a great one"). George Orwell does not appear; Anthony Powell's *A Dance to the Music of Time* is mentioned only to hang the adjective "leaden" on it and to claim (falsely) that no one reads it. Kingsley Amis gets a single mention as one of several "anarchic energies" to have gained applause: "(Yes, Yes, Amis; yes, yes, John Osborne; later yes, yes, *Private Eye*)." So much for those of us who thought Amis as good a comic novelist as ever practiced the trade. One wonders how many of Amis's novels Kenner did or didn't read; then one thinks, how *could* the author of *The Pound Era* have any room in his imagination for the Amis-Larkin disparagement of modernism?

But disagreeing with Kenner's judgments is, after a not very long while, a barren occupation, analogous perhaps to disagreeing with Dr. Johnson's low opinion of *Lycidas*, or with Eliot's judgment about Robert Frost ("his verse, it is regretfully said, is uninteresting"). However major a critic you take Kenner to be, and I take him to be a major one, he is like Johnson and Eliot in that he never writes a sentence that does not show a major style, and that includes "sentences" like the one beginning "(Yes, yes, Amis)." So powerful a style can transform a subject we haven't thought much about—the situation of the Canadian poet, circa 1952—into a memorably creative formulation. A Canadian citizen himself and reviewing an anthology of Canadian poets, he suddenly bursts into a dithyramb on what it is to *be* such a thing as a Canadian poet:

> Situated on a great blank semi-continent whose official culture, as verbalized by the newspapers, isn't a congeries of activities but a kind of *weather* precipitated from extra-territorial cold and hot air—from the most exportable cliches of British and American life: British complacency, lower-class caution, sobriety that makes a cult of mufflers, galoshes, and Sunday; American financial enterprise, urban discipline, and satisfaction in the ownership of "consumer goods."

In these (surprising) terms the Canadian poet is declared to be the most "alienated" in the world. No reader trying to wrap his mind around that sentence is, I think, likely to raise a dissenting hand and claim that, say, the Icelandic or Australian poet is even more alienated. The sentence is just one, admittedly minor, example of what Kenner found distinctive in Joyce's fiction, which is "great, as is much poetry, because the language, which does not merely extend the author but transcends him, has gone into independent action and taken on independent life."

This survey of the work of a voluminous critic—32 books and 856 periodical contributions are listed in Willard Goodwin's heroic bibliography[5]—is too patchy even to qualify as a mini-survey. Indeed, two of Kenner's most original and readable books, *The Counterfeiters* (1968) and *Joyce's Voices* (1978), I haven't even mentioned till now.[6] Instead of doing them justice, I choose rather to close this account of an exceptional writer by noting Kenner's alert generosity to contemporaries he found exceptional. One expects (and receives) handsome valedictions to Eliot, to Williams, to Pound, to Beckett, as they enter the realm of what Dryden called, elegizing Mr. Oldham, "Fate and Gloomy Night." But tributes were not withheld from writers still alive, sometimes unexpected ones like Leslie Fiedler or Tom Wolfe or Norman Mailer ("the most style-conscious, the most *literary* of living novelists"). Each of them was praised in the pages of the *National Review* for the tonic wildness that, it might be said, they shared with Kenner. He admired outlaws when their outlawry was conducted with daring and intelligence. In a review of F. R. Leavis's contribution in *Scrutiny*—which magazine Leavis had referred to as "an outlaw's enterprise"—Kenner saluted Leavis as a writer whom it had been fashionable in many circles to dismiss as a bad writer. No, says Kenner, let us rather seek to record the distinction of those "bad" sentences:

> His expository manner—a fascinatingly taut instrument of registration, like that of an *engagé* Henry James, virtuoso of the trenchant, qualifying clause, the ironically deferred climax, the epithet delicately placed between commas—is like all such complex instruments potentially a body of mannerisms, as I think it became in his late book.

Manner only becomes mannerism, as it were, when it is strong and individual enough to be bureaucratized.

Unfailingly Kenner found original ways to eulogize critics who resembled one another only in being each of them distinctive. John Crowe Ransom, he wrote, "exerted more influence on human learning than anyone in this century. . . . He valued the act of criticism because it can be an occasion for the critic's language to be *about* something it can clarify but not subdue." In a more reminiscent mood he concluded an RIP for his old teacher, Northrop Frye, with whom as a graduate student at the University of Toronto he had taken a Blake seminar: "Oh, 45 years back, the final exam for that graduate seminar was graced with a box of chocolates on the table. Norrie thought we'd earned those at least. What we'd chiefly earned was participation in his intelligence." And in a journal few were likely to see, *Conradiana*, he paid tribute to his old friend, colleague, and professional outlaw, Marvin Mudrick, whose essay "The Originality of Conrad" "drew on a rereading of the whole Conrad canon and a good deal of the major criticism. He reread, as he read, with obsessed intentness, filling flyleaves with pencilled codes that helped him retrieve any beauty, any bathos." Titling his tribute "The Examiner's Eye," Kenner ended by remembering old days with Mudrick at Santa Barbara, also their final meeting in August 1986 when, although "he must have guessed he was dying, he betrayed no sign and was genial as of old: Unable to think how I could have spent better hours than the many consecutive ones I spent in his company, I'm grateful to *Conradiana* for a place to light this candle."

More than once Kenner quoted Pound's injunction, directed at Kenner when he visited the poet at St. Elizabeths, to visit the great men of one's own time as a clear duty of one's education. But Kenner added, "it was also part of a duty to such men, who among them comprise the only reason the time, or any time, may be worth remembering, and civilization is memory." I met Kenner only once, and that most briefly, but his work is something the time, our time, should keep remembering.

HUGH KENNER: SELECT BIBLIOGRAPHY

1951	*The Poetry of Ezra Pound*
1954	*Wyndham Lewis*
1956	*Dublin's Joyce*
1958	*Gnomon: Essays on Contemporary Literature*
1959	*The Art of Poetry*
1959	*The Invisible Poet: T. S. Eliot*
1961	*Samuel Beckett: A Critical Study*
1964	*Flaubert, Joyce, and Beckett: The Stoic Comedians*
1968	*The Counterfeiters: An Historical Comedy*
1971	*The Pound Era*
1973	*A Reader's Guide To Samuel Beckett*
1975	*A Homemade World: The American Modernist Writers*
1978	*Joyce's Voices*
1980	*Ulysses*
1983	*A Colder Eye: The Modern Irish Writers*
1987	*The Mechanic Muse*
1988	*A Sinking Island: The Modern English Writers*
1989	*Mazes: Essays*
1990	*Historical Fictions: Essays*
2000	*The Elsewhere Community*

THREE CRITICS OF POETS AND POETRY

1. The Kenner-*Hudson* connection was made to seem ominous, at least shameful, by Irving Howe in his free-swinging essay, "The Age of Conformity" (*Partisan Review*, January 1950). Howe wrote, "When a charlatan like Wyndham Lewis is revived and praised for his wisdom, it is done, predictably, by a Hugh Kenner in *The Hudson Review*." (Howe later wrote for the magazine, so must have had a second thought.)

2. Kenner wrote about Empson on three other occasions, the first being a review of his *Collected Poems*, mainly admiring ("The Son of Spiders," *Poetry*, June 1950); the second a dismissive review of *Milton's God* ("The Critic's Not for Burning," *National Review*, August 28, 1962.) In the latter review, Kenner referred to Empson as "The Playboy of the Western Word," the last word of which phrase a typesetter corrected, thinking of Synge, to "World." In *Milton's God* Empson had called Kenner "the American Roman Catholic critic" and "a spanking neo-Christian." In *A Sinking Island* (1988), Kenner quotes from Empson's preface to the second edition of *Seven Types of Ambiguity*—"Whenever a reader of poetry is seriously moved by an apparently simple line, what are moving in him are traces of a great part of his past experience and of the structure of his past judgments"—and says about it, "That is wise, and exact."

3. Collected in Tomlinson's *Metamorphosis: Poetry and Translation* (Manchester: Carcanet Press, 2003, 1–20). Tomlinson's first American book of poems, *Seeing Is Believing* (1959), was published by Macdowell Obolensky, with Kenner's urging.

4. In a review of Eliot's *Collected Poems 1909–1962* (*National Review*, February 11, 1964), Kenner spoke of Wordsworth's poetic procedures—"their evasions, their deliberate blurs of syntax, their odd meditative substantialitives"—and called him the "first specialist in majestically cadenced not-quite-sense." Could this not be Eliot writing about Milton's verse?

5. *Hugh Kenner: A Bibliography*, by Willard Goodwin (Albany, NY: Whitston Publishing Co., 2001).

6. *The Counterfeiters* contains an especially fine chapter, "The Man of Sense as Buster Keaton," in which Kenner, with the aid of the classic anthology of bad verse *The Stuffed Owl*, shows how one of its exhibits, Cowley's "Ode upon Dr. Harvey," describes Harvey's discovery of the circulation of the blood in a manner so absolutely clear as to be "exquisitely ludicrous."

Donald Davie, the Movement, and Modernism

A s a poet-critic and a thinker about poetry, Donald Davie used the word "Modernism" confidently ("There is no doubt about Robert Graves; no Modernist, he") but did not occupy himself with breaking new ground in clarifying it—his interests were in something other than achieving a good definition. As a poet and critic whose impulses and inclinations as an artist were formative of the directions taken in his criticism, Davie's relation to Modernism can be approached in two ways: either by looking at how his poetry came to terms with, accommodated itself to, or repudiated the principles and practices of modernist forbears, particularly Yeats, Eliot, and Ezra Pound; or by inspecting his voluminous criticism of these and other modernist poets in order to suggest his contribution to literary discourse—his right to the title accorded him by Christopher Ricks as "the best literary critic in the post-Eliot-Leavis-Empson world." My emphasis will be on the latter approach and will begin by considering his relation to the Movement and its opposition—at least in the work of its most famous members, Philip Larkin and Kingsley Amis—to Modernism.

I.

The story begins in 1956, when Robert Conquest's anthology *New Lines* appeared. Davie was one of the contributors, thus becoming however briefly a member of the Movement even as he began to detach himself from the group. *New Lines* was reviewed the year after it appeared by Charles Tomlinson in *Essays in Criticism:* "The Middlebrow Muse" was a lively attack

First published in *The Movement Reconsidered: Essays on Larkin, Amis, Gunn, Davie, and Their Contemporaries*, ed. Zachary Leader (Oxford University Press, 2009)

on the anthology, deploring the "unconscionable amount of self-regard" shown by many of its contributors, and finding it a sure sign of "lack of genuineness." The only good word Tomlinson had to say for any of the poets was to call Thom Gunn more "promising" than Robert Conquest, and to regret that D. J. Enright and Donald Davie should have shown up as "fellow-travelers" in this band of brothers (and one sister, Elisabeth Jennings). Tomlinson found Davie "the least representative chosen poet here," whose recent work seemed to be developing away from his earlier manner—that manner to be observed in his poem "Remembering the Thirties," one of the poems Conquest included, whose "heavy iambic swat" to Tomlinson's ears was too pronounced to be sustained over its twelve quatrains. Generalizing about the poets in New Lines, Tomlinson said "they show a singular want of vital awareness of the continuum out-side themselves, of the mystery bodied over against them in the created universe, which they fail to experience with any degree of sharpness or to embody with any instress or sensuous depth."

Davie responded, in the Critical Forum of the magazine's next issue, to Tomlinson's charge that ten years ago (the 1940s) the average level of poetry was vicious while at present (as in New Lines) it was merely dull. His defense was minimal indeed, claiming that when the poor or minor poetry of an age is dull rather than vicious, then the poetic tradition is in a healthy state. Although he thinks many of Tomlinson's criticisms of the New Lines contributors are just, the "cultural phenomenon they represent as a group" should not be disparaged. This somewhat contorted attempt to say the least for the anthology and its members, of which he was one, is brought out when juxtaposed, as it was, with D. J. Enright's response to the Tomlinson review. Enright called it "second-generation vulgarisation which today passes as healthy literary criticism," and said it "confidently aped Leavisian and Lawrentian gestures, the blank assertion of authority with little behind it except the 'right' phraseology and the O.K. names (including even Laforgue, that old Anglo-Saxon invention)." Doubtless part of Davie's much more pacific handling of Tomlinson had to do with his having been Davie's pupil at Cambridge; more deeply it reveals at how early a stage he had become acutely uneasy in being associated with the Movement writers.

Further items testified to his dissociation from the group, first a 1957 review of Enright's second book of poems, in which Davie found disconcerting an attitude he called "common-mannerism," an element in the Movement particularly to be detected in Kingsley Amis's critical writing. In Enright's poetry it shows itself in the way references to traditional culture, Oriental or European, are elevated only to be torn down again "with snarls of disgust." Davie deplores how impatience with cultural pretentiousness is turning into impatience with culture itself; this he finds "a very ugly phenomenon." ("Ugly" is not a commonly used word in aesthetic criticism and here it rings with moral disapproval.) Two years later Davie wrote a glowing review of Tomlinson's *Seeing Is Believing*, which had been published, with the help of Hugh Kenner, by Kenner's American publisher, MacDowell, Obolensky. Here Davie throws down the gauntlet by insisting that since Tomlinson's models are mainly French and American rather than English, "he refuses to join the silent conspiracy which now unites all the English poets from Robert Graves down to Philip Larkin, and all the critics, editors, and publishers too, the conspiracy to pretend that Eliot and Pound had never happened." He goes on to add Marianne Moore and Wallace Stevens—presences detectable in Tomlinson's book—as other American poets whose work should have altered the English poetic tradition. One could not find in F. R. Leavis any stronger—or is it any more fantastic?—notion of a conspiracy that unites all English poets, critics, and publishers under the same sinister motive. I'm sure Davie did this with deliberate swagger and overstatement, but it is overstatement such as his criticism would continue to thrive on. He hadn't of course then read some future Larkin poems, notably "White Major," about which Barbara Everett would artfully point out their trafficking with Mallarmé. But what about not mentioning Auden (is he or is he not in the "conspiracy"?), a poet who surely did not pretend that T. S. Eliot never happened and who was attacked by Graves for his modernist irresponsibilities? It must have been heady for Tomlinson, reading the review, to imagine himself as single-handedly bucking a conspiracy most recently embodied in *New Lines*.

Finally there is "Remembering the Movement," a short prose reflection in which Davie buried the thing almost before it happened. "Remembering the Thirties" was about English writers from twenty years before; "Remembering the Movement," if it might to the unwary sound like an affectionate trip down memory lane, was anything but. Its major gist is that "we" sold out ignobly to—in particular it seemed—knowing readers of magazines like *Essays in Criticism*, readers of the "high-brow élite" Davie and his friends were catering to. It was those believers in Leavisian "minority culture," Davie claimed, whom Movement poets were all too ready to woo and placate. As with the stance taken in his review of Tomlinson's poems, Davie is here concerned to make out the very worst case that can be made for the tough-minded (so they thought) no-nonsense Movementeers. Not a bit of it, he declares: "Ours was writing which apologized insistently for its own existence, which squirmed in agonies of embarrassment at being there in print on the page at all." "We were deprecating and ingratiating," he charged—as if self-deprecation weren't a perfectly usable human attitude for a poem to display, or as if "ingratiation" weren't basic to the technique of any poem. (I am thinking of Kenneth Burke's useful definition of literary style as "ingratiation.") Davie notes how frequently "almost" or "no doubt" or "perhaps" or "of course" occur in Movement verse, gestures that might, one would think, reasonably occur in poems spoken by an "ordinary" person. Whether such gestures justify the charge of "craven defensiveness" Davie brings against them, and against the behavior these poets showed in interviews and other publicity, is a question to be asked.

"Remembering the Movement" is significant, not as a balanced assessment of Davie's sometime associates, but for its announcing two principles that would figure largely in his later thinking and writing about predecessors and contemporaries in the poetry scene. The first was his linking the self-deprecating "defensive" nature of Movement poetry—its amounting to what he called an act of "private and public therapy"—with the absence in it of what presumably is a real world outside the poet's head: the absence, in Davie's words, of "outward and non-human things apprehended crisply for their own sakes." There is a relation between this homage to the nonhuman and the wish or hope he had expressed three years earlier at the end of his extremely tendentious criticism of the third of Eliot's *Four Quartets*, "The Dry Salvages." This was a wish for—in contradistinction to the symbolist principles on which Eliot composed the *Quartets*—a different sort of poem, "more in harmony with what was written in Europe before symbolism was thought of." The result would be poetry "which stands on its own feet . . . as an independent creation, a thing to be walked round, and as satisfying from one standpoint as another." It sounds as if such a hope were linked with the one, expressed in the Movement remembrance, for "outward and non-human things apprehended crisply for their own sakes." What's interesting is that the two styles Davie hopes poetry will move away from are, on the one hand, Eliot's modernist verse that does not try to pretend Mallarmé or Laforgue never existed; on the other, the revisionist common-mannerism of the Movement vernacular. Did he change his mind over the three years, or is there a contradiction here? Or is it, most likely, that both Eliot's powerful and intimidating achievement, which can't be a useful model or influence on Davie's own poetry, and the Movement verse he is concerned to dissociate himself from, were equally to be fended off?

The other principle, indeed obsession, that announced itself in the essay was enunciated in its final paragraph containing a sweeping extension of the charge of self-deprecation Davie had brought against Movement writers. This charge could be made about the procedures of most English and a great many American twentieth-century poets. It was being practiced blatantly by Auden and Empson—the "it" being what Davie called "the manipulation of 'tone,'" *tone* being placed within quotation marks. Even such a modernist as William Carlos Williams, who tried to keep his eyes on "things" rather than on the reader, was also guilty of, in Davie's strong language, "the excruciating tone of the *faux-naif*," a tone (and this time the quote marks have been removed) to be found in Williams's American followers as well.

When "Remembering the Movement" was collected in Barry Alpert's edition of Davie's essays, *The Poet in the Imaginary Museum*, Davie added a brief postscript: "The occasion for this piece determined its tone. The anger—with myself, as well as with others—is designedly unbuttoned and topical." A curious way to speak about one's anger, as "designedly unbuttoned," suggesting that it was more a matter of strategy than the eruption of outraged feelings. Some years later in an interview, he was

THREE CRITICS OF POETS AND POETRY

asked by Millicent Dillon whether he thought the "personal voice" she heard in his criticism had to do with his being British rather than American. Davie answered by again using the word "unbuttoned." "A degree of unbuttoned trenchancy, sharpness, a frank avowal of a personal reaction," he said, was more common in British than in American criticism, and he had detected in himself of late increasing sharpness and impatience. It is as if the designedly unbuttoned tone had grown into second nature, where it was impossible to distinguish sincere occasional impulse from habitual procedure. At any rate, this matter of tone continued to raise Davie's hackles. "The Rhetoric of Emotion," an essay of 1972 concerned partly with praising Thom Gunn's *Moly* poems for treating inflammatory subjects with coolness, ends in a moment of unbuttoned (designedly unbuttoned?) trenchancy by lashing out at "our fussiness about 'tone' (most baleful and most insular of all I. A. Richards's bequests to us.)" It will be recalled that in *Practical Criticism* Richards defined tone as the speaker's relation to his audience, "his sense of how he stands towards those he is addressing." On the surface it looks as if, forty years after Richards's work, Davie found a preoccupation with tone to issue mainly in "fussiness"; such a preoccupation was "baleful" because of its "insular" propensities, as if to fuss as any poet might about such matters was to convict yourself of being a Little Englander, one who thinks of poems as rhetorical efforts at wooing an audience, rather than as something more admirable, impersonal, done "for itself," whatever that might be.

2.

Since Davie's death in 1995 there has been an outpouring of essays about him by various hands, mostly published in the magazine *PN Review* he edited for some years with Michael Schmidt and C. H. Sisson. Schmidt's Carcanet Press has brought out four important collections of his essays, most of which had gone out of print, and an enlarged volume of his *Collected Poems.* The essay volumes were *A Traveling Man* and *Two Ways Out of Whitman,* collections respectively of his pieces about eighteenth-century and about American writing, both edited by his widow, Doreen Davie. Two further collections dealt with twentieth-century poets: the first, *With the Grain,* reprints his book on Hardy and essays on a number of recent English poets, notably Basil Bunting; the second, *Modernist Essays,* takes up one or another aspect of the work of Yeats, Pound, and Eliot. These last two volumes were edited and introduced by Clive Wilmer, perhaps the critic who makes the strongest case for Davie's achievement as, in Wilmer's words, "the indispensable thinker about poetry of the later 20th century." Wilmer concludes his introduction to *Modernist Essays* by claiming that, for Davie, "the stature of the three great Modernists seemed to him indisputable but, especially in the case of Eliot, he was never quite at peace with them." Of course, one hastens to add, with whose poetic achievement was Davie *ever* at peace? The temperamental sharpness he confessed to in the interview, the trenchancy of personal response at which he consistently aimed, precluded being simply at peace with what another poet had written, certainly when the poets were twentieth-century predecessors whose status as "major" was generally agreed upon. Not totally so of course, particularly with Pound: we remember Conquest's attack on that poet's "bullfrog" reputation, as well as various comic derogations of Pound and Eliot shared by Amis and Larkin in their correspondence. But it was not just these three Modernist predecessors about whose achievement Davie was ambivalent. Perhaps the most unexpected book he produced in his career was *Thomas Hardy and British Poetry,* in the introduction to which he claimed that the most "far-reaching influence" on British poetry of the last fifty years (he was writing in 1972) was not Yeats, nor Pound, nor Eliot, but Hardy—"an influence both for good and ill." Yet even with that warning, a reader like myself who came to the book looking for illumination as to why and where Hardy was a great poet, rather than a far-reaching influence, was disappointed. After two chapters in which a number of his poems are taken up, sometimes briefly and adversely, the verdict passed is that Hardy's "engaging modesty and decent liberalism" was in fact a "selling-short of the poetic vocation." Hardy was not "radical" enough, did not, as a great poet must, go to the roots, and Davie found it unfortunate that so many of his British successors (of whom the Movement poets were surely central ones) followed his cue. Accordingly the remainder of the book took partial, sometimes skeptical looks at Larkin, at Amis, at Auden and John Betjeman; along with sympathetic appreciations of lesser-known names like Roy Fisher and Jeremy Prynne. The finest piece of critical appreciation Davie bestowed upon Hardy occurs not in the book but in a separately published essay—one of his very best—"Hardy's Virgilian Purples." Even there, though, the appreciation was qualified by a later postscript he wrote to it in which he said that Hardy's "European" allusion to Virgil showed that the poet at his best proceeded in a manner not wholly different from Pound's or Joyce's or Eliot's. But in the years since the essay, Davie noted, recent books and essays on the poet were "still impelled by a wish to prove that Hardy provides a viable insular alternative to the international 'modern movement.'" "I am quite out of sympathy with that endeavour," was his ominous concluding declaration. Surely the shaft is most clearly directed at Larkin's championing of Hardy as such an alternative to the "international."

Davie's relation to modernism as it showed itself in Yeats, in Pound, and in Eliot, is discussed by Clive Wilmer in his introduction to *Modernist Essays* and will be developed here. Of the five essays Davie published on Yeats, by far his most important ones were written early in his career, in the middle 1960s, and focus on Middle Yeats—the Yeats of "A Prayer for My Daughter," "Easter 1916," and other poems from *The Wild Swans at Coole* and *Michael Robartes and the Dancer.* Visionary Yeats of the "great" period Davie more or less ignores, except to discuss "Blood and the Moon" as a "fascist" poem. His interest is in Yeats the craftsman who alludes in his poems to Ben Jonson and finds the Renaissance rather than the Romantic poem something to emulate. Wilmer says that in the early essays Yeats is seen from a "movement-ish perspective" and celebrated for his insistence on the importance of craftsmanship. But "craftsmanship" is surely not an exclusively Movement concern, and Davie's best critical perceptions about Yeats can hardly be accounted for by any common aim "Davie and his associates" (Wilmer's words) shared. Rather, as in the following brilliant commentary on "Easter 1916," we see him at his most rewarding when he takes up the poem's third section:

> Hearts with one purpose alone
> Through summer and winter seem
> Enchanted to a stone

To trouble the living stream.
The horse that comes from the road,
The rider, the birds that range
From cloud to tumbling cloud,
Minute by minute they change;
A shadow of cloud on the stream
Changes minute by minute;
A horse-hoof slides on the brim,
And a horse plashes within it;
The long-legged moorhens dive,
And hens to moor-cocks call;
Minute by minute they live:
The stone's in the midst of all.

My ancient copy of Yeats's poems has its margins filled with the attempt to paraphrase that third section. Davie seizes upon the problem—or the marvel—of these lines and comments thus:

> At this point, in fact, "Easter 1916" goes past the point where exegesis can track its meaning. The imagery of stone and birds, rider and horse and stream, has a multi-valency which discursive language cannot compass—and this accrues to these images simply because of the beams which fall upon this poem out of other poems in the same collection. Because Yeats holds and keeps faith in the discursive language, for instance by the sinewiness of his syntax, as his contemporaries Eliot and Pound do not, a moment like this when perceptions pass beyond the discursive reason is poignant in his poetry as it cannot be in theirs, and we do not dream of grudging him the right to acknowledge his defeat and to retire baffled before it, as he does in the last section of the poem.

It may be recalled that "Easter 1916" is a poem the never-at-a-loss-for-words Harold Bloom found "puzzling," although, or perhaps because, it possessed a "clarity of rhetoric" that made it unlike other Yeats poems. Davie's point about the third section is that it marks a moment when "clarity" is precisely not the word for its effect on a reader. Wilmer quotes a remark Davie made in reviewing Hugh Kenner's *The Pound Era,* to the effect that Kenner was excellent in showing "how words on the page, as they come off the page, work upon us as we read." The praise may be directed even more strongly at Davie's own procedures in exploring the question of "What does it feel like to read X" rather than "What does X *mean,* how should it be interpreted." The payoff for such exploration may be seen in his remarks about that third section of "Easter 1916."

But for all the salience of his commentary on Middle Yeats, Davie's real engagement with Modernism over the years can be seen in his writings on Eliot and on Pound. His first book on Pound, still a notable piece of criticism, appeared in 1964 when Davie was campaigning for a poetry that recognized a world outside the mind as real and available to be saluted in language. In his chapter on the *Pisan Cantos,* he quotes the "Brother Wasp" passage ("When the mind swings by a grass-blade / an ant's forefoot shall save you / the clover leaf smells and tastes as its flower") to note that neither Yeats nor Eliot could have written it:

> In fact, what lies behind a passage such as this . . . is an attitude of mind that is incompatible with the symbolist's poet's liberation of himself from the laws of time and space as those operate in the observable world. In order to achieve that liberation the poet had to forego any hope or conviction that the world outside was meaningful precisely insofar as it existed in its own right, something other than himself and bodied against him.

He would extend and elaborate the difference between symbolist and non-symbolist poetry in "Pound and Eliot: A Distinction," where he complicates his usual procedural question ("What does it feel like to read X") by considering how, in the opening of "Burnt Norton" as in many other passages in *Four Quartets* and in "Prufrock" as well, "we have hardly begun reading before we find the poem talking about itself, appealing to the reader with the question: 'So far as you've gone the experience of reading this poem is rather like this, isn't it?'" Whatever reservations about the symbolist practice Davie may have had, his demonstration of how it works in the *Quartets* is permanent criticism, as is his treatment of that poem in the essay "Anglican Eliot." There he presents us with a bipolar poem, one extreme being the symbolist, Mallarméan, musical, non-discursive one; the other, an extreme prosaicism that also aspires to say something about the condition of England at war. Why should a poet aspire to incorporate, or try to incorporate, such tension in a poem? Davie's conclusion is one of his most memorable formulations, as he supposes such a situation

> might come about if a poet compelled by temperament as well as history to school himself in the ironic reticences of Henry James on the one hand and of Jules LaForgue on the other, should find himself wanting to speak to and for a nation which conceives of itself as cornered into a situation which is wholly unironical because not in the least ambiguous. For such a poet (who may be wholly imaginary) I should feel affection as well esteem.

Again, Davie's criticism at its best, as in these remarkable essays on Eliot, gets its energy and audacity from never being at peace with its subject; by always worrying it one more time.

The worrying, of course, went on longest in relation to Pound, through twenty-some essays in addition to the books, and it's not possible here to praise highly enough the interest of these writings, even for the reader unconvinced by Pound's greatness as a poet. Part of Davie's authority as a critic of Pound is his willingness to write off whole sections of the *Cantos*—like the John Adams and Chinese ones—as unredeemable, and although he struggles hard to make the post-*Pisan* "Rock-Drill" and "Thrones" sections more available, the strain is palpable. So even in an address to the converted, lecturing at a London conference on Pound studies in 1977, he refers to "us," the exegetes, "industriously annotating out of Sir Edward Coke Canto 107, without noticing that the English language is in that canto handled with none of the sensitivity that would make those labours worthwhile." This unwillingness to pass off everything in the long poem as masterly distinguishes him from Hugh Kenner, even though Davie acknowledged more than once that serious study of Pound began with Kenner.

At the close of his address to the Pound conference, he rallied the troops by calling the assembly an act of homage to a great poet and also "a patriotic demonstration against suffocating insular coziness," one of his perhaps too frequent hits at Little Englandism. Eight years later, in a piece entitled "Pound's Friends" he insisted that whatever satisfactions and dissatisfactions *The Cantos* provide, and though they will remain caviare to the general,

> yet there they sprawl, a labyrinthine ruin (to put the case at its worst) plumb in the middle of whatever we understand by Anglo-American Modernism in poetry. Anyone may be excused for deciding that life is too short for coming to terms with *The Cantos:* but if we make that decision we thereby disqualify ourselves from having any opinion worth listening to, about the poetry in English of this century.

Here is the Davie "unbuttoned trenchancy" at its extreme, the gauntlet thrown down most provocatively. If in his later years he mellowed in some respects, as in his seventieth-birthday interview when he indulged in a moment of nostalgia for the Movement, he never wavered in his advocacy of Pound. There's no doubt in my mind that the attachment has much to do with Davie's feelings about his own father, and the matter is made explicit in something he wrote at the end of his life, his last word about Pound titled "Son of Ezra" published in the year of Davie's death. He begins with a military analogy, noting that his father was an NCO and like all NCO's both loyal to his superior officer and most fiercely critical of him. Davie speculates that what first drew him to Pound was "the voice of the NCO in his mess: a voice stroppy and irreverent, yet devoted to authority." "It is this voice that offends others by just so much as it appeals to me," he announces, raising the ante more or less to Davie against the world, certainly the world of English letters. In the final paragraph of the essay, he notes its elegiac tone and declares that he would like his own life in writing to be "considered in the light of Pound's." His own best stab at explaining this allegiance "would have to use fuzzy or loaded words like 'heroic' and 'adventurous,' even—or particularly—'magnanimous.' If in my chosen trade I was looking for authority, he more than anyone embodied it." In other words, Davie had something to live up to, "the stroppy and irreverent voice" of the noncommissioned officer he heard in his poetic father, Pound, and perhaps in his real father, the Barnsley-West Riding one.

3.

Having touched on Davie's relations with the Movement and with his three giant Modernist predecessors, what about the critical attitudes he took or did not take toward some of his British and American contemporaries? It would be naive to expect that any poet can assume disinterested or "objective" attitudes toward his practicing colleagues, but Davie's championing or marking down of a fellow poet nearly always emanates from a critical principle he makes explicit. This distinguishes him from such a critic as Helen Vendler who, especially on the basis of his later poems, admitted Davie into the lists of those she has praised but who has consistently refused to formulate any criteria that would explain her preferences for X rather than Y. By contrast, Davie follows the example of Yvor Winters, for whom criteria were everything. There is as well the example of T. S. Eliot who, in *The Sacred Wood* and with Aristotle in mind, spoke of intelligence "swiftly operating the analysis of sensation to the point of principle and definition."

One of his key principles had been announced in "The Rhetoric of Emotion" when he spoke against "the baleful and insular matter of 'tone'" as all-important determinant of a poem's virtue. Five years later he published an important article on Basil Bunting, the first of a number on the poet. In "English and American in *Briggflatts*," Davie sought to account for Bunting's being ignored by English readers of contemporary poetry, just as, he finds, the American "objectivists" like Louis Zukofsky, George Oppen, and Lorine Niedecker are ignored by American readers. He proposes that in England at least, readers "have got used to being cajoled and coaxed, at all events sedulously *attended to* by their poets." For this he blames, in part, teachers in English classrooms who persuade children that reading a poem is "a matter of responding to nudges that the poet, on this showing debased into a rhetorician, is supposedly at every point administering to you." John Berryman, whom Davie calls "at times a very affecting writer indeed," does so "nudge and cajole and coax his readers,

THREE CRITICS OF POETS AND POETRY

in a way that one can be sure Americans such as Oppen and Zukofsky are offended and incensed by." Davie is on the side of those Americans, and the Englishman, Bunting, who share the "wholesome conviction" "that a poem is a transaction between the poet and his subject more than it is a transaction between the poet and his reader." So the good reader is conceived as someone who merely sits in on or listens to a "transaction" that he is not a party to, rather than someone manipulated by suasions of the poet as rhetorician.

I find this a strange argument, and perhaps it should be taken as one (another one) of the extravagant formulations Davie has made throughout his career, with the hope of jolting complacent readers into entertaining a new thought. But suppose we take it seriously and see to what extent it justifies or rationalizes Davie's preferences among his English and American contemporaries. No disputing tastes of course, yet to this reader Davie's seem extremely odd ones, especially in relation to poets he—at least in his criticism and reviewing—has little or no time for. Among his American contemporaries, and as is evident from their names above, Oppen and Zukofsky are given good marks; Charles Olson and other Black Mountain poets such as Robert Creeley receive some attention, respectful if not wholly favorable. Davie's enthusiasm for Ed Dorn, who joined him for a time during Davie's years at the University of Essex, is patent, and he also admires Samuel Menashe. Of poets in the generation that preceded him, he has good words for Winters and Allen Tate and not-so-good words for William Carlos Williams, who should have been in the "good" Modernist group with Pound and the Objectivists, but whose poems Davie mainly can't abide. This we may call the positive side; on the other one—not so much a negative as an underdescribed side—can be grouped the "confessional" poets Lowell and Berryman, to whom Davie's responses were mixed: the sometimes confessional, surely rhetorical appeals of Jarrell and Theodore Roethke; and Elizabeth Bishop, however one would describe her. Then there is the triumvirate of American formalists—Richard Wilbur, Anthony Hecht, and James Merrill—whom Davie completely ignores.

There are different though related ways to understand his relation to American poets of the last century. One of them has to do with the spirit of place. Davie first encountered America, as it were, when as a postwar student at Cambridge he discovered Yvor Winters's *In Defense of Reason*, wrote to Winters, and over the course of reading Winters's criticism and letters, learned, he said, much about poetry, particularly poetic rhythm and meter. A year spent teaching at Santa Barbara in 1958 futher extended his American "side," which would be seriously developed in the ten years he spent teaching at Winters's university, Stanford, 1968–78. Davie's America was very much the far West (he also spent a term in the 1950s at Grinnell College in Iowa); later would come the ten years at Vanderbilt preceding his retirement and move back to England. Except for one semester at Smith College, he neglected the Atlantic seaboard—the New York/Boston axis where so many poets taught and flourished. My sense is that his attraction to Winters's poetry, and later to the very different but equally unfashionable work (by academic "Eastern" standards) of the Objectivists, Olson, and Dorn, had to do as much as anything with an adventurous desire *not* to cast his vote for poets—like Wilbur, Hecht, Merrill, just to name three—who were at peace with old-fashioned English verse in traditional forms, no matter how freshly and inventively they used those forms.

Yet as anyone will immediately ask, how can admiration for Yvor Winters's poems and critical principles square with the seventy-five or so pages that conclude Davie's *Two Ways Out of Whitman*, containing celebrations of Zukofsky, Oppen, Carl Rakosi, Olson, Dorn, with even a friendly nod to, of all people, John Ashbery? They do not square with admiration for Winters, any more than they do with the pages from this volume devoted to rescuing Allen Tate from oblivion. In 1977, interviewed by Dana Gioia and asked about his association with the Movement, Davie rather wistfully looked back and then around him in America, for some contemporary movement "in which variously talented but serious writers clung to their little things in common for a while." He thought that would be a good thing to have happen; it might do something to make the landscape less "eclectic" and might give poets something to focus on. The Black Mountaineers, he said, were such a movement, but that, like the English one, was history.

Davie's eye was able to find no rallying ground in which sense could be made out of the American—or English—poetic scene in the final decades of the last century; perhaps because of this his celebrations of individual talents have something overblown and undercriticized about them. I noted this way back in 1971 in reviewing a volume of essays, *The Survival of Poetry* (edited by Martin Dodsworth), that led off with Davie on the Black Mountain group. I found him to be "advertising" rather than criticizing the product when he claimed that for those poets it would not do to "dissect" specimen poems in a manner of "the graduate seminar class which spends a happy hour winkling out the symbols and the ambiguities from a dozen lines of Robert Lowell or Allen Tate or Ted Hughes." This special treatment, and pleading, was evident in Davie's willingness, in this essay and others collected in *Two Ways Out of Whitman,* to make large quotations with minimal commentary substitute for a more critical presentation of the poet's work. In "Two Kinds of Magnanimity," for example, he casts a cold eye on Charles Olson's poems, "marred as they are on nearly every page by solecisms and gaucheries, by arbitrary coarseness in diction, punctuation, syntax, lineation." After which he proceeds to make the case for Olson nonetheless.

The moral seems to be that when Davie put himself to "positive" appreciation of the underdog, the underappreciated, he denied himself the right to quarrel with the writer in question, as if to say X has enough detractors already, why should I heap on further adverse commentary? But without such quarreling, so important a feature in his criticism of modernist predecessors, his recommendations of Zukofsky, Oppen, and the Black Mountaineers offer little, to these eyes, in the line of pertinent criticism. One finds something similar happening with regard to the Whitman who figures in the title of his writings about American poetry. The title essay, "Two Ways Out of Whitman" pays stimulating and skeptical attention to then recent work by William Carlos Williams and Theodore Roethke, neither of whose "way" in the volumes to hand Davie finds satisfactory. But the only piece that deals with the great precursor directly is the shortest one in the volume, a 1968 *Guardian* review of a selection of Whitman's work edited by Donald Hall. Titled "Coming to Terms with Whitman," that is exactly what this five-paragraph review *doesn't* do—or does only in the most casually assertive manner. For after noting Yvor Winters's charge that Whitman as sage was "profoundly and dangerously irresponsible" (Winters had gone so far as to argue that Hart Crane's suicide was the inevitable consequence of his taking Whitman and Emerson seriously), Davie executes a striking turnabout. Calling Whitman a confessional poet who must be allowed the right to be irresponsible, he notes that articulate British readers of the poet refuse to make this concession, then states in a new paragraph: "We shall have to learn to do so. For reluctantly and with embarrassment I record for what it is worth my own testimony: reading *Song of Myself* in this selection I found myself reading a great poem, invigorating and liberating." He adds that after this "undeniable" experience, his ideas about poetry and morality will have to undergo a change, at which exciting and surprising point the review ends. He was never to return to Whitman again in print, and as for his ideas about poetry and morality undergoing a change, I fail to see that this portentous vow was ever followed.

Twenty years later, in 1987, he began a review of *The Collected Poems of William Carlos Williams* by declaring, "Williams is the most embarrassing poet in the language, surpassing even Whitman." Davie never changed his mind about Williams and was impervious to the efforts of two critics he greatly admired—Hugh Kenner and Charles Tomlinson—on the poet's behalf. Aside from allowing a few early Williams poems to have merit, like "The Widow's Lament in Springtime" and "To Waken an Old Lady," Davie treated Williams as modernism's Dumb Ox, calling his most famous poem, "The Red Wheelbarrow," a "trivial and self-preening squib"—something that surely needed saying. With Williams, Davie did not need to act as advocate—the poet had plenty of advocates and followers—so was free to provide vigorous and useful demurs and acceptances toward a number of Williams's poems, by way of assessing an achievement more "precarious and perverse" than Black Mountaineers and Objectivists would admit. This, however, does not mean that we need accept his invitation to admire certain of Williams's followers—Robert Creeley and Ed Dorn, for example—more than Williams himself.

4.

Finally let me return briefly and inadequately to this congeries of the Movement, Modernism, and Donald Davie. And to England, the history of whose poetry from 1960 to 1988 he treated in his volume *Under Briggflatts.* This odd and in many ways unsatisfactory book is nonetheless full of interest. In this his last polemic, though he denied in the preface it was a polemic, he proposed to commemorate and promote certain British authors as "however modestly, canonical." He also admits that his judgments are disputable, although he had not come by them lightly. Accordingly I will dispute, beginning with the title. What does it mean? That British poets have written, or should have written, under the aegis of Basil Bunting's poem? Or that *Briggflatts* towers above all other poetry written during the past thirty years? (The latter seems to have been the case, since he would later call Bunting "the master of us all.") For an uninstructed reader like myself who finds that though there are attractive effects in the twenty pages of *Briggflatts,* Peter Dale's judgment that the poem is "tediously dominated by the simple sentence" is incontrovertible. What I should call, without demonstrating it, Davie's overvaluation of Bunting goes hand in hand with an undervaluing of Movement writers—a final putting of them in their place. On the evidence of *Under Briggflatts,* that place in the history of poetry in Great Britain is not a significant one. Messrs Conquest and Wain are mentioned, but not for any poetry they have written. Elizabeth Jennings and John Holloway are absent; so, more questionably, is D. J. Enright except for a tiny mention in a footnote. Kingsley Amis appears once, in the course of Davie's discussion of a Tony Harrison poem whose "combination of formality with coarse sentiment" recalls Amis.

That leaves Larkin and Gunn. The former is acknowledged to be, along with Seamus Heaney and Ted Hughes, the only British poets to command a "public" rather than a "following." (Davie calls Auden and Betjeman "special cases.") On the evidence of his pages about Larkin in this volume, having a public is nothing to celebrate. In the book on Hardy, Davie devoted a chapter to landscapes in Larkin's poetry, with "Water" and "The Whitsun Weddings" as notable examples. *Under Briggflatts* contains nothing comparable, but does contain the following about Larkin: "The career, as distinct from the poetry (some of which will surely endure), calls out for sensitive and searching study." The enduring qualities of Larkin's poetry are nodded at in a parenthesis: evidently the poetry does not demand—or Davie refuses in this history to give it—sensitive and searching study. Why this refusal to commemorate at least by singling out what in Larkin's verse will endure? The answer is, I'm afraid, that Davie sees Larkin less as a poet than as a portent of the English reading public's diminished expectations. If Larkin's subject matter was inevitably "lowering" ("lowering" is a word John Wain used about R. S. Thomas's poetry), Davie cautions that to write in such a "sweetly formal way" and to "set up that way of working as a norm runs the risk of overvaluing a suave melancholy, the poignantly managed dying fall." He adds, "it is a risk to which admirers of Larkin, that poet of very 'lowering' apprehensions, are particularly prone." It seems then that Larkin's public has been seduced by "tone," by a rhetoric that ministers to admirers who were unable to appreciate (although Davie doesn't say this explicitly) the more impersonal, sterner transactions between the poet and something outside him—the nonhuman. In the pages where Larkin figures in *Under Briggflatts*, I find but a single reference (and that parenthetical) of positive commemoration, that to Larkin's great poem "The Explosion."

I conclude with Thom Gunn, with whom Davie felt a kinship. "There is no one of my contemporaries I respect more," he declared about Gunn in a *PN Review* salute on the poet's sixtieth birthday. It was partly their shared admiration for Yvor Winters; partly a matter of their having both taken up residence, for many years, in California. Davie once referred to Gunn as the "scrupulous expatriate," and he would not have minded being so named himself. After Davie's death, Gunn in an interview called him "consistently supportive, very kind to me." But also "very against queers," and Gunn understood him to have said, reviewing *The Passages of Joy*, that unlike Gunn's earlier books, "Davie couldn't admire *Passages of Joy* because it advocated homosexuality." Actually what Davie had said, extravagantly, in the review and in *Under Briggflatts*, was that Gunn's commitment to "Gay Liberation" was such as to alienate him from the seventeenth-century English poets whom he had so fruitfully drawn on in his earlier work. In making "experience" the true test of worth, rather than any anterior moral idea or principle, Gunn had sacrificed "resonances" from pre-Enlightenment poets. But, Davie added, "it could always be maintained that the objectives of Gay Liberation were objectives so obviously just and overdue" that "the

THREE CRITICS OF POETS AND POETRY

sacrifice of such resonances and continuities was a small price to pay." It could be maintained, though Davie didn't exactly maintain it; yet he singled out for praise the "chaste" diction of two poems from that volume, "Expression" and "Night Taxi."

Gunn said in the interview that part of his next volume, *The Man with Night Sweats,* was written to show Davie that "what I hoped he would admit was good poetry could be written out of this kind of sexuality." And in conversations subsequent to the volume, Davie admitted Gunn had made a point. And though, Gunn added, he thought Davie's own point of view was "strangely ridiculous, Davie was not a ridiculous man—he was a good thinker and a good critic." In Gunn's final volume, *Boss Cupid,* published five years after Davie's death, there is a poem to his friend that seems the appropriate place to end:

> *To Donald Davie in Heaven*
>
> I was reading Auden—But I thought
> you didn't like Auden, I said.
> Well, I've been reading him again,
> and I like him better now, you said.
> That was what I admired about you
> your ability to regroup
> without cynicism, your love of poetry
> greater
> than your love of consistency.
>
> As in an unruffled fish-pond
> the fish draw to whatever comes
> thinking it something to feed on
>
> there was always something to feed on
> your appetite unslaked
> for the fortifying and tasty
> events of reading.
>
> I try to think of you now
> nestling in your own light,

as in Dante, singing to God
the poet and literary critic.

As you enter among them,
the other thousand surfaced glories
—those who sought honour
by bestowing it—
sing at your approach
Lo, one who shall increase our loves.

But maybe less druggy,
a bit plainer,
more Protestant.

Index

Index

Index